MW01087953

BOTTOMS UP

SEXUAL CULTURES

General Editors: Ann Pellegrini, Tavia Nyong'o, and Joshua Chambers-Letson

Founding Editors: José Esteban Muñoz and Ann Pellegrini

Titles in the series include:

For a complete list of books in the series, see www.nyupress.org

Bottoms Up

Queer Mexicanness and Latinx Performance

Xiomara Verenice Cervantes-Gómez

NEW YORK UNIVERSITY PRESS

New York

NEW YORK UNIVERSITY PRESS
New York
www.nyupress.org

© 2024 by New York University
All rights reserved

References to Internet websites (URLs) were accurate at the time of writing. Neither the author nor New York University Press is responsible for URLs that may have expired or changed since the manuscript was prepared.

Library of Congress Cataloging-in-Publication Data
Names: Cervantes-Gómez, Xiomara Verenice, author.
Title: Bottoms up : queer mexicanness and latinx performance /
Xiomara Verenice Cervantes-Gómez.
Description: New York : New York University Press, [2024] | Series: Sexual cultures |
Includes bibliographical references and index.
Identifiers: LCCN 2023042422 (print) | LCCN 2023042423 (ebook) |
ISBN 9781479829118 (hardback) | ISBN 9781479829156 (paperback) |
ISBN 9781479829163 (ebook) | ISBN 9781479829187 (ebook other)
Subjects: LCSH: Sexual minorities—Mexico. | Sex customs—Mexico.
Classification: LCC HQ73.3.M6 C47 2024 (print) | LCC HQ73.3.M6 (ebook) |
DDC 306.760972—dc23/eng/20240124
LC record available at https://lccn.loc.gov/2023042422
LC ebook record available at https://lccn.loc.gov/2023042423

New York University Press books are printed on acid-free paper, and their binding materials are chosen for strength and durability. We strive to use environmentally responsible suppliers and materials to the greatest extent possible in publishing our books.

Manufactured in the United States of America

10 9 8 7 6 5 4 3 2 1

Also available as an ebook

for Vincent

CONTENTS

A color insert follows page 126

Introduction

A Bottom's Theory of Exposure

You don't let every man hit your bottom. And your body remembers it. Just like a man will put a woman over doggy-style or maybe get a mirror or something. And then they start hitting that woman from the back or on her back they hittin' her. Then, they start talking. They start saying all kinds of stuff to her while they hittin' her. And, you see, that woman is being seduced. She's being seduced. He's breaking her down, man. He is screwing her into *submission*. He is screwing her into slavery, by using the penis as a weapon to break her ass *down!* And her defenses? I mean, she wide open!
—Alexyss K. Tylor, *The Alexyss K. Tylor Vagina Power Show*

This is a book about being fucked. Surely, we know that not everyone is fucked—as many have come to learn painfully and perhaps with great difficulties. Yet those who *are* fucked can never truly escape its event by succeeding to un-fuck themselves. Once fucked, they are and always will have already been fucked, insofar as the burden itself of un-fucking presents larger stakes of being fucked over by the trauma and violence of fucked-up situations. Befittingly, being fucked becomes almost inevitable. Those being fucked are positioned as a stand-in rhetorical prop for all that is precariously ignorable, destroyable, and ultimately disappearable without a trace. Surely, then, a book about being fucked would also be about sex, and these pages do not disappoint. They are soaked with the performance of the body's sexual encounters with others. Embracing these erotic gestures in the analysis of sexual culture, sex as a modality of relational exposure underscores how the aesthetic and political contours of the one being fucked—the bottom—have been and continue to structure varying contentious negative topologies in critical race studies and queer theory writ large.

This book inserts itself into the bottom, to cultivate an intimate exposure between readers and sexual systems that attempt to contain or quarantine the bottom, where, with, and with whom we would find bodies—well—ass-up, face-down. The bottom cruises sexual discourses produced by the failed projects of "nation building" while nullifying an abject recognition of sexual subject formation. Markedly, the bottom is, or at least becomes, an invisible shared abjective space occupied by those who conduct a sexual labor of an ethics articulated through a relational exposure to an other, or at times many others. I find this theorization to be at the center of the *ethos* of queer theory and a foundational entry point into a critical reading of the aesthetics of sex and politics of death as they conceptualize the bottom as a modality of performance that becomes an affectively charged ethical encounter.

The bottom describes a critical terrain to name something that many of us already do. It describes how to perform quotidian practices. This work mounts the bottom as a noun, verb, and analytic, in which the categories of "marginal" or "sexual dissident" may no longer be sufficient ways to describe how to be fucked beyond the stakes being sidelined. To be "marginalized" is still to *be*, to exist, and leave a record. Marginal logic implies a possibility of being or becoming a form of marginalia, a script in and of itself accompanying the main body of text that it complementarily decorates. These symbols and notes, in many cases, as the proverbial archive reveals, are preserved to perhaps manifest new forms of knowledge production to be discovered. Marginalia become paratextual to the body narrative at hand. But the bodies and subjects at stake in the bottom represent a political corpus prescribed as a destructible or disposable form of cultural script. I would argue that the bottom makes every effort to ensure that their trace remains difficult to be legibly or visually accessible. The bottom prepares itself to be presentable for its own exposure. Therefore, a bottom cannot so easily be represented by signs and symbols of their relationship to the larger body, or bodies, in question. This book locates the systemically and systematically exposable aspects of the bottom as a performance, an ethics, and a political aesthetic. I invite us to go deeper into the bottom.

The proliferation of the cisgender gay male bottom in queer studies, particularly in the United States, is as admirable as it is capacious.[1] Yet paradoxically, one of the biggest shortcomings in many of these inquiries *is* the centrality of the cisgender gay male, who more often than not remains hegemonically legible as white or at least white-passing. On the other hand, there are also meaningful studies of the "female" bottom, directing our attention toward more vulvic ways of sexual analysis.[2] Although inadvertently, often these counter or divergent theoretical genealogies still become repositories for phallocentric binary oppositional thinking, even while centering its disavowal and rejection. Nonetheless, the discourse of fucking remains fucked by its own attachment to both the implicit and explicit cis-maleness of the concept itself, or even more pointedly, an obsession with this penis power in question. *Bottoms Up* conceptualizes and theorizes a particular modality of the body that illustrates what and how it means to perform from the bottom, as a bottom performance, and to perform bottoming. It names a thing that happens *to* people. In doing so, the bottom describes a way of inhabiting this modality of performance in which taking it ass-up, face-down is central as an analytic and aesthetic strategy to be with the effects of being fucked. Performing the bottom, from the bottom, through the bottom accounts for those moments in which we might also stumble across someone fucked, or being fucked, or fucking. This modality of performance deploys the bottom as an aesthetic, ethical, political, sexual, and queer way of being in the world and being with an other or many others. It models a way of living with, navigating, and working with the affects and effects of being fucked in an abjective register.

The bottom exposed itself to me while I was in the audience of the Museo Universitario del Chopo in Mexico City on June 19, 2015, for the annual Festival Internacional por la Diversidad Sexual. I watched curiously as the queer experimental *queretanx* performance artist Lechedevirgen Trimegisto entered the stage and took their mark at the microphone stand. It was the final act to their series on homophobia and Mexican masculinity, *Inferno Varieté*. The music began to play as they opened with their now memorable and iconic scene from the prior three performances: a bloody lip-sync to Agustín Lara's "Como dos puñales." But there was something remarkably different in this version. The lip-sync wasn't bloody. In prior performances, the artist's forehead was pierced with needles across their forehead. Lechedevirgen would then remove the needles, allowing blood to spill down their clothes and body. But not this time. The omission of blood did not seem too bothersome, until the performance progressed. I watched as the artist exposed their nude body while engaging with recognizable tropes of Mexicanness, such as the inclusion of classic Mexican popular music, religious symbolism, posing as a footballer, and even nods to the cultural and political effects of narco-warfare. But without the blood, I felt cheated in a way. Something was taken from me. While it started out as a subtle omission, it unwittingly had long-term chronic effects for the entire performance. The final act was incomplete. Later the artist shared on social media that thirty minutes prior to their start time, they and their team were informed by the museum's visual arts director that they were not permitted to use human blood without prior approval from the Universidad Nacional Autónoma de México. Lechedevirgen explained that they had never been informed at any point prior to this.[3] Later, the antsy feelings I experienced at the beginning of the performance gained more vocabulary once paired with the idea of not just exposing others to human blood, but needing institutional "permission" to bleed one's own publicly. The risk of exposing the public to Lechedevirgen's blood was perceivably too high, and in an attempt to contain that risk, the performance exposes how queerness, even when it is hailed, still needs to be "safely" accessible. In other words, exposure to the body is containable, but exposure to its violent acquired substances, like blood, could or would be too risky and would leave undesirable traces of the queer.

The museum's reaction to Lechedevirgen Trimegisto's use of live human blood reflects a looping history of the violence against art that involves the queer body and the public. The incident with the Museo del Chopo extends a historical and institutionalized cis heterosexist treatment of conceptual performance that pathologizes the bodily substances of sexual minorities as a public health risk. Lechedevirgen's treatment by museum official recalls the uncanny specters that haunted the scandalous blacklisting of artist Ron Athey as a result of his performance *Four Scenes in a Harsh Life* (1994).[4] Athey's piece boldly confronts the sexual politics of religiosity through a ceremonious masochism ritualized with fellow artists Divinity P. Fudge, Julie Tolentino, and Pig Pen. The performance addresses body politics situating the gay male body as a site of reverence and sacrifice during the AIDS pandemic. The piece's mixing of the queer aesthetic with heterosexist religious iconography aims to unsettle the agendas of the religious right. Consequently, these themes by queer artists have sparked long-standing national debates regarding what defines "explicit" art. Spurred by the conservative agendas of the culture wars, the *Minneapolis Star*, joined by other media outlets, falsely accused Athey of exposing his audience to AIDS-infected blood. However, the blood that was central to the live performance was not even from Athey. Rather, it was from performer Divinity P. Fudge, whose HIV status was negative. Nonetheless, the polemic of blood in the performance catalyzed the censorship of and discrimination against Athey's work not only by art venues, but also by the National Endowment for the Arts. The religious right took this a step further by also attacking Athey for blasphemy and sacrilegious acts.

Ron Athey is an icon in contemporary performance art. His often grotesque, experimental, bloody, and exposed portrayals of life and death during the time of AIDS call into question the limits of the artistic practice. This reactionary treatment then sets a dangerous precedent for the use of queer bodies in public spaces and defining it as "art." Lechedevirgen's experience dovetails with the reactive ignorance of a high culture that makes every attempt to not be tainted by fucking the bottom. While representations of queer life can be made visible, its ability to contaminate, infect, and kill entire populations is not worth the risk. These events reveal how an aesthetic of queerness establishes a relational ethics between a contaminant and an infectious body that illustrates the bottom as a figure who gets fucked in the process of their own embrace of the passivity of being a bottom to the world.

Mexicanness: Bottoms in Spanish

Sex and death cannot be so easily disimbricated in the bottom. Rather, when one is a bottom bottoming bottoms-up, they recursively expose themself to direct contact with the libidinal economies of institutionalized violence directed at the bottom. The mutual imbrication and contamination of sex and death reveal the instability of the risky residues that remain and linger after the bottom's exposure. The bottom gets filled with divergent forms of political and ethical knowledge production

in the national and collective imaginary. As a sexual modality of performance, bottoming accounts for how these violent acts originate in
sexualized systems of power. The bottom creates theoretical conditions
for ethics and politics to condense into one another through the pains
and pleasures caused by going deeper in the bottom.

Among the names used to hail the bottom in this book, at their core
is a conceptualization rooted in their name in Spanish: *pasivo*. The word
translates to "passive," but in gay colloquialisms, this is the bottom.[5] The
pasivo offers more to critical bottom studies than just "bottom" alone by
not bifurcating the term from its double meaning. Rather, the bottom as
a figure, action, and spatiality allows both passivity and bottomness to
constitute an aesthetics of performing through and from a fucked positionality. Being bottoms-up reflects a passive positionality giving way
to bottoming. The *pasivo* captures an abject positionality always already
known to sexual subject formation across hemispheric Latinx America.[6]
The *pasivo* reveals both an aesthetic practice (topping-bottoming) and a
relationality (active-passive) that are knowable through the ways a body
can be with itself in fucking. In other words, the *pasivo* keeps the bottom
accountable to the aesthetics of an ethics of relationality.

As an analytic, the bottom is a critical lens that helpfully observes
how sexual identities and practices are captured and converted into political structures. As a signifier and the signified, performing the bottom
exposes patterns of attachment and nonnormative desires, in which the
styles of attachment are recognizably aesthetic strategies through both
politicized and relational sexual practices. Effectively, then, thinking
through the bottom as a *pasivo* actor accesses a modality of performance
that shows how to be with the presence of death. Of course, sex in this
book refers not necessarily—or at least not exclusively—to the literal
penetration of an orifice (whether mouth, anus, vagina) by a phallus. I
advocate for an understanding of performing the bottom through the
bottom bottoming as a means to seize the body in its basic nudity. And
power, be it the state or the political as its own enterprise, has the capacity to systematically dispose of those bodies from the bottom that
bottom.

Perhaps, then, no concept better captures the confounding and con-
fusion of the pain and pleasure of passive bottoming than Mexicanness.
As a case study in hemispheric Latinx American performance studies,

Mexicanness heightens an aesthetic relationality historically mounted on rectal politics. As a framework, Mexicanness may only exist, or at least be tolerable, as long as there is a bottom. With the fictional gay prostitute Adonis García, xenogender artist Lechedevirgen Trimegisto, dancer Bruno Ramri, Mexico City's notorious gay adult film house Mecos Films, gay undocumented poet Yosimar Reyes, feminist dancer Yanina Orellana, and queer Black Cuban artist Carlos Martiel, I contend that the political discourses at the heart of the national and collective imaginary are indelibly intertwined with the affective experiences of being fucked that have proliferated sexual cultures of death in our historical present. *Bottoms Up* underscores the theme of a radical passivity to negativity's exposure through the sexual acts of the bottom. As such, the bottom as an aesthetic, ethical, and political modality defines performance as relational exposure. This relationality produces larger stakes of a nonnormative ethics, understood as an ethics of alterity or otherness, in which those are always already decided to be beneath, beyond, or outside the fictions of the nation-state's sovereign promise of totality to the collective imaginary, while ultimately exposing and being exposed to an alterity of that otherness rooted in the imagination of the self. The passive bottoming of being bottoms-up relates to the one fucked, creating an affective relational exposure between them and the outside world. Darieck Scott describes this invocation as the utilization and conversation of pain into pleasure "for an experience of self that, though abject, is politically salient, potentially politically effective or powerful," which reflects the embrace of a positionality always already imbricated with death.[7] Mexicanness as a national way to perform bottomness exemplifies the concatenation of contemporary expressions of hemispheric Latinidades.

Like sex, the bottom is not an encounter with a literal death, in the sense that this book is not invested in the project of counting corpses—although, if we could, there certainly would not be a shortage. In other words, I depart from examining death and power through a journalistic or even forensic lens, in favor of reading the aesthetic specters of violence exposing themselves in Mexicanness. *Bottoms Up* is not invested in localizing or reclaiming bodies only to be folded into some nation-building project or national consciousness that never accounts for them anyway. The version of Mexicanness I subscribe to focuses on *feeling* the implications, ramifications, and risks of performing a *pasivo* ethics. As Laura Gutiérrez rightfully teaches us, this type of Mexican performance is built on "the idea that representations of sexuality are a primordial element in public cultural debates related to censorship and control, or in more general terms, to politics and the economy."[8] Accordingly, Mexicanness possesses the hemispheric breadth to extend beyond the borders of Mexico, into its surrounding diasporas and landscapes infected with experiences and feelings shared with and inherited by other Latinxs. An idea of Mexicanness is conceptualized with the constructions of queerness as a cultural framework, wherein Mexicanness centers around how one feels Mexican through the ways their sexual body moves in and negotiates with the material death-worlds surrounding them.

Let me also be clear, I do not take this as an opportunity to flatten all global and hemispheric Latinidades to be legible only through Mexicanness. Rather, as an aesthetic of the bottom, Mexicanness is a conceptual framework that gives a way to talk about the borders of a hemispheric Latinx American approach in performance studies. It proposes a theoretical geography, and perhaps the most appropriate case study to demonstrate the relationality between sex and death at the heart of this book. As such, *Bottoms Up* is less committed to proving its own "Mexicanness" than examining the relational abjection of an attachment to sex and death. This book thus positions Black, cisgender, indigenous, feminist, queer, and trans artists and writers from the Caribbean, Mexico, and the United States that fuck with Mexicanness. Taking this hemispheric approach empowers this book to extend beyond the question of nationality to take seriously what national fidelity feels like.

PAZ4PAS: National Myths of the Bottom

In 1990 the internationally acclaimed Mexican poet Octavio Paz was awarded the Nobel Prize in Literature for "impassioned writing with wide horizons, characterized by sensuous intelligence and humanistic integrity."[9] Truly a statement could not be more accurate; the arousing wordplay of the award's own description preserves the titillating performativity of the poet's own writing style. The sensuality with which the poet utilizes sexual semantics across his oeuvre conceptualizes and describes a version of Mexicanness that has remained remarkably sustainable. Octavio Paz's sexual writing style converts an act of reading into an intimate encounter with the author's sensual ways of constructing and designing a cultural linguistics to convey feelings about being a "true" Mexican.

Since the mid-twentieth century, Octavio Paz's "sensuous intelligence" as a writer has impactfully reverberated throughout the hemispheric Latinx Americas. Representations of sexual acts have consistently been folded into modernity's narratives that attempt to construct a national consciousness. Queer Latinx American studies sometimes might need to find itself in a return toward foundationally problematic texts in order to investigate the circulation of sexuality within the libidinal economies of the nation-state. Reading Paz for bottoming accounts for how the bottom is rhetorically positioned as a locus upon which authentic and divergent ideas of Mexicanness are imagined, projected, and represented. As a theoretical anchor, Paz's "sensuous intelligence" is a complementary episteme to queer theory, which better characterizes how esteemed Mexican intellectuals, too, found themselves preoccupied with *fucking* as an essential aspect of the national and collective imaginary.

Octavio Paz writes as a poet amid what he perceives to be a cultural crisis threatening Mexicanness brought about the progressive institutionalization of the Mexican Revolution, which solidified a revolutionary lexicon in social and political exchanges. Unlike his poetry, Paz breaks with tradition with his publication of the seminal nation-building text *El laberinto de la soledad* (1950). In his ambitious account of Mexico's cultural history, society, structures of power, modernity, and relationship to the United States and Europe, he finds a poetic resonance in a version of Mexicanness that transcends the political enterprise with which he has become disaffected.[10] Paz takes a unique approach to conceptualizing what this looks like, by critically meditating on the verb *chingar*, most commonly understood in Mexico as "to fuck." The primacy of fucking in Paz's conceptualization of Mexicanness constitutes what the Nobel Foundation describes as a "sensuous intelligence," in other words, a form of theoretical praxis itself, in which I read Paz beyond the literary, in favor of thinking within the context of how these sexual narratives interface with queer theory writ large. The poet professes, "For the Mexican, life is the possibility of fucking or being fucked. That is, to humiliate, punish, and offend. Or vice versa."[11] Moreover, "The fucked one is passive [*pasivo*], inert, and open, in contrast to the one who fucks, who is active [*activo*], aggressive, and closed."[12] The binary opposition between who fucks and who is getting fucked, or who is "open" or "closed," firmly resonates with the *activo-pasivo* binary that characterizes top and bottom gay sexual positionalities in Spanish.[13] Paz's reflection on fucking as constitutive of Mexican life invites us to read quotidian affairs and politics not just sexually, but necessarily penetratively, or even more precisely, through the ways men penetrate other men.

This penetration paradigm of "to fuck or to be fucked" systemically privileges the one doing the fucking. Yet Paz takes this a step further by being very specific about positionality in ways that sexualize Mexicanness with so much precision and detail that perhaps it may not be so literary or metaphorical after all. It becomes overly obvious that Paz is really anxious and concerned about getting fucked. He describes modesty and nudity, in relation to his larger arguments of what he articulates as the Mexican's solitude and the role of decency as protection from external penetration, which would reveal or enable unwanted access to what is internally protected or kept private. He writes, "We are not afraid or ashamed of our own or other people's nakedness, it is almost a reflection of the physicality between us. . . . For us, the body exists, giving weight and limits to our existence. It causes us pain and pleasure."[14] Paz sets up a possibility, then, to read this oscillation of pain and pleasure more precisely as affective experiences within a sexual encounter with an other or, sometimes, many others.

Paz randomly addresses the subject of sex between men in a rather curious way.[15] Fascinated, though it seems also remarkably confused, by what could be perceived as typical gay cruising practices, he gives an account of what he observed in Mexico City. He confidently explains the uniquely Mexican concept of the *albur*: wordplay or slip-of-the-tongue sexual double entendres exchanged in usually public settings, but not always—more common to masculine homosocial settings. However, Paz describes these exchanges as a unique "game" generating a loser, who will be fucked in front of everyone. He does not explain any other ways in which a man would elect to bottom. He "loses" when it comes to exchanging *albures*.[16] While it would be much easier to discredit what appears to be a laughable ignorance about homosexuality, I would find it more advantageous sitting with his very incisive description of what he believes he witnessed. His reference to sex between men demands a closer reading of how bottoming makes its own claims about Mexicanness and leaves a mark in the cultural history of sexual subject formation.

Since tops tend to be overly virile in general, they will most likely get some anal play on the side.[17] But their indulgence is just that: a disposable pleasure, a matter of excess that does not need to result in anything else but ejaculation. For Paz, it would appear that there is an otherness to the act of anal sex between men that is not innately wrong, just different. As such, Paz does not condemn or disparage the practice at all. Rather, it is discussed as if it is a normal practice, almost common, that he attempts to make sense of for the reader, and most likely for himself. Yet, as he explains, anal sex is indulgent only as far as the *activo* is concerned—but how would he know? According to Paz, the *pasivo* does not indulge himself by participating in these sexual acts as the one who will take it up the ass. Rather, for the Nobel laureate, bottoming appears neither pleasurable nor something a man should necessarily seek. Therefore, it cannot exist in excess form within the realm of masculine sexualities as far as the bottom would experience pain or pleasure. The homosexual *pasivo* is deprived of an indulgent sexuality and his sexual pleasure is neither accessible nor necessary for the penetration paradigm to be set into motion. And just here is where his text veers into the radical—Paz concludes, "As such, masculine homosexuality is tolerated, on the condition that it consists in violating the *pasivo*."[18]

I read this statement as the advocation and prescriptive mandate for sex between men to be not just tolerable, but acceptable, practical, and understandable: as long as there is a bottom! Paz's need for bottoms enables a deeper engagement with the rhetorical gestures and politics of bottoming at play more broadly in sexual subject formation.[19] Without the bottom, there is no top. In this sense, anal sex might be read as an applicably indulgent act for *both* men since he names the bottom as an abject being anyway. It is from here that I turn toward how the bottom leans back into the perceived violence of their forced subjugation, their Conquest.

It is clear that Octavio Paz fears being fucked. He is overly repetitive that men should avoid the possibility of even accidentally having something stuck inside them. Therefore, a man should never allow himself to be too "exposed." Paz's sexual anxiety thus manifests as strict guidelines for the only acceptable reasons a man should ever have his ass out.[20] This version of Mexicanness depends on bottoming. However, Paz clarifies that not all can truly achieve the status of Mexicanness; rather, it is a small elite class. As I said, not everyone is fucked, but those who are become an unlikely critical life source. Paz unexpectedly enters bottom studies by exposing the inherent importance of bottoming for national belonging. Paz offers hemispheric bottom studies a sexual account of *how* the bottom becomes rhetorically positioned ass-up, face-down and converted into a locus onto which authentic and divergent ideas of the national consciousness are imagined and represented. It is also a site where other affects and anxieties are projected and signified. Being fucked risks exposure.

By keeping the inseparability of "passive" and "bottom" intact in *pasivo*, I propose we gain access to divergent forms of a sexual national consciousness that can be read as a queer ethical mode of engagement that analyzes the live wire that crosses sex and the political. The bottom is passive and open to being fucked. It is also a positionality that names an always already fucked state. I argue that through the bottom's exposure, hemispheric performance theory turns toward an affective ethical encounter with alterity.

Abjective Politics of Pleasure

The bottom does not invert a top-down approach into a bottom-up approach, which would be just hegemonic. Rather, "bottoms up" is a call to think ass-up, face-down. That is, the bottom is not exposed hierarchically, but *as* the grounds on which the top necessarily projects their national and collective responsibility to fuck. Mexicanness as a way of bottoming refers to the sexual crossings of the bottom as an aesthetic form of relational exposure in sexual acts. As passive and bottom, doing Mexicanness operates within a political plane of death that fucks the bottom into ways that extend beyond borders that are crossed hierarchically. A bottom, performing bottom, and performing from the bottom throughout this book shapes and characterizes different ways of being with death, each with its own ethical and political nuances, yet collectively these versions of the bottom return to an aesthetics of being fucked, defined by affective experiences constituted by and responsible to an other in that exposure. Studying the bottom through the lens of the *pasivo* enables a way of theorizing a fucked modality of being with others and being in the world, even when it is violent. That risk is reflected through a pain-pleasure matrix. It is a sensation and an urge. That moment the top sticks it in a little too fast and a little too deep. Wince. Or maybe bite the pillow. Bottom lip? Either way it's sharp. The rectum tightens while the penis pauses in motion. The bottom has a choice. It is only a split second as the bottom takes deep breaths: pull out or let the top go deeper? Even if pulling out means adding more lube and trying again, the body already remembers. The bottom teaches us how to be with that pain of being fucked a little too fast and a little too deep. Fucking through the pain may or may not result in pleasure, but sometimes becomes the only necessary response to that acute trauma. A *pasivo* way of bottoming is a way to analyze how the bottom performs being with others while with this painful pleasure: an abjective relational ethics is brought forth.

Propelling this book is a method of thinking that is *negatively* defined. In these pages, we find ourselves exposed to and by figures across a rich corpus of case studies approached through a modality of ethical and political engagement with these aestheticizing signifiers. Passive bottoming exposes how divergent forms of sex and sexuality function as necessary paradigms in the exposure of the assemblages or constellations of violence characterizing contemporary political stages and sociocultural landscapes. The political and ethical attachment to a queer subjectivity to come—that is, to be hegemonically read—which has defined a significant part of queer theory, perhaps may not possess a future for queers of color. Rather, bottoming captures an idea of a social death, describing the negation of a prior meta-moment of plenitude or social life for the livelihood of queerness in the hemispheric Latinx Americas. Queer Mexicanness, then, becomes a constitutive part of violent landscapes as both a symptom and supplement of that violence and, conversely, one of the most appropriate loci from which to critique that violence.

From an analytical perspective, I turn toward a language of negativity rooted in the abject. Leticia Alvarado offers a reading of the "aesthetics of abjection" that form divergent or altering "politicized strategies" for Latinx performance, accounting for how Latinx aesthetic strategies rooted in the abject reveal a "sign of the failure of language to the approximate shifting and ambivalent dynamics" of an abjective Latinidad.[21] The performances foregrounded in the following chapters contribute to and depart from Alvarado's rich vocabulary offered to Latinx performance studies. I offer an aesthetic analysis thought through and from abject performances foregrounding the Latinx body's problematic relationality to the external world surrounding its performance.[22] This abjective political strategy functions and operates within an "affective abject vortex" described by a "queer sensual proximity" to the Latinx body and thus introduces a "contrapuntal political project."[23] The ties between abjection and Latinidad are a shared affective state. This shared positionality becomes central through racialized and sexualized subjectivities, thus creating an account of the unaccountable, deployed as an aesthetic strategy in Latinx performance through shared histories of violence residing in our bodies.[24]

I follow a negatively paved trajectory to my approach to the bottom. As a modality of performance articulated by those who get fucked, the bottom performs a profound experience that exposes structural violence that is always already sexualized. Bottoming as a negative ethics is one structured by the endless deferral of difference in the relational exposure to and from the *pasivo*. This enables a way of thinking about how the bottom activates and exposes bodies to what José Esteban Muñoz describes as "memory performance," or that sensation in which "many of us take periodic refuge in the past." Queer Latinx performance accounts for how "an antinormative affect offers a model of group identity that is coherent without being exclusionary."[25] The negative lexicon guiding the bottom in this book is indebted to Afropessimism and Latinx approaches to negativity addressing questions about the relationality and sociality of those at the bottom. Juana María Rodríguez rightfully argues that "refusal, destruction, failure, masochism, and negativity are not the absence of sociality; instead, they signal the active critical work of engagement and critique that is always already relational." As such, for Rodríguez, "sex can function as both a site of queer failure *and* a site of impassioned sociality."[26] Ramón Rivera-Servera also reminds us, then, to be "mindful of the need to attend to the tensions and frictions that emerge within social spaces that are structured around difference and inequality."[27] This would underscore the "unsettling" aesthetics of performing *mexicanidad* that, Laura Gutiérrez argues, "unsettle a certain sense of comfortableness or naturalness about gender and sexual systems, which have acquired a sense of normalcy."[28]

The artists foregrounded in this book come up from the bottom. These are artists across gender identities, yet arguably all bottoms, whose works challenge any sense of assimilation, comfort, or sufficiency by making profoundly explicit the very instability of their Mexicanness through their sexualization and the types of sexual acts produced as political effects of their performance and its affective encounter with its publics. These pages are soaked with tales of the blood of those lost and murdered lives and those whose blood continues to be shed. The level of experimentalism, gore, and obscenity in these pieces is inspired by a long legacy of how the body's materiality—namely, blood—plays an essential role as aesthetic matter itself in the performance. These artists draw from long legacies of feminist and queer praxis that foreground the body's exhaustion against the oppressive forces pushed against it to perhaps entertain those negative affects about queer of color life when, after all, it's all fucked-up anyway.

Toward a Passive Ethics of Relationality

The capacious conceptualization of sex and death outlined thus far underscores aesthetic and affective qualities of sex and death through the performance of passive bottoming. My analysis of pleasure and violence in the following chapters divulges a closer reading of the different actors at stake in penetration to raise questions and critiques about subjectivity and alterity. Focusing on figures whose positionality always already has a sexual relationship with death, I insert rectal subjectivities into a reading of Mexicanness to understand larger stakes of hemispheric Latinx American sexual subject formation.

The exposed body of the bottom reveals a loop of recognition and misrecognition that calls into question how subjectivity may be understood from an ethico-political angle. As these chapters reveal, the sexual histories central to the construction and critique of contemporary politics rely on a rhetoric of alterity or otherness. *Bottoms Up* examines how representations of sex and death culminate in relational acts of exposure that construct and critique ideas of fucking in the national and collective imaginary. A focus on exposure analyzes affective encounters and political positionalities with sexual figures who are already determined as death-dealing or death-possessing. Bottoming as an analytic suggests a reading practice that accounts for daily encounters with those figures as they are situated within the landscape of what Achille Mbembe has described as the "death-world" of the "living dead," wherein these categories overlap through nationalized narratives about the erasure and repression of life through the omnipotent forces of killing. Mbembe describes this system of violence and death as "necropolitics," in which, within the contemporary state, "to exercise sovereignty is to exercise control over mortality and to define life as the deployment and manifestation of power."[29] My own interest in the study of sex and death dovetails with Mbembe's concerns with figures of sovereignty whose central project is "the generalized instrumentalization of human existence and the material destruction of human bodies and populations."[30]

Prior to Mbembe's coinage of "necropolitics," Michel Foucault's category of "biopower" aided in explaining the domain of life over which power has taken control. The issue of vitality and longevity is at the heart of Foucault's reading of death. He writes, "The power to expose a whole population to death is the underside of the power to guarantee an individual's continued existence." He continues, "But the existence in question is no longer the juridical existence of sovereignty; at stake is the biological existence of a population."[31] For Foucault, the ability to exercise the right to kill just for the sake of killing or just to wield one's power, because the sovereign could, was no longer sufficient to describe the contemporary state. Instead, he redirects our attention to the biological implications of deploying death as a strategic action against a group of people. In other words, the longevity of a population, or the life of a nation, is the reason death would need to be distributed. In a biopolitical system, death becomes a mechanism through which to allow the greater whole to live. He argues, "One might say that the ancient right to *take* life or *let* live was replaced by a power to *foster* life or *disallow* it to the point of death."[32] In this biopolitical reading of sovereignty, Foucault contends that the body functions as a machine, subject to regulatory control to support this political system dependent on a biological imperative. More specifically, it is control over sex and sexuality that mediates this process of power over bodies.

Exposure as it is conveyed by Foucault through the idea of exposing a whole population to death is central to a queer exposure that reads sex, death, and the body. Exposure, in this sense, resonates with illness, contagions, and risky behaviors. Death is pathologized in this encounter of exposure to a body of people. It is something that should be avoided because it can contaminate the whole body when those in power allow it to spread, infiltrate, and penetrate the body. In the Foucauldian capacity, death appears as a threat to sex, life, and the nation. But in the context of Mexicanness, though death is not feared, it is dangerously wielded over populations and regulated through the exertion of power over sexual bodies.

Across both Foucault's and Mbembe's critical readings of life, death, and politics, the category of "death" not only is positioned at the center of political structures, but is also one of the defining contours of the project of "nation" through the control of bodies—including their actions, desires, pleasures, and sexual functions. Yet I do not find Mbembe's theorization of necropolitics—as the domain of death over which power has taken control—to be antithetical to Foucault. Rather, I read the two to be complementary: a biopolitical *and* necropolitical condition of modernity. The ultimate expression of sovereignty in this context is power over the exposure of and to sex and death. This form of sovereignty rests within the freedom of the subject to recognize themselves *as* a national subject: a subject characterized by domination, destruction, and the consolidation of national myths dependent on the sexual expression of power. Yet, for Mbembe, the expression of sovereignty is a question of humanness; he writes, "In other words, the human being truly *becomes a subject* . . . in the struggle and the work through which he or she confronts death (understood as the violence of negativity)." He continues, "Becoming subject therefore supposes upholding the work of death."[33] In bottoming we encounter a context wherein the nation depends on the labor of death as an integral part of its national myth. What follows, then, is a question of how to account for humanness and the process through which subjects are formed and recognized by sexual expressions of power.

Sex not only needs to be taken seriously, but also necessitates being read critically. As Foucault aptly reminds us, sex is a political issue.[34] "Sex was a means of access both to the life of the body and the life of the species," he recalls. "It was employed as a standard for the disciplines and as a basis for regulations."[35] These standards of regulation became an integral part of political operations and economic interventions, most obviously through the control of procreative sexual practices, which "became a crucial target of a power organized around the management of life rather than the menace of death."[36] Looking toward sex supports a biological imperative of the nation, allowing sex to be converted into a type of national desire. For Foucault, a political system oriented around the management of life turns sex forward, whereas a political system invested in the distribution of death would not.[37] Foucault describes how political structures became oriented around and by sexual acts. Sex is informed and was informed by politics: "Power delineated it, aroused it, and employed it as the proliferating meaning that had always to be taken control of again lest it escape; it was *an effect with a meaning-value*."[38] Sex, between whomever, is loaded with political baggage of a biological imperative to talk about life and death.[39] In other words, as this book purports to do, sexuality—and the very act of sex itself—needs to be analyzed as a tool, strategy, and weapon that has been made available and possible through the political structures that not only enable it, but rely upon it.

Foregrounding the role and strategy of sex acts in this analysis, sexuality's location at the center of Mexicanness and death is made more explicit. Mbembe gently touches this topic through his reading of the French philosopher Georges Bataille's conceptualization of erotism. Distinct from "eroticism," erotism is the actual state of sexual excitement of the *eros* (appetite, desire, hunger), which functions as a noun for the arousal and anticipation of sexual feelings. Eroticism, in contrast, describes relational logics of the erotics of power in language and representation. The latter certainly has its place in this book, but erotism *is* anticipation that sex will hurt so good that it arouses the *eros*, or desire and appetite of the body and soul. Whenever humans enact the erotic, they have an impulse to want to abandon the constituted forms given to them by life. Erotism encodes an impulsive sensation and urge to move beyond this life.[40] Bataille writes, "In essence, the domain of erotism is the domain of violence, of violation," in which death is "the most violent thing of all for us, . . . which jerks us out of a tenacious obsession with the lastingness of our discontinuous being."[41] Sex, in this sense and across this current work, signals a rupture of the symbolic order, not as transgression or protest (necessarily), but as an always already disruptive life-shattering event. Mbembe can thus conclude, "Sexuality is inextricably linked to violence and to the dissolution of the boundaries of the body and self by way of orgiastic and excremental impulses."[42] The bottom as a sexual category is loaded with the capacity to reveal some defining quality about violence and death. It gives us access to understand violence in a different way.

The actors at the center of this political theater address broader issues of the misrecognition that inform the larger theoretical concerns motivating this book. Moreover, the dichotomy of recognition and misrecognition emboldens a more developed understanding of exposure as a passive ethical mode of engagement and analysis. Following Judith Butler, the notion of ethics I subscribe to in this book refers to an ethics that responds to an alterity, or otherness, in an other or many others. I theorize an ethics that cannot be known ahead of an encounter with an other, but rather is contingent upon demand through an affective responsibility to respond to their alterity.

Butler's attention to the terminology of "recognition" begins with questions of subjectivity, through which they take up the question of recognizing the subject in relation to the Althusserian notion of interpellation. They articulate how the constitution of the subject depends on the subject being called, addressed, or named.[43] At stake for Butler is an affirmation of ways to be transgressive in ways that do and do not identify with the subject whom that name would install in their response to such an address. Butler specifically describes "a signifier capable of being interpreted in a number of divergent and conflictual ways," such as Black, Chicana, queer, trans, and so forth.[44] Such names and categories could simultaneously function as affirmation *and* insult in the same utterance, depending on the context in which the address occurs, is received, responded to, and thereby acted upon. For Butler, "at stake is whether the temporary totalization performed by the name is politically enabling or paralyzing," and whether it is "politically strategic or regressive or, if paralyzing and regressive, also enabling in some way."[45]

A Butlerian misrecognition provides for encounters with the Other in spaces always already marked by the aporia of these signifiers. In performance, I center misrecognition as an integral part of how sexual positionality and the politics of death could be productively read. A relationship of misrecognition to the bottom and its function in the material reconsiders the social and affective conditions of subjectivity and alterity. The body is a site where we expose ourselves to one another. In that exposure, bodies open themselves up to those people, places, and things that lie beyond their own borders. That opening welcomes, consensual or otherwise, experiences of pain and pleasure. The bottom is a site for recognition and misrecognition—the location onto which to project and perform the policing and transgressions of norms. Accordingly, the body exposed becomes such a vital political and ethical tool in this book, enabling us to understand our own roles in the lives of others who are similarly embodied and exposed.

The signifier of the *pasivo* as Spanish's mutual imbrication of sex and power offers ethics the congealment of a moment of nonnormative responsibility to the Other. In the following chapters, a *pasivo* ethics demands transdisciplinary promiscuity. The aesthetics, ethics, and politics of sex and death permit grounding "close reading" practices traditionally known to literary studies in the ways performance studies engages with the artists and their performative acts through the proximity of affective encounters. A passive ethics describes an aesthetics of political and sexual performances projected from and onto the bottom.[46] From these critical acts of sexuality, this book seeks to cross the borders of the body across geographies to make sense of a need for the bottom's passivity. In this sense, we could think of the bottom, as a *pasivo*, beyond sexual positionality—though never erasing it—and account for the abjective bonds, political affiliations, and social classes that constitute the *pasivo*'s embodied reality.

Through the acceptance of being penetrated, open, and dominated, the *pasivo*—an agent of the bottom—represents a type of passivity that Jack Halberstam describes as a performance of "the subject to actually come undone, to dramatize unbecoming for the other so that the viewer does not have to witness unbecoming as a function of her own body."[47] As such, the willingness embedded in the *pasivo* bottoming, passively, interfaces with the French philosopher Emmanuel Levinas's argument that passivity expresses the idea *a priori* that I am acted upon before I have the opportunity to act or passively accept the actions for the Other. In relation with the Other, the fact that I am "for the Other" is true "prior to activity and passivity."[48] The passive logic described creates a method to analyze a relationship that predicates itself upon a subject being taken hostage by an other. This approach to passivity within the construction of a relational ethics depends upon a passivity as an unbecoming or undoing of subjectivity in queer terms. Levinas characterizes this splintering as part of the ethical experience of "being torn up from oneself in the core of one's unity, this absolute noncoinciding, this diachrony of the instant, [which] signifies in form of one-penetrated-by-the-other."[49] Passivity in this regard offers an idea of antisociality that, as Halberstam describes, "dictates an unbecoming, a cleaving to that which seems to shame or annihilate, and a radical passivity allows for the inhabiting of femininity with a difference."[50] Passivity's imbrication with the bottom thus deconstructs a reading gaze of the duality of the *activo-pasivo* and *top-bottom* binaries that posits a passivity capable of entirely obliterating both partners prior to any sexual engagement.

Bottoms Up argues that through sexual passivity the bottom performs a critical repetition of a relationality that makes bottoming the radical process that it purports to be. During sex we are open to somebody else, whom we cannot seize or fully grasp in our own consciousness. In other words, sexual practice is not an amalgamation of bodies or a coming-together-as-one. Rather, sex is a destabilizing relationship underscoring that which will always remain unknown and inaccessible. In sex, everybody is rendered passive through their inability to wholly grasp the event. It is a passivity that performs a rupture and rejection of identitarian-based political projects. Sex renders all partners passive to one another in their encounter. I consider the inhabitation of being penetrated with the radical passivity of the unbecoming of the subject from the positionality of the bottom as both a sexual position and a conceptual logic. An invocation of passivity annihilates the penetration paradigm through a willingness of all—let's also not assume these are all one-on-one encounters—to become undone by their imprisonment to the Other in sexual encounter. As an affect and effect of bottoming as an ethics, passivity brings self-negation to embrace the unintelligibility and messiness of bottoming deployed by national narratives as a central allegory for Mexicanness's cultural prosperity and social milieu.

The Queerness of Being Exposed

The term "exposure" historically continues to metamorphose in its con-notations, meanings, and signifiers. The evolution of the term's gestures is politicized as it possesses varying relationships within the national and collective imaginary that ascertain or strip the bottom of the pos-sibility of power. In the last century alone, we may recall how examples of "exposure" through these various meanings has had the traction to become political during moments of public health crises—from the onset of the global HIV/AIDS epidemic, to global influenzas, biological terrorism, the coronavirus COVID-19 pandemic, and those yet to come. I bring together figures that amplify a negativity at the center of the concept of exposure. They point to something that is contagious, con-taminating, endemic, infectious, poisoning, viral, and, ultimately, just too dangerous to the public and its safety writ large.

These political gestures and nods result in the power to determine which modes of exposure are deemed considerably "decent" and which are not—that is, to what degree something or someone is palatable and hygienic enough to permeate the national and collective imaginary. Yet exposure's tender touch with a doxa of decency and modesty ascribes a universality to the people, actions, aesthetics, and gestures that are so profoundly contradictory to the normative mainstream that they are labeled "indecent." And in many cases their indecency is height-ened to the level of the criminal, if not fatally worse. The expectation for conformity—that is, hegemonic assimilative aspirations and behav-iors—is equally exposing. The overproduction of the promise of totality mutually contaminates the public and collective imaginary with "decent" presentations of the body that would contribute to fictions of the totality of the nation-building project. In stark opposition to those figures who are too indecent to be accounted for within—and counted with—the larger stakes of state violence. Not so ironically, their participation as passive actors is always already demanded, as it is necessary for these frameworks to become realized in the first place.

Exposure describes a basic nudity of the body, while also generating an idea of being naked or nude, except in exposure there is a vulner-ability to the ontological body in question that challenges exposure as an ethical device. This describes the controlling ways certain nudities are tagged as forms of "indecent exposure." A bottom exposes nudity as a presumed passivity through its vulnerability of being fully "exposed," which expectedly infects those other surrounding bodies that spectate upon its nudity—in other words, a bare nudity that cannot be forgotten by the subject and thus captures their own respective exposure.[51]

The *Oxford English Dictionary* defines "expose" primarily as "to put out."[52] Expectedly, I cannot resist the low-hanging fruit of "putting out" as an innuendo for offering oneself sexually, which, again, *also* is very true for the bottoms discussed throughout this book. Yet the term "exposure" historically refers to the concept of putting one out of their home or depriving them of economic security: to *put them out* on the streets. In other words, to put them out of any form of hegemonic legibility or recognition under the state that would protect the parameters of the Other's alterity that are accessible. The chapters in *Bottoms Up* address these origins of being "put out" as they relate to the risks of exposing the bottom in public. Exposure in this sense is always already outlined and underscored by the power to—that is, the sovereign right to—distribute life and death. At stake is something much more baneful and pestilent. Those at the bottom must "put out" as a means of strategic survival and postcolonial revolt, while also risking being "put out" or otherwise eliminated without a trace.

This book lingers in the temporal space of the not-yet-vanished, with those putting out after being put out. Through experimental works by and about being fucked, this expansion of Latinx performance to the bottom refers to a languor described by Joshua Javier Guzmán and Christina A. León as "a dwelling that inhabits the spaces of ambivalence and ambiguity."[53] The risk of being exposed to residues that still remain tacky and perhaps contaminating after exposure is central. This book is invested in what remains indelibly tactile and threatening about these bottom dwellings—already known for being dirty, grimy, wet, and sticky. Revealed are the dangerous contours of the bottom that remain stuck upon those who are "put out" into the bottom. As such, what happens when we cannot rid ourselves of that exposure to the aftermaths of being (or in) the bottom?

Exposure in the aesthetics of Mexicanness is a modality to perform a sexual positionality that critically and carefully transliterates exposure as a heuristic process of "being fucked." A queer Latinx American exposure activates the multiple meanings of the bottom as an ethical and political modality of performance dependent upon an aesthetics of sex and death dealt by the top. Characterized by sexual practices and cultural signifiers, and as a structural device within the nation-state, the idea of a body exposed captures various acts and contexts of "being fucked." The bottom is positioned and read through, from, and against three approaches of "being fucked." First, I propose thinking sexually through the practices of the figure of the *pasivo* who is being fucked up the ass; whether by choice or force, these bodies are bent over, ass-up, and face-down, taking it hard. Second, using sexual positionality as a template of sorts, this book also considers how bodies get fucked over by the systems of power that purport to protect them—or even to destroy them. Finally, the former two often find themselves folded into fucked situations that leave the body stuck, or irrevocably positioned to never become a full subject within the national and collective imaginary. These different but complementary tenors of "being fucked" are deployed as analytical channels that flow into the same body of Mexicanness at stake.

The versions of sex explored in the bottom are aggressive, forceful, reactive, and perhaps even perceptively violent. These aesthetic scenes of sex build upon a national narrative that rhetorizes heteronormative perceptions of the bottom as a figure who is nonconsensually and violently ripped open, converting them into an abject being and rendering them passive. Descriptors of the bottom's praxis invoke possibilities for calling into question the phallic authority of hegemonic systems. In this respect, the anus and rectum become politicized to poise their potential to reject heteronormative constructions of sexual subject formation that seek to penetrate them. By foregrounding problematic and forceful acts of fucking, this book takes seriously the political affects of penetration as a "power" central to the bottom positionality. The condensation of "power" into bottom comes from a radical creation and use of pleasure as a rejection of the norms of subjectivity. Darieck Scott describes this invocation of power as the transformation of pain and pleasure, "the *taking* of pleasure out of the maw of humiliation and pain, and the utilization of that pain that windows into pleasure and back again for an experience of self that, though abject, is politically salient, potentially politically effective or powerful."[54] This speaks to an embrace of a positionality always already marked by death's awaiting touch, underscoring a political gesture of the *pasivo* as a figure representing the concatenation of contemporary Mexicanness and politics. What follows, then, in the subsequent chapters is a critical and theoretical intervention in the study of sex and death. This book centers male sexual practices as an object for further critique from the perspective of a bottom politics that circumvents a reading of the fucked and exposed *pasivo*.

A second approach taken by exposure explored in this book conceptualizes "being fucked over": a cultural paradigm that converts the exposed body into a rhetorical signifier. Here, the body becomes understood as a meaningful trope within sexual cultures of Mexicanness. Functioning as metaphor or analogy, the body in its fucked position signifies something beyond its own embodiment, thereby producing new cultural signs of meaning within the national and collective imaginary. These signifiers, at least in this body of work, are both politically activating and threatening. In the following chapters, I center artists whose embodied realities as sexual minorities pose a threat to the image of *diversidad sexual* (sexual diversity)—the go-to terminology used by the nation-state's social capital campaign in Mexico to make heterosexuality and homosexuality one and the same. The threat that these artists pose is derived from acts of refusal to be captured by any terminology other than those that speak to how their bodies are fucked (symbolically or otherwise).

One salient example of this aesthetic approach could be found at the height of the North American AIDS crisis. In his seminal essay "Is the Rectum a Grave?," Leo Bersani advocates for a sexual approach to the gay male body in public discourse as a result of its conversion into a cultural signifier for death in a global health crisis. He elevates the pursuit of anal sex as "our primary hygienic practice of nonviolence" in contrast to the relational heteronormative alternatives.[55] Gay men, in particular cisgender and white, can "advertise" this practice of sex not only in response to heteronormative assimilation, but in response to the state's invocation of these normative trajectories of sexual practices and familial models of desire because they are positioned, literally through the act of anal penetration, to "represent the internalized phallic male as an infinitely loved object of sacrifice." In any case, gay men thus advertise their overindulgence in orgasm as what Bersani concludes as "a mode of ascesis."[56] Bottoming wanders and lingers in these cultural spaces, as a marker for that which is threatening to the longevity and livelihood of the whole. Culturally, he is fucked over by dynamics and communities he was always already excluded from. Fucked and looking to the future are the only possibilities left.

Finally, exposure also divulges how "being fucked" functions as a structural device. That is, the exposed body reflects a social position within the configurations of the nation-state. Structurally there are a lot of experiences attached to being at the bottom. Yet the sensation of being both bottom and at the bottom is an aesthetic practice that positions pleasure and violence at the center of the field of vision. This book identifies how violence and pleasure structure exposed bodies in specific scenes within the theater of the nation-state. The body is exposed in all its traumatic pleasures, ensuring that actors can optimally fulfill their roles. It is, after all, a fucked-up situation.

Bottoms Bottoming from the Bottom

Following the methodology through which the bottom is characterized by sexual practices and cultural signifiers, and as a structural device that becomes a modality of quotidian performance, each chapter builds upon ideas of performance by exposing the different angles, frames, and viewpoints of bodies in their "being fucked" position, against the backdrop of those systems of power that restructure and reconfigure their sexual embodiments.

Chapter 1 untangles the cultural signifiers made out of those bodies being fucked through performance art produced by queer nonbinary xenogender artist Lechedevirgen Trimegisto, from Querétaro, Mexico. Here, their body is explored through the public's overexposure to the bottom bottoming. This chapter considers the necessary, but at times forced, risks posed by being exposed for too long, or being in too deep. Lechedevirgen's very experimental and disturbing oeuvre is rich with the grotesque, the uncomfortable, and the unsightly, becoming necessary points of tension that bring to the surface anxieties about the bottom in the national and collective imaginary. Focusing on their piece *Inferno Varieté* (2014–2015), this chapter wrestles with constructions of homophobia as they are deployed to constitute and redefine the parameters of queerness and Mexicanness.

Chapter 2 takes up the sexual practices of "being fucked" in the aesthetic representations and sexual acts of Adonis García, a fictional gay prostitute from the US-Mexico border living, but mostly fucking, in 1970s Mexico City. *Las aventuras, desventuras y sueños de Adonis García, el vampiro de la colonia Roma* (1979) features Mexican literature's first openly and unapologetically gay protagonist. As the COVID-19 coronavirus stretched globally, its author, Luis Zapata, died from virus-related complications on November 4, 2020. In the wake of the author's death, it became clear that Adonis García affects his readers in ways that extend beyond the literary encounter of reading. This chapter thinks *after* we have experienced *Vampiro*, as well as the possibility of remembering Adonis García *after* Luis Zapata. The author created a character with whom readers have an intimate experience. This is a chapter about Adonis García in which his sexual acts pose aesthetic, ethical, and political consequences for the material world. Reading the character against the grain accounts for the spectrum of aesthetic portrayals of Adonis García in the novel's text, in various versions of the cover art, and in the inspired gay experimental film *Siempre Sí* (2018), directed, produced, and written by Chilean experimental author Alberto Fuguet. These aestheticizations of a sexual hero center Adonis García's stories of sexual belonging that operate both on and off the page.

Chapter 3 explicitly exposes sex acts and submission to understand exposure as a structural device within the national and collective imaginary of state violence. This chapter asks, How do we account for the moments when violence rears its head as we gaze into the face of pleasure? Through a pornographic approach, chapter 3 identifies how violence and pleasure structure specific sexual scenes within the theater of the nation-state and its internal and external forms that construct sex and death as necessary actors that entangle with one another. Exposure, in this respect, is understood by how the abject body exposes itself to the nation-state to be used and abused. Mexican artist Bruno Ramri's performance of *Revenge Porn: La invasión de la privacidad* (2014) and the gay adult film *Corrupción mexicana* (2010) by Mecos Films emphatically bind us to moments of abject submission that become central to constructions of the nation-state that make Mexicanness a feeling of being fucked over and over. This chapter underscores how enablement of violence by the nation-state is dependent upon the subjugation of sexual minorities; and in some cases, those bodies lean back into that subjugated positionality.

Chapter 4 turns to an idea of diasporic Mexicanness. This chapter considers what it means for this critical geography of sex and death to directly affect—or infect—its surrounding landscapes. By looking toward Mexico's borders and the diasporic queers who share complicated relationships with the constructions and feelings of Mexicanness outlined, this chapter accounts for how the diaspora embodies and inherits ancestral sexual histories. Centering the historical figure of *la Chingada* (Malinche) as a queer mother who gives space to how borders, bodies, and boundaries are read, this chapter conceptualizes diasporic Mexicanness as a feeling of border crossing. Through queer undocumented artist Yosimar Reyes's performance poetry and multimedia Mexican feminist artist Yanina Orellana's performance *Todos somos hijos de la Chingada* (2017), I attempt to sketch the theoretical coordinates of a hemispheric Latinx American performance captured by the histories and stories of sexual survival surrounding the idea of *la Chingada*, constituted by sexual legacies of pain and pleasure of being a bottom, from the bottom, and being *in* the world as a bottom.

Chapter 5 is the congealment of these themes into a way of thinking with Mexicanness as an aesthetic specter. This chapter demonstrates how the bottom becomes a hemispheric analytic. In its account of Blackness and race in the construction and critique of the passive relationality of being exposed, this chapter explores how Carlos Martiel's aesthetic embrace of blood and risk is central to Mexicanness and exposes the Blackness of the bottom, which always already risks disposability. Martiel's performance as a racialized sexual alterity reveals the broader stakes of the bottom for a hemispheric Latinx American performance studies while accounting for racial negativities beyond the implicit binary of whiteness and brownness. These chapters converge into an understanding of the aesthetics, ethics, and politics of Mexicanness as determined by how sex and death are exposed to one another through the movements and gestures of sexual bodies. Each chapter straddles and mounts each other to blend together an understanding of exposure in a transdisciplinary model of reading sexuality, politics, and performance. As such, exposure might function outside the boundaries of any highly structured discipline.

1

Like a Dagger

Lechedevirgen Trimegisto Risks Aesthetics

You're a dagger!
—Spoken in English by classmates to Lechedevirgen
Trimegisto

Figure 1.1. Lechedevirgen's bloody lip-sync to Agustín Lara's "Como dos puñales." *Inferno Varieté: Devoción*, 2014, Teatro de la Ciudad, Monterrey, Nuevo León. Photography by Herani Enríquez HacHe.

The sight of Lechedevirgen Trimegisto's bloody lip-sync performance of Agustín Lara's "Como dos puñales" is the iconic and signature image of *Inferno Varieté* (2014–2015). The artist enters the stage, dripping in sequins and bright patterns, with over-the-top gestures, and with their forehead pierced with needles as they look directly into the audience. As they make eye contact with their spectators, the music plays and Lara's voice sings:

Quiero sentirte mía, inmensamente mía
Que asesinen tus ojos sensuales,
Como dos puñales, mi melancolía.

(I want to feel you mine, immensely mine
Your sensual eyes slay,
Like two daggers, my melancholy.)

Lara's cover of this classic *bolero* conjures the dark romantic imagery of the piercing and painful seductive gaze of the feminine subject with eyes so dark that they slay like two daggers right through the man's melancholy, and that urge to feel the pain that might come with the risk of falling prey to her eyes. As the artist mouths Lara's melancholic lyrics, they carefully remove each of the needles piercing their brow, allowing blood to spill down their face and stain their clothing as it drips to the floor. A sensual ballad takes a sinister turn as each needle introduces a new stream of blood to the verses. If *Inferno Varieté* purports to be about homophobia and versions of Mexican masculinity, the audience is inadvertently trapped in confined spaces with the aftermaths of that violence. Lechedevirgen takes on a literal interpretation of the *bolero*, allowing their face to be stabbed by tiny daggers (needles) piercing their brow. Laura Gutiérrez describes this type of aesthetic as a mode of performance that deploys "parodic mimicry," which enables audience members to "identify at the same time they disidentify themselves." This, she contends, exposes the pervasive universal false narratives about gender and Mexicanness that circulate culturally and libidinally.[1] In this moment, Lechedevirgen invokes an aesthetics of risk, creating a political and social polemic about the social milieu's (dis)comfort, safety, and proximities to these "dangerous" issues, imposing fear that one cannot get *too* close.

The spirit of *Inferno Varieté* interfaces with these competing themes of counter identification that make the queerness of Lechedevirgen's transdisciplinary genre all the more provocatively queer. The imagery of the *puñal* as a uniquely Mexican term carries the performance and its audiences into an affective encounter with an aesthetics of risk. Both the verb form, *apuñalar*, meaning "to stab," and the noun, *el puñal*, literally translating to "dagger," connotatively endow the term with a violent

Figure 1.2. Lechedevirgen's bloody lip-sync to Agustín Lara's "Como dos puñales." *Inferno Varieté: Devoción*, 2014, Teatro de la Ciudad, Monterrey, Nuevo León. Photography by Herani Enríquez HacHe.

resonance. Metaphorically, though, the term *puñal* refers to the sneaky homosexual male who you can't turn your back on because he's lurking behind straight men, waiting to make his move—he just may come up from behind when you're not looking and "stick it in." This imagery of the *puñal* invasively and forcefully penetrating the body leans against Octavio Paz's cisheterosexist image of Mexicanness discussed earlier: the *gran macho* must never allow himself to be *rajado*, or cut open. If *Inferno Varieté* is a performance about Mexicanness and masculinity, the *puñal* is positioned as part of those Mexican forms of masculinity and masculine forms of Mexicanness. Moreover, by forming part of this spectrum of masculinity, the *puñal* inserts himself as a haunting figure within a broader constellation of erotic, virile masculinities that these narratives of Mexicanness necessarily demand to be manifested.

Accordingly, Lechedevirgen claims the *puñal*, not just as a sexual identity, but as a necessary political orientation toward a racialized and Mexicanized queer negativity in the face of quotidian violence against those at the bottom, not exclusively against sexual and gender minorities. The artist professes their alterity through the sexual embodiment of the figure of the *puñal*, who is now literally bleeding on stage. By adopting the *puñal* as a performative sexual politics, or what Laura Gutiérrez describes as "strategies of pleasure," Lechedevirgen performs a queer critique of daily encounters with violence that invasively and violently penetrate Mexican political and cultural landscapes by becoming that which poses a risk to the national and social collective.[2]

This chapter advances a critical turn in hemispheric Latinx American studies toward queer bodies that actively mobilize and *do* something with their sexuality in and among the topologies of theory and practice. Through contemporary performance art, I read for an understanding of the body and narrative, wherein the body reveals the flesh as script carried as a trace of the exposed bottom. I observe what I argue to be an intimate risky exposure of and to the othered body and public. This exposure signifies various risks and violences attached to bodies in their centering *as* performative entities or aesthetic matter. Performance, at times, undertakes a political act in constructing paradigms that make sense of the aesthetics, ethics, and politics of exposure explored throughout these pages. These paradigmatic shifts cast the body of the Other into a net of accessibility that, on a queer register, exposes the range of violence against the sexual body in a way that becomes *too* legible and yet still untranslatable—even to themself.

Performing the bottom from the bottom, as a bottom, attends to an idea that bodies have the capacity to challenge regimes of power and social norms by being positioned at the center of artistic and aesthetic practices as a locus for political and ethical discourses. This idea suggests that bodies wield the possibility of performing and conveying cultural memories of their violent and sexual histories across space and time, while making knowable the aesthetics, ethics, and politics of sexual alterity. In these crossings, the body becomes a rhetorical surface onto which other fantasies, fears, and discourses are projected and performed—perhaps that too is embedded in the risks taken before the artist's bloody body.[3]

This particular breed of reading trauma, however, has already been well documented in queer studies.[4] Over and above such analyses of trauma, queer performances just may implicitly commit their own acts of queer violence. These performative acts are ethically and politically charged, beckoning us to rethink how sexual bodies are conceptualized, but also misappropriated in the queer political and collective imaginary. Accordingly, this chapter proposes a reading of performance that highlights the risks of encountering or being exposed to the sexual bodies in question by thinking with how Lechedevirgen Trimegisto introduces a necessary trans intervention into *pasivo* masculinities as a xenogender artist, that is, a gender that cannot be contained or limited to *human* understandings of gender.[5] Rather, it is an "alien" (*xeno*) gender, one that is always already not human enough, nor does it strive to be, and thus is a gender nonconforming and nonbinary gender identity, experience, and performance.[6]

Enigmas in the Promiscuity of Art and Performance

Lechedevirgen Trimegisto was born and raised in Querétaro, where they continue to reside. After completing a master's degree in contemporary art and visual culture, as well as a degree in visual arts from the Faculty of Fine Arts at the Universidad Autónoma de Querétaro, Lechedevirgen formed part of the Thematic Network of the Transdisciplinary Studies of Body and Corporealities "Cuerpo en Red" of Mexico's National Council of Science and Technology (CONACYT). The artist's name is the condensation of the legendary figure of Hermes Trimegisto (father of the alchemists in classic antiquity) and a mythological substance capable of curing and transforming everything—that is, the source of eternal life, the philosopher's stone: *la leche de virgen* (the virgin's milk). The name itself is performative of the bodily and transcendental themes their work portrays. Parting from alchemy, the artist needed a name to camouflage themself. Since the start of their career as an artist, the content of their performances was always explicit, and nothing like they had done before as an art student. Presenting and debuting their performances in their hometown, where their family continues to reside, they were in search of a name that would protect their family's anonymity and themself. "Lechedevirgen" gave the artist access to perform at an underground level. With a name so unique and difficult to pronounce, audiences would remember the *performance*, but could not so easily recall the name of the artist. As such, the artist, their work, and the relationship configured with audiences underscore a disidentification strategy foregrounding the body as that which is the object of art—as opposed to the artist as an identifiable subject who could receive a direct address.

Collaborating with fellow artists, students from their performance workshops, choreographers, musicians, videographers, and religious practitioners, *Inferno Varieté* takes on, as the title of the piece suggests, a variety show aspect. I locate Lechedevirgen's work at the intersection of theater and performance art, wherein we observe accents of vaudeville, cabaret, burlesque, and variety shows in the structure of *Inferno Varieté* itself. The performance brings to the fore the influence of aesthetic genres that have often been historically considered forms of low or popular culture in comparison to the high culture of theater writ large by being painted as mere entertainment and devoid of conceptual or profound content and meaningful value. Lechedevirgen ultimately takes a queer camp approach to Mexican masculinity by making it so obsessively zoomed in, that its excess is not only palpable, but a very essential part of Mexico's cultural production. In her study of the performance of Mexicanidad in the work of *cabretta* Astrid Hadad, Laura Gutiérrez reminds us that in the Mexican context, a "camp sensibility *has to be political*."[7] She argues that these types of performance "critique the same cultural forms that both included her (as sexual object) and excluded her by historically denying women access to modes of representation."[8] Lechedevirgen approaches the sexual ecologies of violence related to masculinity and Mexicanness by creating a variety show in which the definitions of theater, cultural narrative, and experimental art can be problematized and extended through their critique of the body's own process of rupturing gendered performances of Mexicanness. In the artist's words, *Inferno Varieté* "recovers and reinterprets the theoretical and historical approaches of artists, activists, academics, and representative figures around the themes of masculinity, violence towards sexual minorities, gender performativity, decolonization, and body art."[9] Because *Inferno Varieté* has primarily been presented in museums, galleries, and forums, the recovery they describe in the performance is an apocryphal act contrasting these "formal" spaces with performances that explicitly problematize the formality of the theater through using the bodies as a locus for narrative to be produced. Moreover, the political charge to *Inferno Varieté* catalyzes art-based performance activism by using tropes of the theater to center these themes through the body.

Lechedevirgen's oeuvre finds its rich genealogy in *posporno* and queer art, intimately intertwined with Mexican mysticism and folklore, which sets their work apart from the more traditional or popular forms of Mexican contemporary art. Since the 1990s, Mexican art witnessed a change in tone, composition, and overall political message. While art critics have purported that most of the art since the 1990s is apolitical and devoid of Mexican culture, we can see a radical transition from object-based practices in painting to more action-based experiential pieces, such as *Inferno Varieté*.[10] Accordingly, the rise of the genre of "conceptual art" becomes relatively new to certain areas of Mexico. Yet the work of Lechedevirgen inserts itself at the interstices of theater and conceptual artistic practices. I would describe this theatrical contour as an extension of 1950s Mexican theater, in which theatrical works began to preoccupy themselves with social issues and realist aesthetics to construct a critical space from which to problematize, question, and examine cultural, economic, and political conditions. In this vein, theater and art have the capacity to bring varying anxieties felt at the national and local levels to the stage by conveying a theatrical and aesthetic critique of their political and social moments. As such, in Lechedevirgen's performances, audiences are confronted by the smell of sweat, the sensuous tactility of the body, the feeling of the heat of the space, and the visual encounter with human blood and bodily fluids; these sensorial and bodily materials are juxtaposed with established tropes of Mexican national and regional cultures as well as more controversial subjects, such as allusions to narco-warfare and the violence it engenders, religion, and Mexico's cult of death. This imbrication of body and the visuality of cultural narrative positions spectators in close proximity with social and political anxieties as they are carried out and experienced in the daily lives of Mexicans.

Shifting toward the pornograph as a methodological device, Lechedevirgen Trimegisto builds on and departs from queer frameworks already established within hemispheric Latinx American scholarship that address these themes, namely, what Uruguayan Fabián Giménez Gatto describes as *pospornografía*, to conceptualize Mexicanness through a hemispheric pornographic analytical lens. The *posporno* bears a tradition of being a countercultural movement, attempting to revolutionize the concept of pornography through deconstructive and poststructur-

alist practices—hence the name *posporno*, which signifies the condensation of poststructuralism into pornography. This paradigm critically
reflects on pleasure and pain and the idea that the violence performed
on the body functions as a possible tool for reimagining identity and the
body through a form of regeneration and sexual catharsis. As a deconstructive practice, what occurs through the *posporno* is a transformation of how we read libidinal economies in ways that do not necessarily
deconstruct gender and sexuality, but rather, transform the reading gaze
itself. Drawing on Jean Baudrillard, Giménez Gatto argues that the use
of *posporno* strategies "will attempt to force the obscenity that characterizes gender beyond the narrow definition of porn, the emergence of
new registers of sexuality that will not stop at the boundaries of the skin,
transgressing the codes of representation of the pornographic device."[11]
In other words, *pospornografía* approaches reading sex by addressing the
accessibility and proximity the spectator has to the body, while not shy-
ing away from the explicit, carnal, and savage characteristics of the sex
work itself. It is not about stripping away the excess of sexual images, but
rather moving beyond the expected male ejaculation, which has become
the pornographic image *par excellence*—though it is still there. Rather,
as Giménez Gatto explains, "Postpornographic bodies are penetrated
not just sexually, but also scopically; the voyeur is thrown into the body,
sucked into this drive of extreme visibility."[12]

Noting this context, I locate within Lechedevirgen's work the production of an *aesthetics of risk* veiling the nexus of exposure, sex, and death
explored throughout this book. By risk, I refer to a close proximity with
hazardous or toxic matter that prevails in the artist's scoring of their
body and the bodies of others. This risk is a two-way channel: first, the
artist faces *their own* risks through their performance. Their risks function as an ethico-political mandate based on an affective responsibility
of the artist to pose a *necessary* intervention in both public and private
spheres. Guillermo Gómez-Peña describes this necessary risk as a decolonial act for bodies that have become occupied territories—namely, the
queer, the brown, and the migrant:

> It's not that we are exhibitionists (at least not all of us). In fact, it's always
> painful to exhibit and document our imperfect bodies, riddled with cul-
> tural and political implications. We just have no other option.[13]

Gómez-Peña further describes this as a "matter of life and death" in the face of the "cloud of nihilism" haunting an artist.[14] The risks taken by an artist are acts of vulnerability and exposure. To riff off of Diana Taylor's reading of performance and transference, these risks are characterized by a willingness to expose oneself to the audience in an attempt to convey and transmit cultural narratives, but also a willingness to accept interference or intercepted signals.[15] Of course, while assessing risk, one cannot help but think about the worthwhileness of it all. And in some cases, not all risks are worth taking. But as we will see with Lechedevirgen, the artist still continues, negotiating adjustments, and redefining what may be considered a "risk" or otherwise.

The second channel of risk captures and converts the audience into a perceivably risky situation in relation to the artist and their object of performance. While the artist bears a social vulnerability to the audience (at the level of his own risk), the startling access we have to this vulnerability as an audience is, at times, disorienting and troubling. Given the amount of blood and bodily fluids used in Lechedevirgen's artwork, the work itself becomes a risky space in which to find oneself. Perhaps we've stayed too long and have gotten *too* close to the work. Jennifer Doyle theorizes this risky experience as feelings of "difficulty." She explains that through our endurance with the difficulty of an artist's body, "the work is hard because it forces us to keep company with vulnerability, intimacy, and desire."[16] This is mediated through close proximity with the artist, but also with the social and political implications that the body represents. It is a confrontation with latent forms of violence that encircle the artist, only to be redistributed back through the public by way of the queer artform.

This formation of a conspicuous violence represents a displacement and dislocation of the queer Other in response to narratives of sex and death, a concept that speaks to the figuration and disfiguration of the body. I seek a reading of queer aesthetics that names the risk of violence as a critical contour of the affective realization of bodies constructed by their attachment to the political structures of sex. In other words, the aesthetics of risk that undergirds the unwieldiness of Lechedevirgen's performance is bound to his desire for the translatability of violence. This act of translation poses the risk of lifting that opaque veil that keeps sex and death private, thereby making these forms of violence too exposed, too legible, and too intelligible—and I call this queer. The audience risks seeing too much, yet is irrevocably unable to un-see what has already been exposed.

Puñal Poetics from the Bottom

The artist's critical manifesto, "Pensamiento puñal" (*Puñal* Thought), polemicizes alternative, contradictory, and disparate ways of feeling and performing sexually through an aesthetics of Mexicanness. Deploying violent overtones provoked by the mere presence and exposure to a *puñal* reveals a political dynamic toward nonconforming bodies from the bottom that are perceived to be too dangerous. And danger is neither resisted nor avoided in Lechedevirgen's performances. Rather, they boldly underscore risk as a confrontational subject that is right there, in front of the face, unavoidable, and yet somehow still ignorable. Unexpectedly, however, the audience members have already been exposed upon even entering the space of the *puñal*, and risk becoming the ones *rajados* (cut open). A *puñal* also visually makes its presence known (literally and figuratively) in the normative thoughts of erotic masculinities. This manifesto thinks beyond the limits of mainstream gay and neoliberal queer politics that have yet to capture the unique Mexicanness of the *puñal* that makes them too dangerous—to others and themselves—by naming those distinctions in ways that are necessarily untranslatable. Yet, in the performance, audiences observe an artist attempting to perform translation. In their manifesto, Lechedevirgen writes, "From the cuts, from the cracks, the deeps cuts of a failed empire, from the mystical and ambiguous space of the fourth world, from intertextual cut-up of post-identities, because now you read me, this is what I am: text." Here, the body is presented as text, as a *puñal*. The *puñal* is text. Lechedevirgen writes for "el target," those "cuerpos ocupados" (occupied bodies), gender-divergents, trauma survivors, prisoners, the HIV-positive, and for all the names by which sexual minorities are known, that is, when their sexual Mexicanness is called out in terms that remain necessarily untranslatable as they roll off the tongue:

> Putitos, Vestidas con tacones de aguja, Chichifos deliciosos con vergas
> erectas empalmadas al abdomen, Mariquitas con angel-face, Jotas, Pelu-

queras, Vaqueros, Locas, Azotadas, Mayatones zumbantes, Muerdealmo-
hadas emplumados, Soplanucas sudados, Chácales rabiosos, Padrotes
jorobados, Machorras en motocicleta, Bigotonas, Traileras, Machas,
Marimachas, Tortilleras, Guerreras, Guardaespaldas, Quimeras, Trans_
formers, Operadas, Momias, Maniquís, Mantícoras, Nosferatus con
maniquiur.[17]

It is worth noting that throughout the text, Lechedevirgen strategically
deploys the *x* to neuter certain gendered terms in Spanish. Yet this does
not follow the same historical trajectory as the condensation of *x* into
"Latinx" in the United States; rather, the use of the *x* in the writings
of queer Mexican artists and activists predates the US Latinx usage by
over a decade. Artists were not seeking to "decolonize" the Spanish
language—as is often one of the dominant defenses of the *x* usage in
broader US Latinx spaces—rather, as Lechedevirgen explains, "We just
wanted to fuck with gender because as artists, we could. It kept the
[Spanish] reader on their feet." For artists like Lechedevirgen, this turn
in speech acts did not imply claims to identity, let alone decolonization. Rather, if anything, it implies the opposite: the failure of language
to be finite or bear any gendered truths about identity that could be
captured by any language in *this* world. In other words, it is the invocation of a xenogender—an alien nonbinary gender not limited to the
confines of language. They recalled in one of our interviews, "It's funny
how Americans want to fight over this [*x*] so much. But as artists, as the
activists, we've been doing this here already for a long time!" However,
the US usage of the term shifted, capturing the non-binariness of gender, which is truly necessary. Yet the term changed from what began in
the United States as an identitarian term for gender-divergent people
of Latin American descent in the diaspora, and was soon robbed from
queer Latinxs only to be appropriated as an umbrella term for entire
fields and bodies of work. The appropriation of our queer of color ver-
naculars into white mouths, even by white Latinos, is certainly not a
new project, just a lazy one. Nonetheless, Lechedevirgen cannot help
but chuckle and say, "The problem is, when it [the *x*] became a big thing
in the United States and got repackaged before they sent it back to us—
neoliberalism—people were trying to gender-neutralize everything!
Writing, '*sillx*' instead of '*silla*.' We were like, 'Are you kidding? *Sillx* with

an *x* doesn't even make sense! A chair doesn't have a gender!' But isn't that how art works anyways?"[18] Not only did it force untranslatability, but its ability to be unpronounceable indicated a level of impossibility for the human tongue to ever name aloud what we would call the Other, an alterity that is ultimately inaccessible in any human language.[19] In their manifesto, the artist proclaims,

> I am undercover *puñal*, insider-outsider, entering-leaving the flesh, the categories and capitalist presuppositions of the established order, because I'm an outlaw and refugee, because I don't fit their standards, because they forced me and I learned to be fluid, I learned to inhabit the limits, to keep myself vulnerable. . . . Because I'm infiltrated, because I'm a terrorist, because I traffic weapons with my body, because I traffic myself.[20]

The *puñal* is invasive and destructive. Their otherness is excluded from dominant forms of both political and libidinal economies. A *puñal* is always already feared and a body onto which other fears are projected. Their radical alterity incites violence, avoidance, and misunderstanding. Yet, even in that embodied violence and aesthetic of risk, they are also vulnerable. The *puñal* employs a passivity in which subjectivity becomes undone by the very instability of the identity-based discourses that they represent and call into question. The critique of politics brought forth by *Inferno Varieté* exposes a violently gendered constitution of the political landscape, imposed by the state, the institutionalization of narco-warfare, and even the complacency of private citizens—including other sexual minorities—who participate freely and willingly in these sexual systems of discipline and control.

The *puñal* is violently hyperaware of their dual status as that which is politically activating while also opening the body up to be inhabitable to violence. Lechedevirgen is diligent to articulate this, inviting necessary transgender and trans-gender critiques to be made about these forms of erotic masculinities:

> I am *Puñal* and wounded. Penetrator and penetrable. Body full of borders, of lines, of fissures and wrinkles. A cartography of sutures and scars, piece of flesh divided up by imaginary and tactile lines, intersectional, trans-border, subaltern.[21]

Repositioning the body to be bordered while also being a border subject makes space for the necessary trans gestures needed to critique how death operates queerly. Sayak Valencia argues that necropolitics produces violence against "minoritarian becomings," which she defines as "a process that does not essentialize identities but is performative; that is, one is not essentially minoritarian but *becomes* so."[22] As such, this process of "becoming"—Black, woman, trans, queer—does not translate to "a passive reproduction of subalternization but to the creation of other imageries and political potencies that build queer alternativities that create networks of affection and survival in highly normative and violent contexts."[23] Death's relationship to Mexico is gendered through the ways death follows and haunts trans and gender nonconforming lives and the lives of women. The dead are feminized, while their killers are masculinized. The *puñal* fucks with this dichotomy in a deeply Mexican way through linguistic performance of speech acts in deadly contexts—that is, thinking with Judith Butler, Valencia tells us, "radically denying them their 'right to appear.'" Accordingly, then, violence and death are indelibly intertwined in the "coloniality of gender."[24]

The presence of blood in Lechedevirgen's performance captures the representation of life and death in the same image. This use of blood and bodily material is consistent with hemispheric Latinx American conceptual art traditions—such as in the notable works of the late Cuban American artist Ana Mendieta and Mexican forensic artist Teresa Margolles—in which blood represents a magical and powerful element that may aesthetically evoke nonnormative sexualities, but only while simultaneously revealing the masculinist sexual violence that is converted into political structures. The body's contact with bloody material within the Latinx American aesthetic imaginary is certainly not new, as it dates back to Mesoamerican and pre-Columbian indigenous theological understandings of the body and bloodletting in which blood signifies a magical or alchemic substance, capturing the spiritual and physical materialities of the body into one substance. For the Nahua-Mexica, for example, blood sacrifice (including bloodletting—namely, human sacrifice) was one of the highest blessings and offerings to the celestial world. These ceremonial sites were part of the quotidian affairs of urban life, becoming part of the infrastructure of culture and society.

With Lechedevirgen's blood, the audience may encounter a living, breathing, mobile body, made of cells, muscles, and blood vessels. Their active bleeding on stage becomes a reminder that they can still shed blood. Yet the blood may also signify the real violence that is carried out against queer bodies and the sexual spaces they inhabit. This, of course, is complemented with the idea that the blood of gay men and queer artists in our post-AIDS and HIV moment is read as life-threatening. Their blood synchronously emerges as toxic matter, a risky substance, and a reactive agent. In this sense, the blood of the *puñal* that Lechedevirgen openly exposes to audiences also serves a material role to destabilize the power of masculinist discourse by weaponizing sexual otherness as a *puñal*, one that assaults or poses an aesthetic risk to the hegemonic and heteronormative image of Mexicanness consumed by national and public cultures.

Experimental artists like Lechedevirgen move beyond what is deemed comfortable, in favor of a difficulty that amplifies what Jennifer Doyle describes as "the absence of a disciplinary discourse on its value, and that has been aggravated by the fact that US institutions are wary of going near it."[25] This wariness carries across borders as we think from the position of a diasporic queer bottom studies, as it is a condition of the neoliberal institutionalization of body narratives in art. Doyle locates this difficulty in the work of American artist Ron Athey, which is apt in a reading of Lechedevirgen since the two experimentalists have collaborated in Lechedevirgen's hometown in Querétaro and Mexico City. These transborder artistic exchanges are already occurring. The work of difficulty in the Americas is a hemispheric feeling shared across experimental artists. What occurred with *Inferno Varieté* is uncannily similar to the treatment of Ron Athey for his *Four Scenes in a Harsh Life*.

Describing Athey's repertoire, Doyle writes, "We are given startling access to the body. The body is presented aggressively to the viewer. . . . Sexualized violence and corporeality are associated with a defacing, . . . [addressing] a latent social violence toward the body, furthermore, and link that violent defacing of the body with sex."[26] In this vein, Lechedevirgen's *Inferno Varieté* also features the rhetorical incorporation of a video of a young Ugandan man brutally attacked, alongside the body of the bloody *puñal*. The video necessarily produces an aesthetic critique of comfort and discomfort that makes the image difficult to digest, to make sense of, or even to overlook. The aesthetics of risk in the performance reach a boiling point in which the audience has already seen too much, but also, they can never un-see it. Their proximity is already tightened to the visual imagery of quotidian violence in the face of a queer person.

The aesthetics of risk that bring audiences "too close" to the *puñal* position the public in a difficult, disturbing, and yet vulnerably intimate relational proximity with the artist. That intimacy, then, continues, as the scene fades to black and opens to Lechedevirgen naked on the ground. In *Inferno Varieté*, the audience is faced with the Other. Yet, on a more sexual plane, to follow the flow of Doyle's vein of difficulty, the work curates an encounter for the site of sexual alterity through the body of the artist and collaborators. The role of nudity in this work draws clear ties to the sexualization of the body. Nudity is far from neutralized. Rather, as a matter of rhetorical performance, the materiality of the body introduces a necessary affective encounter with sexual embodiment and practice.

The rhetorical gesture in question is best exemplified in the third act of the *Inferno Varieté* series, *Enigma*, performed on January 28, 2015, at the Museo de la Ciudad in Querétaro. The sexualization of the artist's body, nudity, but also their performance of a gay man—all while informed by and subjected to the violence such a body experiences in its quotidian affairs—becomes literalized through sexual positionality. Lechedevirgen's exposed body is placed into a pillory and joins performance artists Crisna Donají and Roja Ibarra dressed as topless executioners, with one wearing a strap-on dildo. The bloody Lechedevirgen is then bent over, while still secured in the pillory, and Donají lubes up the dildo, inserts it into Lechedevirgen's anus, and begins to penetrate the artist repeatedly, thrusting harder and deeper. They scream loudly. Their voice echoes between sounds that could either be pleasure or pain. After this aggressive act of what could be perceived to be a form of public anal torture or a punishment, or even a public act of humiliation, Lechedevirgen is unshackled and left on the ground, as the executioners exit the scene. The artist tells me that it was an act of atonement.

As a *puñal*, this moment of gendered fuckery with anal punishment brings to the fore the duality of the bottom performance embodied by the *puñal*, who weaponizes that precarity in strategic and meaningful ways. Lechedevirgen writes,

To be abject, to betray my country, my government, my mother and my father's wishes, biology and genetics, academia and the fucking "Fine Arts," racism, classism, sexism, to say NO to being a Macho, because like the male goat, I only have my leg to the left, to not be a "real and straight man," to not procreate without creating, to not hit women, to not kill *jotitos*, to not know how to drive or ride a bicycle, to deny myself to reproduce systems of control over my body and life.[27]

These shared abject embodiments bring together the mixing and promiscuity of the *pasivxs* that wander throughout this book. The *puñal* ideology invoked by Lechedevirgen's manifesto provokes a reading of passivity that extends beyond the normative trajectories of reading most forms of mainstream queerness, *because* of the Mexicanness felt sexually through sexually violent and violently sexual words that demand sustained attention to larger issues at stake for performers exposed at the bottom.

Black Translations of Violence

Inferno Varieté includes a very questionable scene wherein the artist displays a viral video from social media of a young man being brutally beaten and burned alive on the street for his alleged homosexuality, days after the Ugandan parliament passed the Anti-Homosexuality Act of 2014, more widely referred to in the media as the "Kill the Gays bill." The anatopistic presence of the attack on the young Black Ugandan man in *Inferno Varieté* is as shocking and problematic as it is haunting and sinister. From a broader queer aesthetic imaginary, perhaps this visual reference could gesture toward an idea of a collective solidarity for the violence that occurs against the sexually oppressed across the global South. Yet, in one of our interviews, Lechedevirgen explains that their primary intent was to "translate" the visual aesthetics of sex-based violence into the Mexican context, wherein they find there to be a dearth of images of anything comparable in their own country. This advances a labor produced by the act of translation that may pivot from the intention of expressing solidarity and raising awareness. In this particular sense, translation becomes an act of exhuming the same imagery of brutality and violence always already stained by the bottom.

Such a project might even address an interdependent transcontinental relationship between violence, sexuality, and politics that is often
overlooked in Mexico's historical present, but not absent. Within the
same timeline, the capital's notorious gay neighborhood, the Zona Rosa,
had witnessed its own share of violent attacks against men in the area.
In the "gayborhood," during Gay Pride (which the city officially calls the
Festival por la Diversidad Sexual [Festival for Sexual Diversity]), we can
expect the crosswalks painted into rainbows and the streets lined with
rainbow banners with the official seal of the city at the center. Yet the
rise of sexual inclusivity in the nation's capital is part of larger attempts
at pinkwashing the parallel occurrences of state and local violence in the
name of social capital campaigns. In other words, beyond these rainbows, the Zona Rosa is also known for its reputation as the place where
sex, drugs, and dirty money coalesce. It is not regarded as the "safest"
place in Mexico City—with sex workers lining the streets all hours of the
night, club bathrooms occupied by drug dealers, men cruising, and the
sight of people overdosing on drugs and falling out of bars and pouring
into the streets. While its seediness is charming for some, local authorities have handled crime in the Zona as just part of its already perceived
delinquent subculture. A year prior to the Ugandan cell phone video,
several well-known businesses and people in the Zona were targets of
violent killings that occurred in public.[28] Within blocks of these attacks
are the Secretaría de Seguridad Pública del Distrito Federal, an agency
of the Ministerio Público for sexual crimes, and the Órgano Descon-
centrado de Prevención y Readaptación Social.[29] The interface between
these government agencies, the sexual culture of the Zona Rosa, and
these crimes raises questions about the intersectional violence that occurs within Mexico. However, the local authorities have dismissed these
attacks as the result of narco-related violence, with no mention in the
media of the possibility that these attacks could be linked to acts of sexualized violence or homophobia.[30] Given the sexual landscape, it would
be negligent to not consider the sexualization of the violence that occupies the quotidian affairs of Mexican life.

Overlapping narratives of drugs, violence, and sex are not easily sep-
arable in the context of Mexico or even in the broader global landscape
as we think about the assemblages of violence, sexuality, and the state.
The attacks in Zona Rosa could be read as a microcosmic representa-

tion of the sexualized spaces that become infiltrated and penetrated by masculinist systems of domination and power. These categories of identifiable tropes of negativity should not be regarded as isolated events. Rather, the intersection of these categories reflects what Mexican feminist cultural critic Sayak Valencia has described as "gore capitalism": the profitable enterprise of death as a money-making business, because we as a culture are consumers of gore at all levels, curated by those in power to benefit from this economic wealth—the state, the police, and *narco* cartels. What this creates, then, is a market-driven, hyper-consumerist, and hegemonic masculinist narco-state, which really began to take form in the late 1970s but has radically attained its monopoly of power in Mexico in the last couple of decades through profitable death.[31] The workings of masculinist institutions that have constructed spaces of violence wherein crime is committed against marginal bodies are not foreign to Mexico. Accordingly, violence, censorship, and the complicity of the state in these events, when thought about alongside Uganda, might point to a transcontinental experience in which homophobia and sexism dictate political narratives about the sexual economies of the body.

I am hesitant to make any overarching generalizations about the violence enacted upon sexual bodies across the divide of cultural contexts. Although we could witness similar instantiations of violence in Uganda and Mexico, these are two quite different histories and are not reducible to a singular narrative about sexualized violence. Rather, to borrow from Valencia's gore capitalism, the translation work that Lechedevirgen's performance purports to do localizes the aesthetic visualization of quotidian violence within the sociopolitical contexts that enable such landscapes to exist in the first place. Valencia argues, "Gore capitalism has infiltrated our lives and from our position as simple consumers/spectators we cannot isolate ourselves from that fact. Many of the phenomena that are daily for us are anchored in organized crime."[32] Accordingly, my own engagement with the work of Lechedevirgen Trimegisto necessarily emphasizes how the bodies of sexual minorities become central to the visual production and critique of the politics of death and national belonging, in which the Ugandan cell phone video is always already part of that critique. From Lechedevirgen's strategic use of bodies, I argue that the artist offers a necessary queer intervention in contemporary art by positioning the "body" as script: a locus from which narratives should be derived. They ultimately return us to the materiality of the body—including its fragility and blood—as artistic matter in and of itself.

Taking into account Lechedevirgen's intention to invoke the work of translation, I want to pause to think a bit with the etymological implications of attempting to invoke what the project of translation promises. Dating back to the fourteenth century, the verb "translate" signified "to remove from one place to another" and "to turn from one language to another," from the Old French *translater* and directly from the Latin *translatus* (carried over), serving as past participle of *transferre* (to bring over, carry over), from *trans-* (across, beyond) and *lātus* (borne, carried). The temporal lag of the grammar of what the act of "translate" purports to do (to bring over, to carry over, to remove from one place to another) cannot be ignored when thought alongside and through a Black body presented in suffering through the Uganda attack video that finds itself always already without the primacy of consent to be publicly displayed a screen. A Black body is being deployed as a translatory device that interpellates the young Ugandan man into the project of the grammatology of Slaveness: literally and figuratively to be brought over across the Atlantic border to perform various types of labor (physical, sexual, and symbolic).

The conversion of the Ugandan young man's body into a script distilled through the grammatological paratexts of Slaveness reduces the body in this performance down to basic nudity. Hortense Spillers distinguishes between "body" and "flesh" by contending that "flesh" is that which always precedes the body, or "that zero degree of social conceptualization that does not escape concealment under the brush of discourse, or the reflexes of iconography." In this sense, "flesh," which Spillers tells us may be thought of as a "primary narrative," aids in reading how historical trauma remains embodied within and contributes to how Blackness becomes both a symptom and constitution of the violence carried out against Black bodies. For Spillers, this is the result of an ontological process of "pornotroping," in which the body in suffering "becomes the source of an irresistible, destructive sensuality," while signifying an alterity that embodies "sheer physical powerlessness that slides into more general 'powerlessness,' resonating through various centers of human and social meaning."[33]

Suffering signals a sensual encounter with an alterity in the Other, in which the others are reconstructed and represented through exotic rumination and fantasy—making their suffering digestible and empathetic. Alexander Weheliye tells us that this type of pornotroping "reveals spectacularly how racial slavery and its afterlives in the form of the hieroglyphics of the flesh intimately bind blackness to queering and ungendering." He continues, "Usually these scenes are presented in the form of flashbacks and feature nubile black bodies in pain."[34] We may see how these flashbacks are conjured in the presentation and re-presentation of the video of the young Ugandan man's violent murder. The visual aesthetics at work in these memories and re-presenting are set in motion by a spectrality of historical violence that haunts the present in ways that may possess violent futures. At the center of the *ethos* of queer theory is a way of accounting for the not-fully-human or even the non-human—that is, the body's inability to inhabit and act on the libidinal currents that undergird all acts of political domination. Queerness, in this sense, flows into the currents that are occluded and masked by visual and textual renderings of the human aesthetic. The body's suffering is sensualized and converted into a sexual object. This sexual object becomes a political entity, precisely through what both that sexual object and the violence against it represent. I describe this nexus of sexual objectification and violence as necessarily queer—insofar as I understand "queer" to be defined as the capture and conversion of sexual practices into political structures. Moreover, if Blackness converts the human into the sexual not-fully-human or non-human, racialized bodies are not a protected category under the hegemonic masculinist regimes contributing to their death.

It is important to note that the violence that produces Blackness cannot be fully represented, either visually or verbally. Rather, it is either illustrated or textually represented as a sexuality or directly presented as violence in another register: one that is adjacent, such as the inclusion of the video of the young man in Uganda in *Inferno Varieté*. With the passing of a law sentencing homosexuals to death, violence against a minority population was vigorously incited and documentable, and the image remains readily accessible. Lechedevirgen's decision to include the video in *Inferno Varieté* was in the interest of translating the themes of violence and the state as they relate to sexual minorities, because, as they claim, such a clear and accessible image of this violence does not exist for Mexico.

As I continue contemplating the relationship between Uganda and Mexico, and truly between Blackness and Mexicanness, as a result of inaccessibility and the probable impossibility of speaking about queerness and queer politics in a Mexican context, I am struck by the difficulty of contextualizing and translating violence. Following this line of thought, then, including the video to correct the dearth of images of homophobic violence in Mexico seems like a difficult solution. Yet I contend that this concern with translatability is not necessarily about the translation of violence—aesthetic images of brutality and violence are already part of the Mexican national and collective imaginary. Rather, and more pressingly, I posit that it is the translation of *queerness*.[35] The juxtaposition of the violence against and alongside the bloody exposed body of the artist produces a difficult image. Its difficulty is shaded in by the dearth of images that capture queer violence in Mexicanness. The transcontinental reach of translation necessarily creates a fissure in narratives about violence that exposes the sexual structures in place that enable such violence to occur. This raises questions, then, about the impossibility of speaking about queerness and politics in a Mexican context. The difficulty posed by the video lies in the way images of violence in Mexico are tampered with or otherwise made inaccessible: missing students, uncounted corpses of women in the Sonoran Desert, mass graves of undocumented migrants, and mass shootings at gay bars.[36] The image of death is pervasive to the daily life of Mexicanness. It is at this point of difficulty that a queer performative intervention within *Inferno Varieté* takes form by forcing such questions to their limits.

Thinking with the grammatology of translation, importing the Ugandan body is a rhetorical device, and Blackness is interpolated into the libidinal economies of Mexicanness. Jared Sexton describes the libidinal economy as "the economy, or distribution and arrangement, of desire and identification (their condensation and displacement), and the complex relationship between sexuality and the unconscious." In other words, it is "the whole structure of psychic and emotional life."[37] Frank Wilderson expounds upon this: "It is linked not only to forms of attraction, affection, and alliance, but also to aggression, destruction, and the violence of lethal consumption."[38] The project of translation finds itself at these interstices by surrounding Blackness with what Wilderson describes as a "grammar of suffering" in which the body of the Slave (represented here by the Black Ugandan young man) is "generally dishonored, perpetually open to gratuitous violence, and void of kinship structure."[39]

The inclusion of this Black body in suffering does not foreclose ways of reading a hemispheric bottom and the forms of violence associated therein; rather, it galvanizes how this book accounts for the topologies of grammatological structures that always point toward a form of alterity that performs captiveness and Slaveness, and thus informing how one is to read the bottom in all its theoretical contortions. As such, as Amber Jamilla Musser rightfully argues, "To think with pornotroping is to acknowledge that some people circulate as highly charged affected objects, while simultaneously being positioned outside of the parameters of normative sexuality and subjectivity."[40] I localize my reading of Afropessimism alongside performance studies amid the theoretical waters that lead us to where we might wade in the viscosity of these performative utterances in the grammar surrounding sexually racialized/racially sexualized bodies.

Call Me *Joto*: Threatening Sex and Misrecognition

The role of identity within Lechedevirgen's work is a mode of exposing the instability of categorical identity markers. He destabilizes not only narratives about Mexicanness, but also narratives surrounding normative sexual diversity and practice within "safe zones" of exposure to sexual alterity. It is a mode of reading the subject against the grain to necessarily reveal the insufficiency of identity-based discourses to capture the messiness of human sexuality embedded in politics. In doing so, their performance functions as a critique of the production of power in the name of those identities. Lechedevirgen playfully resituates that overexposure to masculinity and sexual discourse. At work in *Inferno Varieté* is an exposure of the body for public consumption. It is an announcement of an identity-in-difference and positions the audience in an encounter with the sexual other. As such, Lechedevirgen performs a radical alterity.

Emmanuel Levinas describes an encounter with the Other through the figure of "the face." Lechedevirgen presents "the face"—a very bloody one—of their alterity from the positionality as an artist engaged in a bottoming performance. They create a space to look into the eyes of an other as the violence spills down their face. Lechedevirgen invokes a politics of relationality through a disidentification of the *puñal*, asserting alterity that cannot ever be fully realized or understood. They repeatedly, across their works, reject homonormative or even hipster permutations of a "queer" politics of free love. Rather, their sexual and political alterity as *puñal* is one resistant to being wholly calculated or grasped; after all, if we could understand the Other and know the Other, then that wouldn't be the Other. The ethical gestures at work in the queer formations of performance take into account the possibilities that emerge in thinking through the ways in which Lechedevirgen reveals an interdependent relationship between sexuality, violence, and the ethico-political. There is something risky about being this close to the *puñal*.

As the artist lies on the ground, they begin spray-painting their exposed body with a stencil that reads "JOTO," as the voice of undocumented Mexican poet Yosimar Reyes encompasses the space, reciting his poem "Quiero que me llames joto."[41] As the audio comes to end, Lechedevirgen pauses. They linger. Suddenly, the artist bursts into a frantic cry and pours the liquid remnants of a container on himself, violently erasing the JOTO markings from their body. In Yosimar Reyes's words, cited here in Spanish to preserve its rhetorical untranslatable intention,

> Quiero que me llames JOTO
> Pero no con coraje y odio
> Si no con amor y compasión
> Quiero que me quieras
> En español
> No quiero ser Gay o Queer mucho menos Xueer with an X
> quiero que tu amor sea tanto que hagas olvidar
> El rencor que le tengo a esa palabra

"Joto," which translates as "queer," "faggot," or "sissy" but also has an affective resonance that is not fully translatable outside Spanish, is imprinted onto the exposed body of the artist, a body covered in blood, carrying the embodied memories of trauma and violence enacted upon it. The word "joto" carries multiple registers of power when placed upon

Figure 1.3. Lechedevirgen painting "JOTO" on their body. *Inferno Varieté: Devoción*, 2014, Teatro de la Ciudad, Monterrey, Nuevo León. Photography by Herani Enríquez HacHe.

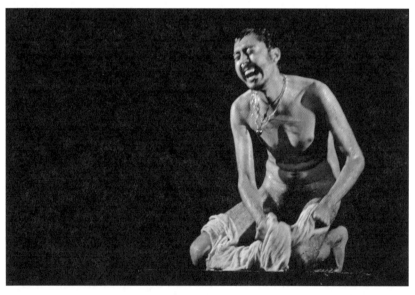

Figure 1.4. Lechedevirgen erasing markings. *Inferno Varieté: Devoción*, 2014, Teatro de la Ciudad, Monterrey, Nuevo León. Photography by Herani Enríquez HacHe.

the body. For Mexicans in the diaspora, like Yosimar Reyes, the term is endowed with new meaning and thus reclaimed as a theoretical, philosophical, and ideological possibility.

The first-person voice in this narration of the poem, speaking to the *tú* (you) subject, to "call me *joto*," interpolates the spectator into an encounter with the Other. This desire to be addressed, to be recognized, to be legible, but also to be untranslatable, performs a complex ethical interaction with the face of the other. The materiality of the body introduces a necessary affective encounter with sexual embodiment and practice. In the Levinasian sense of the encounter with the other through "the face," Lechedevirgen presents the bareness of "the face" from the position of their sexual alterity. For Levinas, the face is not any particular individual, but the very essence of the other human, prior to any cultural coding: "a bareness without any cultural adornment."[42] While Lechedevirgen invokes identity through self-identifying as a *puñal* and *joto*, these signifiers assert an otherness that cannot be fully realized, understood, translated, or recognized. After all, if we could understand the other and know the other, then that would not be the Other. I do not want to neglect that the poet writes this poem to his grandfather, making a demand of the gaze of generational masculinities that are erotically charged as they also and conversely are traumatically informed.

While *joto* is empowered with new resonance in today's tongues, it still labors with the residues of traumatic events. Hence, the aggressive and reactive erasure of the term from the artist's body. The term is thus capable of operating at both registers of empowerment and disengagement at the same time. I suggest that such a duality is a moment of what Judith Butler describes as "misrecognition," in which signifiers like *puñal* or *joto* are capable of being interpreted in a number of divergent and conflictual ways. As Butler explains, "If that name is called, there is more often than not some hesitation about whether the temporary totalization performed by the name is politically enabling or paralyzing, whether the foreclosure, indeed the violence, of the totalizing reduction of identity performed by that particular hailing is politically strategic or regressive or, if paralyzing and regressive, also enabling in some way."[43] Effectively, then, while the categories of *joto* and *puñal* may be deployed as political and performative identities that are central to the artist's aesthetic critique of the violence enacted by hegemonic masculinity, these identities are always already characterized by the risk of a passive vulnerability. These sexually identifying terms are imbued with and incite violence, even in their reclamation. In turn, Lechedevirgen's performance of the *puñal* and *joto* reveals the instability of identity-based discourses to "properly" name those sexual bodies who suffer under the quotidian violence that paints the Mexican political and social landscapes.

These gestures capture what José Esteban Muñoz describes as a disidentificational mode of reading subject formation, in which performances like *Inferno Varieté* "transform a cultural logic from within, always laboring to enact permanent structural change while at the same time valuing the importance of local and everyday struggles of resistance."[44] In other words, what emerges is a strategic queer process that neither assimilates nor opposes, but rather, reimagines ways of negotiating power. Lechedevirgen's project underscores how violence against the bodies of sexual minorities becomes central to the representation and critique of Mexicanness.

The audience comes face to face with Lechedevirgen's otherness through an encounter with their sexual embodiment: they are exposed to his own exposure. They do not attempt in any way to sterilize gay male sexual practices nor to hypermasculinize the image of male homosexuality by making themself the *activo* or top in these interactions— which has become a common trope in Latinx American representations of gay men, wherein the top in male-to-male sexual relationships retains a sense of passability within the cultural coding of accepted gendered and sexualized political practices. The act of being penetrated on stage works on two levels: first, Lechedevirgen reminds us that the *joto*, *puñal*, *maricón*, and *homosexual* has anal sex, and that men bottom—and here is the presentation of his anus as a confrontation with those forms of sexual alterity. There is no undoing of this process. This performance is not a redemptive or decolonial practice: no un-traumatizing or un-fucking can and will ever occur once already fucked.

Lechedevirgen mobilizes other bodies to do the work of critique and knowledge production. These transnational and transcontinental presences, however, tear into constellations of representational violence in the historical present that encircles the livelihood and longevity of bodies that are always already marked as death-dealing. The body of the young Ugandan man bears the weight of translating the indelibly intertwined narratives of violence, sexuality, and politics. And, through the audible voice of queer undocumented poet Yosimar Reyes, the artist allows the voice from the Mexican diaspora to narrate feelings of trauma and sexual alterity. Nonetheless, how might we attempt to read an artist's body that is meant to be enigmatically abject, among this amalgamation of other abjective bodies (re)traumatized in these acts of exposure? To begin answering this question, we must return to the iconic image of the bloody *puñal*.

Overexposed Publics: A Body Too Risky

Inferno Varieté's last act, *Actos de fe* (Acts of Faith), was performed on June 19, 2015, at Museo Universitario del Chopo, an institution of the Universidad Nacional Autónoma de México (UNAM) in Mexico City, as part of the annual Festival Internacional por la Diversidad Sexual. The room was entirely packed, with over two hundred audience members in attendance. By this time, Lechedevirgen's work had gained a significant amount of popularity, so the large audience was not surprising. The artist took the stage and began performing their famed lip-sync to "Como dos puñales" by Agustín Lara, but this time without their forehead pierced. Unlike every prior performance, not a single drop of blood was shed during that entire performance at the Museo del Chopo. Perhaps it was intentional, I thought. The artist retained the nudity, so the omission of blood was particularly curious. It seemed like such a minor detail at the time, but its absence became confusing and began to take on tremendous significance. The images did not produce the same affective experiences in me as they did in prior performances—it felt incomplete.

According to the artist, thirty minutes prior to their performance, they were informed by the museum's director of visual arts that they would not be allowed to bleed on stage or use actual human blood during their performance.[45] Given Lechedevirgen's portfolio, including photos and videos of past performances of *Inferno Varieté*, surely the museum officials would be well aware of the aesthetic of the artist's repertoire. The artist was surprised by the prohibition. The museum officials explained that they were under the impression that it was paint or fake blood in the photos and the artist would have needed to file a petition to receive special permission to use human blood, even bleeding their own.

Figure 1.5. Lechedevirgen lip-syncing to Agustin Lara's "Como dos puñales." *Inferno Varieté: Actos de fe*, 2015, Museo Universitario del Chopo, Mexico City. Photography by Herani Enríquez HacHe.

The Universidad Nacional Autónoma de México has a policy requiring special permits for the use of such "hazardous materials" within university properties. The artist and their team responded that they were not made aware of these policies prior to the event by either the museum or the festival organizers.[46] But no exception was made for Lechedevirgen to perform the piece as it was intended. Faithful to their commitment to present the audience with the face of systemic violence in real time, they let themself perform under the censorship.

I suggest a reading of this moment as an act of prohibition that becomes part of the performance in and of itself, and perhaps the most appropriate intervention to be made in the last act. The censure of their performance ruptured through as the result of the risky exposures present within *Inferno Varieté*. The action on the part of the museum inadvertently produces an extra-performative act transcending the original performance that the audience views on stage. As such, the absence of blood signals a performance occurring outside the frame, beyond what can be curated on stage. The performance in question, then, the prohibition, is intimately in concert with acts of censorship: an act of regulating a dangerous body before it can expose itself too much. In the interest of "protecting" the audience from "hazardous materials," the decision on the part of the museum officials to prohibit Lechedevirgen from bleeding affirms the claims I have made about the weaponization and risk factor attached to the artist's body as a *puñal* and *joto*, but also as a figure of vulnerability whose risk of being exposed can be controlled by the bureaucratic machine of the state.

The blacklisting of Ron Athey that resulted from *Four Scenes in a Harsh Life* set a dangerous precedent for how bodies, particularly queer bodies, are to be acceptably presented in the public sphere to be considered "art." By that logic, high culture profoundly asserts that art should not risk the lives of its audience. The artist is not the problem; their body as a contagion and death sentence is. The two artists have collaborated several times in Mexico, reflecting that history of the inherited violence that comes with queer performance art. The ability to keep the body contained becomes prescriptive to the ways queer history is legible or accessible.

The *puñal* and *joto* both straddle risk and the political. Lechedevirgen's body, most significantly their blood, possesses the qualities of being politically activating while simultaneously operating as an open threat to the public imaginary, as observed by this interaction at the Museo del Chopo. To think about this aporetic, dare I even say paradoxical, constitution of the *puñal* and their bodily substances—blood, urine, and so forth—it is worth articulating Jacques Derrida's *pharmakon* as it relates to the ambivalent movement of the substance itself—that is to say, the threatening detours a substance may take when doubling as "both remedy and poison":

> If we didn't have eventually to come to recognize it as antisubstance itself: that which resists any philosopheme, indefinitely exceeding its bounds as nonidentity, nonessence, nonsubstance; granting philosophy by that very fact the inexhaustible adversity of what funds it and the infinite absence of what founds it.[47]

Since the double meaning of the *pharmakon* is incapable of being separated, then it is unnecessary to master its ambivalence and, furthermore, "even beyond the question of pain the pharmaceutical remedy is essentially harmful because it is artificial."[48] The *pharmakon* as remedy is as unnatural as poison because it is disruptive to the normative trajectories of life itself. As such, the unsubstantial and artificial externality of the *pharmakon* lies in its ambivalent ability to affect and infect. In the case of Lechedevirgen's embodiment of the *puñal*, the bloody substance of said body riffs with Butler's claim to the aporetic contours of such signifiers. The blood shed by the *puñal* is emancipatory (medicine) while also bearing the possibility and impossibility of being damaging and dangerous to the existence of life itself (poison).

Jacques Derrida opens a semantic space for these bodily signifiers to read the reactionary treatment against Lechedevirgen's "dangerous" blood by the museum officials as a form of what Mel Y. Chen has described as "toxic affect," or the human hierarchies that form around the treatment of toxic matter. Chen argues that, on one hand, a toxin threatens, but it also gestures, directs, and allures the animate subject that absorbs it; though it is not alive, a toxin incites fears of mortality and death. The concern with the use of human materials—in this case, human blood from the artist—as something that requires special permission is a concern with protecting the illusion of public safety, as if the audience could be protected from the discourse itself. Chen argues the productivity of the affective implications of the toxic within methods of queer reading.[49] The bloody naked body of a sexual minority comes to be treated as a dangerous object that arouses the possibility or threat of death. As a result, the audience must be "protected" from such materials: the body of a *puñal*. However, toxic matter and substances as affective triggers are not "containable or quarantinable" and, because of this, they more readily appear as a threat, rather than poise their ability to generate movement, to agitate, to confront, to provoke shifts, and to gesture.[50] The material and symbolic presence of blood in Lechedevirgen's performances through the artist and the visual representation of real violence unfold visceral responses in spectators and participants: an intense interiority and exteriority that simultaneously contextualize and humanize those moments of violence.

This begs the question, then, Whom is the museum protecting? Historically, museums were not created for the poor or the uneducated. So a more accurate question would be, Who is *worth* protecting? This is a question about audience that gives important meaning to the fact that *Inferno Varieté* has been primarily performed in galleries and museums. While these spaces in Latinx America have become more receptive and inviting to experimental art, the work of Lechedevirgen functions more as an act of trespassing. The political act of trespassing provokes a visibility of dominant structures, which can then be mapped onto social and political spaces. They impose their own toxic matter in spaces that are meant to be protected from such confrontations, thus implicitly rebuking systems of power that seek to establish control of bodies, such as requiring that the artist have "special permission" to bleed their own blood. The relationship between censorship and toxicity really depends here on the audience and becomes a question about spectatorship. The idea is that high culture cannot actually get exposed to the toxicity and must be protected from toxic matter by any means necessary. In other words, in the case of the performance at the Museo del Chopo, the show can go on, as long as it does not affect those in and with power.

Inferno Varieté provokes an aesthetic strategy of violence that often goes unrecognized, disregarded even, or at the least ignored. The interdependent relationship between violence, sexuality, and the state is excessively prevalent and yet underexamined. Censorship or not, one only has to look through the recent history of cases of violence and death in Mexico to see this relationship. In other words, Lechedevirgen's body became *too* risky for the national stage that the university museum represents.

Lexical Power of the Negativity of the *Puñal*

Lechedevirgen Trimegisto accesses another lexicon of power within discourses on queer negativity, drawing upon an archive of affectively abject experiences derived from narratives of trauma that threatens sexual bodies. But *Inferno Varieté* does not embody any kind of project of nation building. While Lechedevirgen may gesture to certain elements within their work as points of difference from a "native" or more "authentic" form of Mexicanness and Mexican sexuality, these identifying tropes are never anchored in any sort of nation-building project. The presence of established tropes of Mexican national and regional cultures may be looked upon nostalgically, but not as a means of returning to or reclaiming those ideologies, or even of "queering" them. Rather, they generate a narrative of death that accompanies these landscapes—a narrative that emphasizes the idea of there not being an origin to return to, nor a future that could ever be promised in the first place. These references within the performance are sobered up by an implicit and historical recognition and reminder that sexual minorities tend to be excluded from these cultural spaces. The insistent emphasis on the exposure of and to the sexual body, through nudity and blood alike, elicits a desiring gaze that interrupts, diverts, and overtakes the sublimation of corporeal desire into national desire.

As a *puñal* in the bottom of Mexicanness, Lechedevirgen performs a queer terrorist act as a central feature of the *puñal* and the precarity of what the blood of a sexual minority symbolizes in the neoliberal arena of the nation-building project. The otherness Lechedevirgen embodies and exhibits within their performance is more than provocative: it is read as confrontational. The sight of their bloody, exposed body is not just shocking, nor is it merely an aesthetic or sensationalized enhancement to the performance; rather, it reflects a critical encounter with the aesthetics of *risk*. Their body proposes a risky proximity to the sexual other. Exposure to human blood and the exchange of bodily fluids during a public performance are unsanitary, but also address broader public health concerns. Nonetheless, their blood comes in direct contact with other artists and audience members during their performances. In one of the acts, the artist dances with and kisses audience members, while their face is covered in their own blood. On a surface level, the level of risk I am describing does not appear too obvious. Audience members seem to receive the performance well and no one appears to be too uncomfortable while participating. Yet, as I have described, the *puñal* mounts that live wire crossing political activation and the precarity of impending violence.

The specters of violence haunting political and artistic stages enable acts of censorship within the national and collective imaginary by the institutionalization of narratives about social inclusivity and social capital in the name of the nation-building project.[51] The agenda at the center of the work by experimental and underground artists in Mexico like

Lechedevirgen is to stage the normalcy of the complicated culture of violence and death that already permeates the quotidian lives of Mexicans. Moreover, this work magnifies it to the degree of the fetish it has already become and that necessarily begs closer analysis. The culture of death as a Mexican national totem is taken for granted as part of the cultural fabric, and, as a result, is not regularly questioned or problematized. Instead, narratives of inclusivity and sexual diversity overshadow loss and death tolls.

Inferno Varieté refuses to conform to the homonationalist project of folding sexual minorities into the nation-building project—such as through the banal pursuit of same-sex marriage. Rather, as a sexually charged "terrorist," Lechedevirgen hijacks audiences to be visually assaulted by and exposed to a heavily sexualized image of death's Mexicanness. I want to note that this work is not dystopic or just merely outright pessimistic with regard to sexuality and queer politics. Lechedevirgen refuses to be captured by the normative trajectories of how sexual bodies should possess Mexicanness, by problematizing and extending the category through a resistance-based sexual politics felt in their repertoire. Audience members attending the annual Festival Internacional por la Diversidad Sexual at the Museo del Chopo who seek in *Inferno Varieté* something like a literal story about homophobia in Mexico are somewhat challenged or disappointed because the artist challenges normative ideas about how homophobia is read.

Lost in the criticism of homophobia is a close reading of the inherent homoeroticism at the center of those violent encounters. In the contemporary state, as Achille Mbembe argues, "the ultimate expression of sovereignty, to a large degree is in the power and the capacity to dictate who may live and who must die. . . . To exercise sovereignty is to exercise control over mortality and to define life as the deployment and manifestation of power."[52] Lechedevirgen thus produces a spatial experience to engage with how we are exposed to such a necropolitical experience. The performance space represents what Mbembe describes as the "death-worlds" of the "living dead," to position a reading of the relationship between sex and death in Mexican cultural production, dovetailing with Mbembe's concern with the figures of sovereignty whose central project is "the generalized instrumentalization of human

existence and the material destruction of human bodies and populations."[53] As such, *Inferno Varieté* looks toward how the disposability
and erasure of bodies become a queer issue: the idea that certain bodies
are marked as determinedly marginal because they refuse to participate
within the normative workings of the state, has been and continues to
be a queer issue.

The restrictions imposed on Lechedevirgen's body, prohibiting them
from bleeding their own blood without special permission, underscore
the attempts made to regulate the image transmitted and received by
using the body of the sexual other as an object that can be manipulated
or tampered with to disseminate the propaganda of the state. However,
for those, like myself, familiar with the work of Lechedevirgen, such
a controlled omission produces a sense of exclusion—it is an imposition on our access to the body and an interference with our experience
with the artist. And our experiences are sexual ones. We engage in a
sexual act through our own voyeuristic urges to access information
from their body. Through the sexual tropes informing Lechedevirgen's
work, they position their body to be penetrated, not only by Donají's
dildo, but by our own spectral curiosity with their body. The interference on the part of the museum officials regulates the image within the
normative narratives about the sexual labor of the artistic project cri-
tiquing homophobia: the supposed ejaculatory ending we have become
accustomed to expect of sexual images. Instead, a sanitized image is
enforced as a more acceptable form of queerness to which the public
can be exposed.

As I describe earlier, Lechedevirgen's decision to include a brutal
video of an attack in Uganda in *Inferno Varieté* was in the interest of
translating the themes of violence and the state as they relate to sexual
minorities, because—as they claim—such a clear and accessible image
of this violence does not exist for Mexico. Yet this is due to the fact that
other images of violence would have been tampered with and thereby
available only in hindsight. Rebecca Schneider has argued that the explicit body in performance, like that on display in *Inferno Varieté*, "is
foremost a site of social markings" wherein we begin to have the faintest
glimpse of the "ghosts of historical meaning, markings delineating social
hierarchies of privilege and disprivilege."[54] In Lechedevirgen's oeuvre, as
in the body of works explored throughout this book, the spectrality of

these markings encircles, haunts, and presses on those difficult affects around what Leticia Alvarado so poignantly describes as "those uneasy feelings around the successes of national incorporation or easy assimilation [that], ultimately, wail against respectability politics."[55]

To use an example within the larger Mexican cultural historical context, we could recall the afterimages of the 1968 Tlatelolco massacre, in which the killing of an estimated thirty to three hundred students and civilians by military and police on October 2 in the Plaza de las Tres Culturas in Mexico City, simply do not exist.[56] The death toll does not have a clear result. To this day, what happened that night remains unresolved. However, the documented images that have been curated for the public are the images of the 1968 Olympics hosted in Mexico City. Fast-forward over forty years, as I discuss in the introduction, on the night of September 26, 2014, forty-three students from the Escuela Normal Rural de Ayotzinapa went missing in Iguala, Guerrero. They continue to be unfound, and human remains that have surfaced since remain to be identified. A 2015 investigation speculates about what happened that night, but much is left unknown, and even more so, unseen.

As such, it is indeed difficult to produce an "appropriate" image of homophobia in Mexico when other images of historical violence continue to be tampered with or otherwise pinkwashed to preserve an illusion of the totality of the nation in the name of inclusivity and social progress. What came out of the 1968 Tlatelolco massacre is a precedent that assumes that masses of bodies can be disposed of without any intervention from the state, much as we witnessed in the disappearance of the forty-three Ayotzinapa students. This describes an aesthetic and political pandemic. There is no consistency in determining which bodies are worth protecting: from small-scale efforts like protecting a museum audience from the blood of Lechedevirgen to calls for the national protection of a group of bodies from certain forms of violence. This inconsistency describes the daily violence of Mexico.

Through performance, we feel the tensions of this landscape. In these works, they become sexualized to localize the intimacy we have with violence. Moreover, sex reaffirms our thirsty desire to confront and see what is often hidden away from the public eye. Sex demands an undressing and vulnerability to expose certain truths. Surely, these are performances about homophobia. But what does that statement even mean?

These are not performances about homophobia in any traditional sense of being "about" something: they do not tell a story, nor do they memorialize the fallen homosexual. Instead, they absorb us into the structure of the performance to reframe any attempts to contextualize the narrative without our own social milieu. This is how the performance can do the affective work that needs to be done. These are not political acts, but rather sexual interventions.

.

2

After *Vampiro*

Fucking Like Adonis García

The Secretaría de Cultura del Gobierno de México and the Instituto Nacional de Bellas Artes (INBAL) lament the passing of Luis Zapata Quiroz, who died this Wednesday, November 4, at the age of 69.

This recognized writer was a notable translator, playwright, director of film and theatre; moreover, through his work, he opened the path for the visibility of LGBTTTIQ movements in the country.

El vampiro de la colonia Roma (1979) is one of his most-read works in Mexico, the United States and Latin America, including various translations to other languages, published in English under the name *Adonis García: A Picaresque Novel.*
—In Memoriam: Luis Zapata (1951–2020)

"Fuck! Of course, *vampiro* still dies in the end," I solemnly whispered to myself as I read this press release featuring the headline "Writer Luis Zapata Dies, Icon of Contemporary Literature," at the rise of the global COVID-19 pandemic.[1] I also could not stop thinking about how this is an official press release on a government website. Zapata is almost effectively formally recognized by the nation and state as canonical. Moreover, one of his perviest novels, about an anti-patriotic gay prostitute, is hailed as an international treasure. It would appear that only in his afterlife could he be worthy of being inducted into the "official" Mexican literary canon, in the company of other great men like Salvador Elizondo, Carlos Fuentes, José Gorostiza, and Juan Rulfo, among others. Every once in a while, other men fucking men also entered the boys' club: Salvador Novo, Amado Nervo, Xavier Villaurrutia, Carlos Monsiváis, to name a few. But Luis Zapata, the famed gay writer, is now truly felt to be in a league of his own in comparison to his literary counterparts. It is possible, then, that

65

he and his work would be remembered by readers under the influence of the state's performative bereavement. In the press release, Lucina Jiménez López, general director of INBAL, is cited as saying, "Luis Zapata opened doors to sexual diversity and liberation through his literature and contributed to the rise of independent cultural movements in Mexico." My cringe tightened to think of Zapata and his characters being likened to the Mexican state's neoliberal agenda of *diversidad sexual* (sexual diversity), which ultimately replaces individualized sexual identities—straight, gay, lesbian, bi, and so on—with an umbrella term collapsing the distinction between heterosexuality and otherwise. This consequently inhibits a necessary critique of heterosexuality if it technically does not exist under the banner of the nation-state's social capital surrounding sexual culture. Yet the secretary of culture, Alejandra Frausto Guerrero, on the other hand, describes the late author as a "pioneer of LGBT+ literature in Mexico" and also a "creator of experimental [*experimentales*] and emotive novels, who will be remembered for the brilliant *El vampiro de la colonia Roma* and the monumental *En jirones*."

This description resonates with a version of Luis Zapata and his writing that I had also experienced. Here, the dual meaning of both "to experiment" and "to experience" evoked in the secretary's description might be the most apt description for how Zapata uses language and literature to experiment with how readers experience text, characters, and even themselves. Zapata is associated with affecting the reader with profound experiences. These are also felt by the state, but it seems only posthumously, when at one point (and still), the characters he created are from the most bottom parts of society that would agitate the state and actively say, "Fuck you!" to the government—as expressed by the protagonist in his famed and celebrated gay picaresque novel. The novel has long been regarded as a canonical work in Latinx American LGBTQ+ literature for decades, being the first Mexican novel with a very openly and unapologetically sexually active gay protagonist. This is one of the first novels in Latinx America in which a homosexual protagonist speaks so explicitly, openly, and mostly proudly, and understands his subject formation explicitly by identifying with gay sex. On a literary level, the novel is narrated through a series of stories in a first-person stream of consciousness, presented to the reader as a transcription of what appears to be an oral interview of sorts.

Each chapter is listed as a *cinta* (tape). Scholars and readers have interpreted this as evidence that the book is a type of testimony, interview, or confession. The form of the novel itself is unique and performative of this interview style: it is fragmented and broken, literally with unexplained holes and gaps in the printed text (perhaps suggesting an interviewer or listener, but also maybe he could be talking to himself), no capitalization, and no punctuation. It is speculated that the novel had been derived and inspired by Zapata's own conversations and interviews with a sex worker he befriended in Mexico City. It is never explained, but what remains significant is that it is a story read aloud.

The narration follows a very nonchronological narration of the alleged "life story" of Adonis García. There is no plot. Yet that is beside the point to be made about *El vampiro de la colonia Roma*. This chapter argues that the novel, or rather the *protagonist*, does something to the reader that cannot be solely captured by more traditional forms of literary analysis. It was obvious that the character of Adonis García became a central stake in mourning his great author. As such, the word *experimental* could not be more appropriate to describe what happens when the reader is exposed to Adonis García. It is an experiment of a novel that forces an experience with the characters as if they were to affect us in our material worlds.

This chapter reads the bottom in relation to the aesthetics, ethics, and politics of Mexicanness conjured by the sexualization of the national consciousness through gay sex. On the surface, *El vampiro de la colonia Roma* tells the fragmented life story of a gay prostitute from the US/Mexico border living and cruising in 1970s Mexico City. The significance of just these few details already speaks to why this unique novel becomes such an important text for queer Latinx readers, not just on a literary level, but also on a sexual one: the book is regularly seen displayed in adult shop windowfronts in Mexico City's Zona Rosa. I propose that if we read against the primacy of *fucking* that guides this book, Adonis's shared fictional—but also highly probable and realistic—sexual stories throw the results of this aesthetic nexus of politics and sex into sharp relief.

In the wake of the author's death, I read through various commemorative think pieces, social media posts, and responses from other queer Mexican and Latinx American writers. While everyone lamented the loss of a hero in queer literature, the vast majority of these pieces turned to his seminal groundbreaking gay picaresque novel. In these reflections, people—mostly gay and queer Latinx men—nostalgically spoke of the protagonist with such fond melancholy, recounting their cherished memories of reading *El vampiro de la colonia Roma*, the impact the novel had on them, and even some of their favorite quotes. US Latinxs reminisced about their visits to Mexico City, recalling the same sights and sounds they shared with Adonis García. Yet, surprisingly, the majority of these reactions seem to grieve a character, rather than the author. Luis Zapata made an impact through the ways his characters affect their readers. That November 2020, author and character seemed to have died together. And it is so that, fuck, of course, even the *vampiro* still dies in the end.

Adonis García advances the sexual imagery at stake through his practices, worldview, and, most vitally, the stories he tells about them. Adonis García's character could be described as perceptively invincible, immortal, and unstoppable, and readers found themselves mourning a character who seemed infinite. As I describe in the introduction, the Mexican Nobel laureate Octavio Paz warns against a *pasivo* positionality of being fucked, invoking fears of being violated and humiliated. Yet queer theory and alternative cultural narratives offer an intervention in such a fearful reading of Mexicanness from and through the positionality of the *pasivo*. Thinking through the bottom as a *pasivo* who engages in penetration, if even for the sake of passivity, then sex after *vampiro*, after fucking, and after his signified death, I propose a reading of bottoming that captures the deadly rectal plane that deconstructs and exposes the limits of the oppositional cisgender top-bottom binary projected and performed through the gay male body. In doing so, the passive bottoming underscores the different ways gendered and sexual practices could orient the body, including those that gesture toward a self-pursuant annihilating ideology of the national subject rooted in a desire to be exposed. As a writer, Luis Zapata reimagines Mexicanness through writings on sex, exhibiting a subjectivity constitutive of the "fuck" rhetoric espoused by Paz that I describe in the introduction: one thwarting the body and the state toward their own finitude, enacting a passivity revealing an end of Mexicanness.

Readers had different and conflicting interpretations about *who* Adonis García is. He is presented as an enigma; by their own individualized narratives given to Adonis, readers could collectively mourn a character that was always already created to do something to them. But this is grief for the death of a fictional person, a figure who possesses his own competing views of who he is, or who he might be, or may become next. This is made even more apparent through his use of Mexico City's street slang of the time. Adonis's speech reveals the realities of being poor, uneducated, and perhaps also living with untreated syphilitic insanity and maybe other undiagnosed sexually transmitted infections—he is never exactly clear—in addition to untreated depression and suicidal ideation. Nonetheless, these rhetorical choices on a textual level coincide with the class differences between those in power and the sexualized Other—which queer Latinxs have been able to vicariously experience through their encounters with this character. The performativity of language in the realm of Adonis García thus becomes an event of a performance that has the ability to weave together the political and sexual through literary commentary and the body's relationship to the characters. *El vampiro de la colonia Roma* is arguably a hemispheric polemic for sex, negotiating a sexual crisis to consolidate an understanding of Mexicanness and sexual sovereignty that consequently roused parts of the sexual revolutions in late twentieth-century Mexico.

Two main ideas became clear in the wake of Luis Zapata's death. First, readers had been affected by Adonis García. Second, and perhaps most salient in this moment of grief, we each experienced a *different* Adonis. Exactly which Adonis García are we mourning, then? *El vampiro de la colonia Roma* is a simple book but left with a plentitude of gaps that have been filled with different fantasies and ideas of who Adonis García is—what he might look like, what his chest might smell like, what his cock might feel like, what his cum might taste like. The protagonist leads the reader on a sexual escapade in which the act of reading itself becomes a sexual experience as if we, too, are fucked by Adonis, like his many satisfied clients. Yet there is no definitive image or sustained description of Adonis García in the novel. In a close reading of Adonis García, I consult cover art, the racialization of Adonis García by and for US Latino gay men, the inspired experimental film *Siempre Sí* (2019) by Chilean author Alberto Fuguet, and of course, my own analysis of *El vampiro de la colonia Roma*. This chapter sketches the theoretical coordinates of a critique of the penetration paradigms that signify how one performs an aesthetics of the national consciousness that advocates not apologizing for wanting to fuck or to be fucked. Adonis García brings to light the political consequences one might face as the result of the type of sex he has, wants to have, and really enjoys having.

Gay Sex Is the Bottom's Literature

To understand the political and sexual stakes of reading *El vampiro de la colonia Roma*, we must also think with the cultural and political context that the book portrays, which is to give an account of the material world surrounding a character like Adonis if he were to exist. What made this work so revolutionary at publication was the event of its arrival nearly thirty years after the publication of Octavio Paz's *El laberinto de la soledad*, as explored in the introduction. Turning toward the latter part of the twentieth century, scholars have argued that the radicality of *El vampiro de la colonia Roma* is characterized by the novel becoming a commonly argued counternarrative to Paz's construction of masculinity.[2] But at a literary level, the bottom has always been a stake. What made Luis Zapata's famed novel so "pioneering" is its spotlight on uninhibited and uncensored gay sex. The politicization and sociality of the bottom graze the pastures of queer theory that redirect attention to an innate abjection in the act of being penetrated. Adonis García advances and embodies an image of Mexicanness through his gay sex.

Following a modernist vision, Mexico in the 1960s and 1970s was a nexus of political and economic change that created an anxious cultural climate for Mexicans in Mexico and the United States. In this formative period, the leadership of the Partido Revolucionario Institucional (PRI) had co-opted both liberal and conservative political social identities, creating an illusion of a Mexican totality—a totality represented in the country's one-party autocracy. The intended effect of this homogenization was to ensure that ideological rifts, particularly at the level of the elite, would not weaken or threaten the hegemonic political structures created by the PRI. As Beatriz Magaloni explains, the PRI positioned itself as a hegemonic party generating the reputation of total "invincibility . . . and a public message that only by joining the party could a politician stand a chance of attaining office and that outside of it there is nothing."[3] Under the PRI, profits generated by the oil industry during the López Portillo administration, as well as the prestige the nation's capital, Mexico City, had gained by hosting the Olympics in 1968 (and later the World Cup in 1970 and 1986), positioned Mexico to compete as a modern nation on an international stage alongside the First World powers of the United States and Europe. This initial prestige led the state to forcibly portray Mexico as a democratic society of economic and political progress.

Mexico's major political concern in the second half of the twentieth century was how to define itself as a modern nation by enforcing control of the image of its growth and longevity. The economic and political shifts of the latter half of the century created a culture of death in Mexico that hinges on Achille Mbembe's notion of "necropolitics," or the ultimate sovereign power to make decisions about who deserves to die. Such a question about life and death becomes dependent upon masculinist understandings of domination that begin with the construction of the image of the Mexican subject, almost exclusively conceptualized as cisgender, heterosexual, and male—and very horny. This construction of the Mexican subject, this Mexicanness, sits at the intersection of politics, death, and sex in the national and collective imaginary. Through sex, the necropolitical contours of the modern Mexican nation-state reveal it as an erotic, hypermasculine system of power. Reading the sexual-textual practices in this way reveals a paradoxical resistance, on the part of such texts, to the illusion of a totalizing nation.[4]

Literature finds itself compelled to respond to the archetype of the virile Mexican man that has been canonized by public intellectuals like Octavio Paz, Samuel Ramos, Roger Bartra, and others who foreground a penetrative way of reading Mexican subjectivity. Sex forces literature to change because it pushes language toward and beyond its own limits to reimagine and rewrite what a sexual linguistic power might look like. Mexican gay writer Sergio Téllez-Pon argues that the "visibility" of homosexuality beyond homoeroticism is a defining key term of the twentieth century, one that should be deployed paradigmatically to approach what literature sought to achieve, intentionally or not. However, the theme of gay sex, he tells us, "emerged stealthily, aided by the personalities of other latitudes that flourished throughout various eras: Greek and Latin poets, Shakespeare, Miguel Ángel, etc."[5] The literary world introduces the pervasive and invasive presence of homosexuality and other dissident forms of sex that have been exacerbated since the

formative 1960s. The historically infamous "1968" of Mexico is decorated by the massacre of university students on October 2 at the Plaza
de las Tres Culturas in Tlatelolco, Mexico City, by military and police.[6]
Not only are death counts inconsistent, but there are also no sustainable
images of the massacre itself. Rather, Mexico pushed to have the visual
aesthetics and politics of the nation portray it as a cosmopolitan country,
hosting the Olympic Games and slotted to host the FIFA World Cup two
years later. The rise of student and young people's activism, however,
gave rise to other movements led by young people fighting for civil lib-
erties, among them a more humane visualization of homosexuality in
Mexico. Téllez-Pon reminds us that this is a moment in which gay writers across Latinx America in their twenties are beginning to write more
about their sexuality, such as Cuban writer Reinaldo Arenas, Argentine
writer Néstor Perlongher, Puerto Rican author Manuel Ramos Otero,
and Portuguese writer Al Berto, among others, who lived and performed
the sexualities of their gay adolescence in the shadows of this sexual
theater of the nation-state.[7] Téllez-Pon explains that "although inevitably
marked by their social circumstance," the approach of these writers is
not "militant," nor is there "a hint of social commitment. For some, the
only commitment they have is with the poetry itself, with language, with
the construction of their poetic oeuvre."[8]

At one time Doris Sommer's *Foundational Fictions* argued that the
symbolic construction of the nation as an imagined community (riffing
off Benedict Anderson) occurred in nineteenth-century Latin America
through literature's use of heterosexual relations as an allegory for national consolidation. While this reading may have once provided a useful entryway into the problems of sexuality during a crucial period in
Latin American history, Sommer's analysis neglects homosocial bonds.
I argue that there is more at stake in centering these encounters as a
parallel strategy for reading the construction of the national and collective consciousness.[9] *El vampiro de la colonia Roma* makes it possible
to trace a counter genealogy to the tradition of "foundational fictions"
that Sommer argues for in her seminal book. If, as she argues, novels of
the nineteenth century like *María* and *Sab* allegorize the desire for national consolidation, *El vampiro de la colonia Roma* imagines a counter
tradition, one that necessarily "unwrites" identity, while allegorizing the
impossibility of identity or representation more broadly.

The novel arrives at a moment in Latinx American literary history that could be described as exhaustion with the Boom literature that had defined most of the 1970s, with authors like Carlos Fuentes and Gabriel García Márquez. Zapata puts pressure on this exhaustion by offering a very nontraditional text that resists—in several ways—being associated with the likes of the Boom writers. The novel in a sense might be read as a response to this exhaustion. Latinx American cultural studies theorist Alberto Moreiras captures this through the framework of an "exhaustion of difference" that haunts Latinx Americans through a dissymmetrical gaze caught between what he describes as "restitution" and "appropriation." This structural dissociation is not just the Orientalizing burden of Western constructions of the Other, because it extends to the Other's construction of itself. Appropriation, then, becomes a process through which alterity enters and contributes to the hegemonic discursive economies of Latin Americanism as a global machine for the representation of alterity. Restitution would thus be its counterpart as a process through which alterity manifests as an "irruption" or an "event" or a "radical opening" within representational thought, which, unable to restitute otherness as direct presence, at least points to the residues of its absence or disappearance.[10] Under this structural determination, the true radical work of Latin Americanism is limited to "step[ping] out of itself in order to arrest itself" as a global representational machine.[11] From this position, we might be able to confront these cultural figures whose "literary" texts completely obliterate the limits of (Latinx American) literature and cultural production. This allows the field to work toward more non-essentialist forms of identity, whether it be Latinx American, Latinx, or Mexican, in favor of a relational hemispheric abjective encounter with alterity.

Three Versions of a *Vampiro*

Through broken narrative, Adonis García is invited to share his life story, to which he responds immediately by naming himself an irrelevant outsider: "fuck! tell you my life story? for what? who'd even be interested?" There is very little information about who Adonis is, where he comes from, or any relevant background information to understand the protagonist of this groundbreaking novel. By piecing together the scattered information he provides, we know the following: His father was a Spanish refugee of the Civil War. Both his parents died when he was young—his mother when he was ten and his father when he was thirteen. Adonis is telling these stories around the age of twenty-five. And it is a story that reads very much from the perspective of a Mexican gay man in his twenties living in Mexico City. We also know that Adonis was born at the Texas/Mexico border in Matamoros, Tamaulipas, growing up in Colonia Santo Tomás near the southwest Nuevo León border. Around age fifteen or sixteen, he moved to León, Guanajuato, to live with his half-brother and attend secondary school. But in his third year he dropped out and relocated to Mexico City. This is the extent of background information the reader receives about Adonis. The rest of his backstory is never recovered nor revealed because those details are presumably irrelevant, unnecessary, but mostly unrecoverable by Adonis García in these tapes. His actual name is even unknown. Rather, the name "Adonis" is bestowed upon him by his lover René.[12]

As the protagonist of a picaresque novel, Adonis represents the genre's renegade deviant who operates outside the law: he is the *pícaro*, or the trickster. Acting outside the law because he is always already outside the norms of society, he creates his own social contract. Adonis does and says things that are unconventional and without recourse, which includes his uninhibited sexual labor. At first glance, the novel appears to be just a collection of sex stories by a gay prostitute—and in many ways, it *is* just that. Adonis García is a character blithely aware of his isolated otherness as a self-described *vago* (bum), constantly questioning his own social milieu. He remarks,

> i don't think i ever had a destiny or if i did
> i got lost along the way
> i mean i've spent all my life here   in the city you know?   in the streets
> with my friends
> like chillin, you know
> working sometimes
> but hustling almost all the time.[13]

From the outset, it is clear that this is an unreliable character; within a few pages, his story is already inconsistent. Perhaps as readers, we should proceed more cautiously. But it is clear that Adonis operates outside mainstream society's expectations in the same way the novel functions outside the normative limitations of linguistic and literary conventions.

By constantly describing himself as a *vago* who associates only with other *vagos*, he is always in a state of transition—neither present nor forgotten; neither here nor there. He is uncounted, unaccounted for, and unrecognized as far as Mexican elite society is concerned. On the other hand, Adonis is also not concerned with trying to identify or qualify himself as any authentic form of Mexicanness, just as a figure who only represents sex. In fact, there are very few moments of self-identification in the text in which Adonis attempts to name *who* he is in relation to the normative majority. Yet one of the most sustainable moments of self-consciousness in the novel is as comical as it is complex. About halfway through the novel, Adonis recalls attending a very elegant party hosted by his client Zabaleta. As Adonis is getting dressed for the party, he experiences a "transformation" of sorts: a bodily and identity shift. While changing into a tuxedo to be presentable—that is, "passable"—in the presence of "pretentious artists and politicians," he describes becoming another man:

> i was unrecognizable
> completely
> that when i looked at myself in the mirror   i couldn't identify myself i
>   didn't even recognize myself and said
> "who's that sexy guy?"
> Heh
> "so i can cruise him"
> seriously i was someone else
> the *vampiro* of colonia roma had died for a day
> i had put down my leather jacket and my jeans and my super skintight
>   pants and i became a real man[14]

This is the first time in the novel that Adonis refers to himself as the *vampiro* of Colonia Roma. In 1970s Mexico City, *vampiro* was street slang for "hustler" or gay male sex worker, a term used to describe the men of the night who would prey on bodies and exchange bodily fluids. Thus, referring to himself as a *vampiro* in this moment, Adonis acknowledges that he performs an identity imprinted upon him by his sexual labor in which he can code-switch his drag to be the type of gay man he is needed to be. In this instant of self-identification, he names the sexual embodiment he performs through a role that is expected of him as a service provider. However, in this ephemeral moment at the mirror, the *vampiro* dies for a night to perform a certain level of passability within the theater of the national space—represented by "pretentious politicians and artists."

Through Adonis García's self-disavowal and his social status as a *vago* and gay prostitute, he is positioned as a figure who is not supposed to be taken seriously. To some extent, he does not even take himself seriously. His devil-may-care attitude eliminates any credibility. Much is still to be learned from Adonis. His character captures the knowledge production of a minoritarian subject, in which he exemplifies the exigency of a social identity-in-difference to the majoritarian public sphere. From here, we can narrow in on how his experiences that are shaped by the powerful elite and his rich clients lend themselves to be read as an exposure of the aesthetics and politics of sexual world-making and Mexicanness. In other words, just because he is not taken seriously does not mean he doesn't have something to say.

An issue that remains is the lack of clarity about who Adonis García is. A plausible explanation would be that he does not even know who he is, which is arguably very true, since he will not even say his actual name—perhaps he doesn't have one. It was clear in the wake of the author's death that Adonis appeared as someone different to each of his readers, all experiencing Adonis, but different versions of him. Discernible from his own self-realization being mirrored back to him is perhaps an explanation for the competing versions of Adonis each of us wants to protect and remember. That is, there are different versions of Adonis García because he gave us different and inconsistent versions of himself. Nothing about him is given as "real" or "authentic." He becomes who others want him to be, or who they need him to be.

Latino Adonis García

Two weeks following Luis Zapata's death, Daniel Hernandez, a staff writer at the *Los Angeles Times*, published an op-ed with the extremely audacious title "Why Luis Zapata's Breakthrough Gay Mexican Novel Demands a New Translation." His "demand" raises a number of questions. For one, who is making the demand? Is it Hernandez as a proxy for a gay US Latino readership? Is it the novel? Is it Adonis García? If anything, the latter two would rebuke any attempt to be translatable or legible, because Zapata creates an enigmatic space for sex to be performed and reperformed by the sexual Other, who will always already remain unknowable and untranslatable. Hernandez oddly begins with a very nostalgic and lengthy rumination on the Mexican chain Sanborns, specifically, the Sanborns del Ángel, a restaurant and café that Hernandez claims is ground zero for Mexico's sexual underground. The *LA Times* writer briefly reminds readers in a sentence that the author had recently died, before immediately going into his deeply romantic ideas, fascinations, and curiosity with Adonis García, not Luis Zapata. He also returns to his own personal memories of Sanborns, which reinforce his point that this is *the* queer headquarters. Hernandez provides a mostly historically inaccurate literary history of the novel. Nonetheless, he emphasizes how the novel's publication made an important intervention as a new type of literature that interrupts the Mexican literary canon. Hernandez revisits his bold demand in his last point. He whines that the 1981 English translation by San Francisco publisher Gay Sunshine Press is essentially obsolete because it tries to mimic "1970s" gay slang to keep with the tone of the original. I would agree that the 1981 translation is dated and some of the rhetorical choices are quite embarrassing, but humorous. Hernandez argues, "The only barrier for 'El vampiro' is language. All it would take is one brave soul to shoulder the task of re-translating the voice of Adonis García in a way that matches (or challenges) the sensibilities of contemporary American English." As such, "in today's literary climate, the translator would also have to settle on a single form of American slang to sustain the character." Hernandez, then, boldly ends with, "Anyone? ¿*Alguien*?"[15] It appears, perhaps, that it is Hernandez who makes this "demand" to access *El vampiro de la colonia Roma* in American English. I am trapped by the neocolonialist intention of such a "demand." It demands not just that Adonis be translatable, but that he be so in "contemporary American English" through the use of a singular form—normative—of English to be called American English. In other words, there is an expectation that Adonis can be molded to pass for an American readership. Fantasies and requests are given to his role as a sex worker, to do the sexual labor of translation for Americans. Yet left unanswered is a sufficient explanation by Hernandez as to why Adonis needs to be legible to the white imperialism of American standards of English. There is no consideration of the genre itself, the literary risks, and the sexual cultures of Mexicanness that perhaps make the text so resistant to longeval translatability.

Daniel Hernandez's *LA Times* contribution reminds me that the novel does something to people. He makes this evident by including a photo of his own personal copy of the novel, which matches mine, both expressing the same exhaustion and weathering evidence of reading, rereading, and re-rereading Adonis's sick and twisted tales. He and I both tout the novel's third edition (published by Debolsillo in 2008), whose cover is illustrated with a dark-skinned brown man with black hair and large dark eyes who lurks in the shadows, as if his entire body also begins to dissolve into the darkness. Streetlights are visible over his shoulder, along with an adult theater and a seedy hotel. His huge midnight eyes stare very straightforwardly, as if they follow the reader. He has a gold chain around his neck with a cross and his hand upon his cocked waist in his oversized slacks and loose white long-sleeve shirt. This illustrated portrayal of the *vampiro* on Debolsillo's third edition dovetails with the exoticizing Latino aesthetics of the cover image to the 1981 English translation, *Adonis García: A Picaresque Novel*, published by Gay Sunshine Press in San Francisco (figure 2.1). The cover displays an actual photograph of a brown-skinned man, shirtless in a leather jacket, denim skinny jeans gripping his legs with the imprint of his dick and balls hanging to the right. He stands in the dark doorway of what looks like a seedy bar, while he poses his hairless brown body—not overly muscular or toned. His thick straight black hair is coifed to the right, while he, too, places his hand on his cocked waist. Tagged on the wall of the building, in all caps, is "ESTA NOCHE" (tonight), with an arrow pointing inside. In comparison to the illustrated version, it would appear that the English translation's cover is *vastly* more literal in the way race is sexualized by comparison to the Mexican editions.

Figure 2.1. Cover of English translation, *Adonis García: A Picaresque Novel*, published by Gay Sunshine Press in 1981.

Cover Model Adonis García

The photograph selected for the English translation flows from the same waters as the impulse to demand access to Adonis García in contemporary American English. It is a photograph that attempts to make the Mexican sexual subject legible and translatable to the US American reader. The cover itself is reminiscent of the sex tourism guides of the time—which really began to be much more available in the 1980s, leading up to the advent of the AIDS pandemic—that would feature similar images on the cover to entice American (white) men to go south of the border for a little spice.[16] The guides would share information about the hottest clubs, especially those with dark rooms, bathhouses, adult stores with *cabinas*, and the hottest cruising sites. Adonis García is personified by a very brown Mexican man and sexualized in a particular way based on his appeal to a particular audience. Reactions by US Latinx readers to these covers also speak to how Adonis García is browned by his diasporic audience. Hiram Pérez describes this as a cosmopolitan desire for brown gay maleness that occurs on a global register in which, "universalizing from his own experience, the gay cosmopolitan spectator projects himself into the life of another nation, displacing and obscuring local histories."[17] As such, "race consciousness continues to function as the false consciousness of establishmentarian queer theory."[18] The desire to consume the brown body is rooted in a false universal of brownness that originates in whiteness, which has already penetrated most decolonial ethnic studies projects. These racialized sexualizations and sexualized racializations become reproduced, then, despite the field's urge to dismantle these sexual economies.[19] The brownness sought is a "repository for the disowned, projected desires of a cosmopolitan subject[;] it is alternately (or simultaneously) primitive, exotic, savage, pansexual, and abject."[20] Brownness comes with ambiguity.

Adonis García is a migratory figure, like many of his readers in the United States, though in the academic literature he is not typically read as such. He shares perhaps a similar childhood with his readers (if we can even trust his stories). Adonis is from the Nuevo Laredo US/Mexico border, so a presumed *norteño* Mexican and Tejano masculine disposition might be expected of or projected upon him.[21] The novel also migrates, hence crossing many borders in its various implications. It

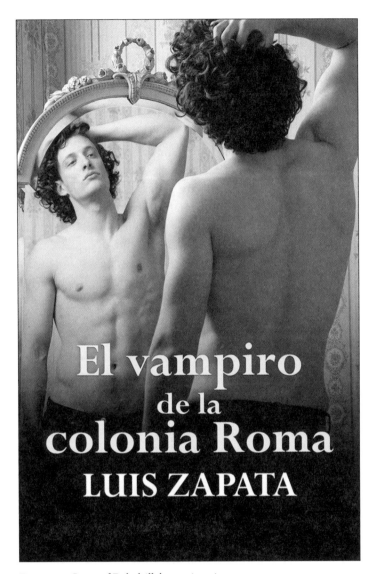

Figure 2.2. Cover of Debolsillo's 2012 imprint.

would appear that there is a political necessity to read Adonis as brown, but overlooked are a few key details that might suggest that Adonis is otherwise. In 2012 Debolsillo released a new imprint of the novel with a brand-new cover model (figure 2.2). Like the English translation, the cover displays a real photograph, but this time it portrays a translucent porcelain white man, checking himself out in a full-length mirror as he runs his hand through his dark curls. His muscles and abs flex through his pale skin, contrasted against his black skinny jeans. The mirror is ornamental and detailed. The ivory and pale pink paisley wallpaper suggests that he is perhaps in a home of wealth. This just might be that moment at Zabaleta's party in which Adonis barely recognizes himself in a tuxedo. To be fair, I barely recognized him—at first. There are details about Adonis that seem unaccounted for or overlooked.

Adonis García is half *white*. He never describes himself as being dark-skinned or tanned. But he does share with his reader that his father is a Spanish refugee. I want to rightfully name the presence of whiteness that is central to how Adonis performs his sexuality. He is also remarkably bottomphobic, femmephobic, racist, sexist, and transphobic. It would appear most likely than not that Adonis passes as not only white, but also as straight. This would perhaps explain why he is regularly in demand to escort rich men to parties with "pretentious artists and politicians."[22] The 2012 cover is most likely the Adonis García whom we are reading.

Perhaps it is easier to ignore these details about Adonis García for a gay readership, but it would be negligent to assume that he is just the exotic brown arm candy for white American men. He is on the arms of fellow white *Mexican* men. His US Latinx readers, it would appear, attach part of themselves to an Adonis that experiences the sexual power in displacements of racialized sexualities. These attachments, though, are neoliberal representations that make gay Latinos seek to see their sexuality in a crusader, gay Batman, vigilante *puto* sparking a sexual revolution. But Adonis is quite clear in the text that he has *zero* interest in any forms of sociality that would be politically motivated because he does not participate in the national and collective imaginary. His gay readers fall in love with him, they get angry, frustrated, confused, resentful—or at least, I do—because Adonis is problematic, but we need him to be; it might be the only solution for alternative and more deviant forms of queerness.

Norteño Adonis García

The desire to brown Adonis García as part of his sexual aesthetic continues, even in South America. The *vampiro* is portrayed in the character of Héctor Vásquez of the contemporary Chilean writer Alberto Fuguet's *nouvelle vague rampage* film *Siempre Sí* (2019, translated in English to *Always Say Yes*). Titled a "Mexican picaresque film" dedicated to Luis Zapata, *Siempre Sí* was filmed on an iPhone through the application Instagram's camera feature. Scenes repeatedly slide through the app's infamous cool- and warm-toned filters throughout the shots. The film cleverly uses on-screen notifications of Google Maps' dropped pins with addresses, his Spotify playlist, WhatsApp audio messages, and so on. This is a film that takes place *on* the apps, which find themselves becoming participatory actors in the sexual theater of the city's sexual culture. With the accessible translation of the pedestrian "real" experience, captured by the Mexican slang in the original, Fuguet intelligently fulfills Hernandez's demand in the *LA Times*. Rather than preoccupying himself with the translatability of language, he focuses on the translation of how sex is experienced in this era. It becomes "real" by translating the simplicity of everyday life that occurs on a screen for most people.

Figure 2.3. Video still of Héctor's Instagram profile. *Siempre Sí*, dir. Alberto Fuguet, 2019. © TLAReleasing. Reproduced with permission.

Siempre Sí follows Héctor, a medium, brown-skinned gay man with an average build from Hermosillo, Sonora, as he enjoys and laments the sexuality of Mexico City. He comes to the nation's capital to pose for an erotic photographer. Ready to take more risks, he pursues a new sexual chapter in his life. On his trip to the capital for a nude photo shoot, the audience is taken on a tour of present-day Mexico City's gayest and "cruisiest" places to fuck and be fucked. Meanwhile, the film regularly pauses and overlays quotes excerpted from Luis Zapata's novel onto freeze frames. Héctor checks in to the notorious Hotel La Riviera, one of the city's seedy hotels for cruising in Colonia Buenavista. As he settles in, he unpacks a copy of *El vampiro de la colonia Roma* displaying the 2012 cover. The camera pauses. Héctor is arguably a modern-day Adonis, or at least aspiring to be like him, as made overly apparent throughout the film's intertextual relationship with the novel. Inspired by the Adonis lifestyle, Héctor is determined to play out all his various fantasies about public sexuality, but in real life, without any inhibitions.

At the start of his adventure, he promises himself that his answer to every new encounter, every new cock, every new ass, is *siempre sí*. The film and its distributors give a plethora of warnings, on the posters, the covers, and the first several opening screens of the film, that the film contains graphic scenes of *actual* men having sex with one another. Unlike Adonis, Héctor tells us from the movie posters a bit more about who he is and perhaps what we might expect. However, like Adonis, Héctor uses social media to curate an image of himself that conditions our preconceived notions about the type of character the audience meets in the beginning chapters of the film. It also reads like someone who admires Adonis García in ways read by others: a sex hero for gay Latinx men. In other words, what would it feel like to *be* Adonis? To fuck like him? To be fucked *by* him?

I offer a more sustained reading of the film later in this chapter, but here I want to fixate on the aesthetics of Héctor as the portrayal of Adonis García, who is positioned to be emblematic of or at least performatively walking in the life of Adonis García during his weekend in Mexico City. Héctor is in construction, average-build, not muscular or toned, slim, full pubic bush, and *activo*. The audience is provided with a brief look at his Instagram profile. He even says in these opening scenes that he does not think he is attractive enough to be photographed, but he will let the public be the judge of that. He listens to a voice message from another character, Serrano, that is very telling of the brown aestheticization wanted of a figure like Adonis:

> I have a thing for the ones from the provinces. There's something that's, I don't know, rough around the edges. I don't know. The truth is, I'm bored with the *fresas*. You're like a mix of innocent and naïve, but I see a little perv in you. The truth is, I'm into it. You turn me on. So, you tell me what you want to do . . . and when you come, don't smell like any deodorant.

As we can hear from Serrano's voice message, there are preconceived notions about someone who looks like and sounds like Héctor. He speaks with a Northern accent, so he is more likely than not to stereotypically be perceived as poor and uneducated. He even arrives in Mexico City outfitted with a cowboy hat, a Western-style plaid long-sleeve shirt, tight jeans, and boots fitting the *ranchero* and *norteño* stereotypes. His character fulfills every fantasy one could have about *norteño* men. One of the prevailing gay cultural narratives in circulation about *norteños* is that they are more sexually advanced and hornier than other Mexicans, but very provincial. Such a barely contained animalistic sexuality gives *norteño* men quite a reputation in larger cities.

The pressure to make Adonis García brown is prevalent, but I ask why it becomes so necessary. A hero is created out of somebody who does not want to be a hero. Yet Adonis's character maladies are easily overlookable, even if overlooking them might come with the risk of being fucked by Adonis. I argue that Adonis García is presented to the reader in the novel as a fuckboy: he fucks you, then fucks you over, leaving you in a fucked-up situation. Nothing about Adonis is real or sincere, which would include his happiness. These multifarious readings of Adonis García and of the novel can only truly promise to reveal the instability of ever ascribing or claiming any determinate absolute truth about Adonis. Once we can assume to know Adonis, his character will always end up contradicting himself. Adonis is unique and leaves an imprint because the author created a character with so many gaps that the reader fills them with their own fantasies of what and who they need Adonis to be.

A Broken Mexico from a Haunting Futurity

El vampiro de la colonia Roma goes beyond narrating the curiosity of coming out and sexual discovery, and even goes out of its way to reject the neatly packaged neoliberal consumption of identity-based gay documentation narrative projects that have dominated Latin Americanist LGBTQ+ literary and cultural studies for decades. The novel draws attention to a performance of sexuality through affective encounters with sex that compete with a compulsive and impulsive drive for ideals that register with the primacy of fucking. Adonis does recount his early childhood sexual trysts, his moment of homosexual consciousness, and early failed and questionable attempts at sexual cruising, including his first anal sex experience, of course.[23] However, while retelling the story of how he lost his virginity, Adonis describes a significant event in which he became self-aware and self-conscious of his own sexual materiality:

> it was the first time i ever had my cock inside anyone and i came like
>> never before
> wow
> i never knew someone could feel like that
> all my masturbatory thoughts and fantasies were nothing like being
>> faced with a real hole
> you don't even know i melted into sperm
> i became pure cum
> and then thought that my life was now complete
> nothing else could ever surprise me
> you know?
> it came to me
> well that probably came after
> that life is only worthwhile for the pleasures it can offer you that
>> everything else is bullshit
> and if you're not happy that's just stupid.[24]

Sex liberated his body to perform its true intended purpose: the pursuit of pleasure. Through anal sex, Adonis claims that life is worth living only if we can receive and dissolve into the pleasures of the sexual experience. This link between bodily fluid and subjectivity redirects a seizure of political power by becoming reproductive matter. He produces a sexual-based, particularly an anal or cum-based, subject formation that dovetails with the primacy of fucking expected of men—as long as there's a *pasivo*, right?

But "homosexuals" were often, and still at times are, regarded as sexual dissidents and thereby political criminals since they go against the "natural laws" of reproduction needed to sustain the nation-state.[25] I contend that Adonis inverts this through the anal penetration narrative when he becomes the sperm. By experiencing the pleasures of the flesh, he transcends the body and becomes the materiality of the sexual exchange itself through the fluids it leaves behind. He refuses to participate in any reproductive labor of the state through his sexual practices. It is a sterilizing sexual praxis, in which the continuity of human experience would cease to exist beyond the singularity of the sexual event.

This scene dramatizes a process of sexual subjectivities becoming undone in ways that exemplify an encounter of passivity. It is only in front of an actual anus, by fucking the *pasivo*, beyond any preconceived fantasies and ideas of anal sex—that physical contact with the rectum—that Adonis's humanness and ability to act as an autonomous and sovereign subject fall apart. A part of him dies through orgasm. All that is left is a shell of who he was. And he can never return to any prior state of being that existed before this experience—whatever that state may actually be, since he never makes it accessible to the reader. The anus disarms him and renders him powerless. It is a passive act, even if he tops. It also reflects back the power the *pasivo* has to disarm and unsettle the man, the penis, and the orgasm.

Power resides within the walls of the rectum of the bottom, enough so that it brings our gay crusader to his own end: a perfect gesture toward a *pasivo* ethics. Through the recollection of his sexual experiences, Adonis writes a queer history of 1970s Mexico City with detail, but also sarcastically indifferent, yet not without a touch of romanticism. He creates a sexual map of the city, describing landmarks familiar to locals in Colonia Roma and Zona Rosa: the Sanborns on the corner of Calles Londres and Amberes, El Ángel de la Independencia, Calle Hamburgos, El Caballo, and so on.[26] Mapping his sexual experiences onto a cartographic history converts Mexico City into a sexual space oriented around and toward universal narratives of Mexicanness that these monuments symbolize.[27] However, the novel's publication predates both the 1985 Mexico City earthquake and the 2017 Puebla earthquake, both causing massive destruction to Colonia Roma and Zona Rosa.[28] *El vampiro de la colonia Roma* is a text that produces a sense of nostalgia, but also an inevitable queer slow death as described by both the late Lauren Berlant and José Esteban Muñoz.[29] It is a glimpse into a specific moment of a sexual history in a city that does not exist anymore.

One of the only symbols of the old Zona referenced frequently throughout the novel that remained after the 1985 earthquake is the monument El Ángel de la Independencia, which did not originally survive the 1957 earthquake, but after being rebuilt, remained indestructible. And surely so, as it also survived untouched by the 2017 Puebla earthquake. Throughout Adonis's story, El Ángel serves as a central landmark for his descriptions of the city. The monument was originally erected in 1910 during the presidency of Porfirio Díaz—arguably Mexico's long nineteenth-century dictator, who pushed for Mexico's global industrialization—to commemorate the centennial of the beginning of the Mexican War of Independence. Later, the monument became a mausoleum for those war heroes. Today, it remains one of the most recognizable landmarks in Mexico City, becoming a rendezvous point for celebration and political protests, the central location for the Gay Pride parade, a perfect selfie opportunity, or even a place to engage in more salacious acts. In this sense, the figure of El Ángel and its recurring reference in the novel represent a particular type of political order. The monument symbolizes a nationalist vision and an ideal for a whole and complete Mexico: a class of Mexicanness that remains impossible to achieve for people like Adonis. Anchoring El Ángel and Mexico City's other national monuments such as the Caballito and the Torre Latinoamericana (which he describes as big dick with huge balls) as public erotic cartographic centers for the mapping of Adonis's sexual practices in the lines of his narration calls for a reading of the relationship between sex and nation written by autobiographical sexual stories.[30]

The fragmentary nature of Adonis's stories is complemented by a queerness toward a negative futurity—as opposed to romanticizing an idealized or politicized past or future that cannot ever be fully rerealized, or perhaps was never even fully realized in the past either, or perhaps never may be afforded in the future. Yet, as many have experienced with Adonis, there is still an attachment to Adonis as a *vampiro* figure that yearns for immortality and invincibility. There is a sense in the trajectory of Adonis's narration that tomorrow *might* be better or there is a more fulfilling promised future ahead. Yet that future is not Mexico, or at least it is certainly not Mexico City. Perhaps what is wrong from the past might still linger in and haunt the present, which could be reconcilable by something that lies ahead. But at the same time, there is also a radical acceptance that such a futurism is never promised to *vagos* or *vampiros*. Adonis belongs to a broken Mexico. His negative outlook, however, does not negate queerness's utopic futurity. In other words, the future—symbolic or otherwise—can only appear to be a proposition, because the past and present have failed, nor were they ever promised to disenfranchised queers.

Utopia, José Esteban Muñoz tells us, "understands its time as reaching some nostalgic past that perhaps never was or some future whose arrival is continuously belated—a utopia in the present."[31] He continues, "It is also a picture of utopian transport and a reconfiguration of the social."[32] Adonis García's stories could very well be read to follow this trajectory, since to some degree a significant number of his readers (including myself at one point) idealize the lifestyle of a man who is free of inhibitions, nor does he apologize for who he is. It is idyllic, but also missing something—or a lot of things. Nonetheless, Adonis's stories cast a very open and explicit image of anal sex, but in the same event of a utopic languor, it is truly that thing that is never absolutely promised to people like Adonis or even the queers who idolize him. A Muñozian utopic logic is descriptive of experience, not (re)productive of prescriptive narratives about utopic longings. Thus, a queer of color utopia is characterized by "flux, a temporal disorganization" that describes how utopic longing structures resistance. Through storytelling, Adonis García illustrates a life story and trajectory that are always going to be filled with gaps, irregularity, and disorderly ways of speaking about a hemispheric Latinx queerness.

Adonis conducts his sexual acts openly in a space marked by a people's desire to escape this plane of existence and the pains of the tragedies that plague the city by experiencing an indiscriminate and uninhibited interaction with the flesh of other bodies. Yet I do not neglect to notice that Muñoz speaks in the subjunctive and of a queerness *to come*, that is on the horizon, *yet* to arrive in an already untimely present—which thus includes the possibility that this queerness *could not* arrive. If anything, as clinical psychologists have warned for decades, sometimes "future tripping" should be avoided as it bears the possibility of inducing or creating further trauma—or even new ones. I thus locate a violent end to which Adonis García navigates the world around him, haunted by a broken Mexico through which its material residues will haunt the future, because they remain to be specters in our already untimely present. Adonis is haunted by the ghosts of a queer utopia that has yet to come and thus may never actually be realized. At the same time, he is also haunted by the specters of the nation-building project of Mexicanness, grounded in reproductivity, even for gays.

Accounts of Mexico City and a higher class of clients give context to a social and political milieu serving as a backdrop. These details create a context from which he comes to understand and accept his role as considerably both *activo* and *pasivo*—since Adonis actively chooses to both top and bottom during his sexual encounters, depending on the client. Adonis's story also predates the initial outbreak of the AIDS epidemic on the North American continent, which will quickly eliminate thousands of lives in the United States and Mexico, having its effect in the Mexico City scene.[33] The promiscuous ethics of his uninhibited practices can understandably be taken up as a romanticized sexual revolution calling for bodies to reject systems of sexual control in order to have sex with whomever they wanted, whenever they wanted, and how they wanted. For Adonis, this means developing his own sense of a code of conduct for *how* he approaches sex. In other words, the broken Mexico to which Adonis belongs reflects his own willingness to *also* be just as broken and fragmented. If the longevity of the nation-building project was and may never be promised to him, knowing this finitude in this plane of reality, Adonis creates his own praxis of ethics and politics: it is a bottom performance.

What remains thus is a question between the Other and those specters of the future haunting Adonis throughout Mexico City. Read with deconstruction's attention to *l'avenir/avenir* (to come/future), a conceptualization of queer of color futurity is always already open to the possibility of negativity. For Jacques Derrida, the future reflects determinateness as something that *will be*, in other words, "predictable, programmed, scheduled, foreseeable," as opposed to a futurity, *l'avenir* (to come), which, Derrida remarks, "refers to someone whose arrival is totally unexpected." Accordingly, the "real future" is characterized by that unknowability, the inability to anticipate the arrival of the Other (the future) *a priori*—that is, "the other who comes without my being able to anticipate their arrival. So, if there is a real future beyond the other known future, it's *l'avenir* in that it's the coming of the Other when I am completely unable to foresee their arrival."[34] Put another way, queer of color futurity must be "inventive or it is nothing at all." Moreover, it must facilitate a way out of the impasse and void of the present toward an unforeseeable future signified by *l'avenir*. Derrida thus proposes the practice of deconstruction as a form of writing "liable to the other, open to and by the other, to the work of the other; it is writing working at not letting itself be enclosed or dominated by [the] economy of the same," which allows "the adventure of the events of the entirely other to come."[35]

The significance of alterity varies according to the contexts of its application, however; Derrida attaches a specific attribute to this term when he stipulates that the "call of the other is a call to come and that happens only in multiple voices." Herewith, then, is a "passage toward the other" in multiple voices, especially the sexual: a sampling of assessments, extrapolations, interpolations, and appropriations attesting to the extraordinary breadth of Derrida's legacy as it pertains to larger themes of the project of performing from the bottom as a bottom exposed in queer Mexicanness and Latinx performance more broadly.[36]

Acts of Refusal: Adonis Gets Fucked

Adonis García develops and deploys a set of strategies that bring the *pasivo* ethics of bottom performance to bear on his broken landscape. In other words, he follows a sexual code. For one, no repeats after three times.[37] He also unapologetically rejects any normative approach to relationships. Yet it is also a rejection of the twentieth-century ideals of the Mexican family within the national and collective imaginary— that is, the transmission of a future-driven Mexico made in the image of reproduction through normative family structures of monogamy, marriage, and childrearing, the defining factors of the modern capitalist state. The rejection of the Mexican ideals of futurism through sexual terms embraces a freedom that Adonis represents as the acceptance of the radicality of being a sexual figure in the worlds he navigates.

Adonis also prefers to bareback. He comically recalls a story about a client who *always* used condoms, which for Adonis was odd, but also entirely unnecessary:

> if you're *activo* it's very uncomfortable because your dick is all sliding
> around and if you're *pasivo*
> it's worse because it sticks to you and scrapes your poor asshole to
> pieces
> condoms are horrible
> they shouldn't be used between men who knows how it is with
> women
> but between men it's really bad and they shouldn't be used
> they don't work[38]

Adonis's arguments against condom use suggest that such barriers deny the body the right to fully experience the pleasures of anal penetration. In this story, he recounts how the client did not have a condom handy, so the two men spent the entire day in search of condoms. But every store seemed to be sold out of condoms on that particular day. The dismayed Adonis finally asks the client why he is so adamant about using condoms. His client discloses that he has a fear of contracting and transmitting genital warts to his girlfriend. Adonis is perplexed by this obsessive fear of sexually transmitted infections and reassures the client that he has never had genital warts, just gonorrhea. He recalls another trick with similar fears who once placed a condom on Adonis's penis and, as he describes,

> grabbed my dick with his hand and started to suck it
> sucking it
> imagine?
> it didn't even get fully hard
> it was so funny
> that is the height of the fear of venereal diseases.[39]

Adonis's reaction, shaming others for their fears of contracting venereal diseases, comes from a position of knowing his own social location in contrast to the world around him. He is certainly not exempt from contracting STIs; he describes an unpleasantly painful experience with gonorrhea in the novel and also suffers from untreated syphilis.[40] To his credit, he did attempt to treat both homeopathically. But to the point, Adonis is able to question and shame fears about the mortality of the body because he presents himself as fearless and all-knowing of the broken Mexico in which he lives. His character has been looked up to as an authority figure who knows sex in ways that others do not. He acts as if he has somehow tapped into a naïve knowledge about sex that keeps sex as *just* sex—untainted by something as mundane as communicable diseases.

Adonis's character comically plays with the qualities of the *activo-pasivo* rhetoric of Mexicanness. He performs a straight-passing persona, despite his homosexual identifiers. That is, he does not exhibit the monolithic or "naturalized" characteristics of "gay," which have been determined by dominant stereotypes and are co-opted in national narrative novels, usually as a key effeminate character, because they are de-sexualized in their effeminate representation and thus less threatening to mainstream sexual cultures.[41] But that is not the case with Adonis. In fact, he is highly critical of effeminate men, *locas*, and *travestis*. Adonis reinforces a version of masculinity dependent upon the symbolic gestures of "fucking." However, Adonis both tops and bottoms, just not with equal interest and enjoyment.

He does talk about bottoming for other men. In another anecdote, he recalls going to Acapulco with his regular client, Zabaleta, when he was around seventeen or eighteen years old. The two of them are having a very drunk conversation about sex and Adonis expresses his hostile and resistant feelings about bottoming:

> and so i told him that i didn't like being *pasivo*
> cuz i don't feel anything
> i've never felt anything
> "ah" he says
> "it's that the body has to be relaxed and then
> in certain positions the cock rubs against the prostate and that's
>   when it feels good"
> "yea" i tell him "but i've never felt it"
> he says "well it's because they haven't been able to hit your prostate
> once they hit the prostate you're going to feel all that pleasure"[42]

Feeling compelled by Zabaleta's confidence as a top, Adonis decides to bottom in order to try to hit his prostate—or rather prove that it is not even possible. With plenty of Vaseline, they try several positions trying to hit his prostate, but with no success. Adonis says, "he kept fucking me in one position and then another he sure gave me the fucking of a lifetime but i never felt anything pleasurable thank god he finally came."[43] Ultimately Adonis is unable to achieve prostatic orgasm, nor does he find pleasure in the act of bottoming. His prostate remained nonresponsive to the deep thrusts of Zabaleta's topping skills, which Adonis finds a humorous curiosity: "with all that fucking it was incredible that he *hadn't* hit my prostate."[44] There are several readings that might emerge from this sex act between Adonis and Zabaleta. On the one hand, Adonis's willingness to bottom and the actual act of doing so introduce a sexually versatile positionality into the conversation that throws a wrench into the oppositional binary workings of the primacy of sex between men for Mexicanness to be realized: a prescriptive top-bottom duality.[45]

What if, however, Adonis refuses orgasm? What if he bottoms in order to actively suppress the power of prostatic pleasure? His rectum becomes a graveyard filled with trapped orgasms: his own. He introduces an act of refusal to submit to any type of phallic power when it is being wielded over him. In other words, it is a bodily rejection of the penis's potential to assume responsibility and take ownership of his pleasure. When Zabaleta asks Adonis, "you like that?," Adonis responds, "no i don't feel anything." He denies the phallus the satisfaction of being the source of his pleasure. And it is a painful rejection that comes with a cost that Adonis is willing to physically pay. He says all he can feel is, in Spanish, "nomás un dolor de la chingada" (just the fucking worst pain).[46] Not just pain, but through his colloquial Mexican slang, a pain rooted in the legacy of *la Chingada* (Mexico's historical "fucked woman," as I discuss in chapter 4). The trace of the *Chingada* as a traitor and sexual pariah resides in the walls of the rectum, and by being ripped open, that trace is painfully released. The act of bottoming not only rejects the egocentric, phallic power of the top, but is also a self-annihilating act of "fucking" himself over—to bring in the double meaning of *chingar*. The proposal of this reading accounts for how Adonis, yet again, performs ethical aesthetics of relationality. Adonis's versatility is less of an identification as both top and bottom than an antisocial performative act of a both/and neither/nor relationship that exists in tension between both categories. Refusing to allow himself to experience prostatic orgasm is a refusal to assume identity. Bottoming in this instance is understood as an act of misrecognition. Adonis's lack of orgasm models a misrecognition of Mexicanness. His refusal "to be" is a refusal to perform the role of the socially accepted homosexual other within a system that demands either his subjugation or domination.

In Adonis's sexual practices as a hustler, playing a role in his active choice to be the *pasivo* that would thus undo his own subjectivity, he introduces a rectal subjectivity defined by rejection of identity-based impositions of the national subject. In Mexico, sexually versatile men are identified as *internacionales* (or *ínter/inter*, for short), signifying a "foreign" sexuality. Adonis's own positionality, then, does not even place him within the borders of Mexico, so he always already does not belong to the nation. These borders and their crossings operate at not only the sociopolitical level, but also a corporeal one. His body and sexuality are experienced by readers in the diaspora, who form sexual relationships with Adonis that must cross figurative and literal borders to travel with Adonis's own migratory status.

We can think about this refusal of the self not just as an act of defiance, but as a powerful bottom performance complicating how we recognize and reorganize positionality in relation to subjectivity. Adonis García's sexual practices refuse to perform as Mexican. The representations of sex in *El vampiro de la colonia Roma* build toward a narrative on the end of Mexicanness. This end of state-imposed class difference exposes certain bodies as solely bodies to be penetrated by dominant systems of power. Moreover, to linger in the semantic space opened by *internacional*, we can thus see a need to read Adonis's sexuality as diasporic in its own movement beyond borders.

The bottom bears sexualized constitutions of Mexicanness. Taking bottoming acts seriously as an aesthetic, ethical, political mode of engagement, we gain a new lexicon and theoretical framework through which to read not only the disruptive nature of sexual acts in nationalist literature, but also the allegorical qualities that posit an ethics to address the sexual Other within the construction of these nationalist paradigms. Adonis García emblematizes and epitomizes a desired sexual freedom and liberation that many seek. He has inspired many men from *el norte*, Mexico, and the United States, who turn to Mexico City to provide something authentically "gay Mexican" to them, in ways that reading about Adonis fucking all over the city arouses their spirit to express the sexuality of their own imposed brownness. In other words, it is as if the reader seeks to pick up Adonis García's clothes as he takes them off and try them on for ourselves, and become the *vampiro*, if only for a night.

Visiting 4 Now: Always Yes

The contemporary Chilean writer Alberto Fuguet takes a literary cue from *El vampiro de la colonia Roma* in a literal way in his experimental gay film *Siempre Sí*. As an author, Fuguet is most notably one of the founders of the 1990s McOndo literary movement in Latinx America, seeking a more realist approach to literature and writing, leaving behind the steamy enchanted tropical jungles of the Southern Cone that dominated the magical realist literature of the 1970s Latinx American literary Boom, a globally accessible and manufacturable form of literature. From the body's senses, Fuguet, however, creates a more realistic experiential encounter with literature by depicting an urban Latinx American life and alluding to popular culture's poverty, crime, and dissidence, the local economic and political consequences of globalization, and social class division. A body language, and thus a body literature, emerges, forming part of the corpus of this post-Boom shift.[47] Faithful to the contemporary world, the themes of sex and sexuality are deployed through a very unapologetic approach to film and performance on a literary register. Sex scenes in Fuguet's writing tend to be described and explained realistically and are so detailed in some cases that they reach the point of coming off as pornographic. Sex is not a theme that is unnecessarily romanticized. Moreover, gender divergence and sexual deviance are not ignored, but rather, often times underscored. While these roles and definitions are not laid out in a concrete manner, they are presented and portrayed as part of real contemporary issues, and something that forms cultural production.

His postmodern, experimental, but highly realistic approach is applied to film as well, as evident in my descriptions of *Siempre Sí* thus far. Fuguet brings the literary to film in a unique and intertextual way that, much like his McOndo aesthetic, uses the contemporary aesthetics of real life to make these experiences plausible. As he is one of Zapata's contemporaries, it is understandable how the two figures and the worlds they create for their readers and viewers are meant to do something to our bodies on the other end on a realist level, especially in their exposure to one another. *Siempre Sí* comes with warnings—many of them. Like his novels, the film gives viewers a story through a realist lens not just to experience the film, but to experience fucking like Adonis García.

The realism of the explicit anal sex in the film is facilitated through the point of view of the Instagram camera, shifting between its various cool- and warm-toned filters. The phone's camera lens filters *how* the viewer sees the world. But the film goes one step further: it never stops reminding us that we are on a phone. Scenes will pause and shift back and forth between Instagram filters, as if the director is deciding on the most appropriate one, sometimes with an insufferable amount of time moving back and forth. Also, applications like Google Maps, WhatsApp, and Spotify overlay the screen with Héctor's phone's display, in which the viewer is given startling access to Héctor's personal life. The shots, at time, become dizzying and unstable.

The story begins the day Héctor arrives in Mexico City—in the "Nashville" filter—with plans to pose nude for an erotic photographer. He is ready to try new things and to surrender himself to the city. After checking in to the notoriously cruisy Hotel La Riviera, he immediately connects his phone to the Wi-Fi, with the camera closing up on his phone's screen. This is not only a reminder that the film is captured through a mobile device, but also perhaps one of the most Mexican nods at quotidian life, in which most Mexicans use pay-as-you-go phones and thus rely almost exclusively on Wi-Fi for all mobile data. Mexico City, for example, offers a free (albeit highly unreliable) citywide Wi-Fi. The viewer is subtly reminded of class status in this scene. Among the first of his belongings to be unpacked is his copy of Luis Zapata's *El vampiro de la colonia Roma*, displaying the live model cover. The frame freezes and zooms in on the cover for a couple of seconds before returning to Héctor getting settled.

Héctor vows to just always say yes to the city: #SiempreSí. One of his first stops is to the Baños Finisterre, another gay Mexican landmark. It

Figure 2.4. Video still of Héctor overlaid with the photo from the 2012 Debolsillo cover of the novel. *Siempre Sí*, dir. Alberto Fuguet, 2019. © TLAReleasing. Reproduced with permission.

would appear to Héctor that he has arrived at a gay Disneyland, ready to enjoy all the attractions. As the attendant gives him soap, towels, and a beer, Héctor begins to undress. Shirtless, he walks up to the full-length mirror in his room and begins to admire his body. As he touches his untoned chest and stomach, the image of Adonis García admiring himself in the mirror from the 2012 cover is overlaid next to Héctor. If there was any doubt about the intertextuality, it is cleared up in this moment. Yet in this mirror moment, Héctor does not become a "real gentleman;" rather, he comes to see his own sexuality. As if picking up Adonis's clothes as he undresses in front of the mirror for Zabaleta's party, Héctor comes to discover the erotic borders of his body and the ways he wants them to be crossed. He sees himself as a sexual person, capable of being someone like Adonis García.

After many failed attempts to find a personal tour guide, Héctor begins to walk around the capital on his lonesome. The film gives long silent shots with melancholic music playing on his Spotify playlist, displayed on the screen. Héctor realizes that he is alone. He goes out alone, attempting to hype himself up, but still not quite having the weekend he anticipated. Upon returning to his hotel, he is cruised by another hotel guest; this time he says yes. He hooks up, which briefly cheers him up, but he returns to the solace of drinking alone.

He arrives at the base of the Ángel de la Independencia to relax and enjoy a cigarette, when he receives a WhatsApp audio message from his lover Carlos Rivera ending their relationship. Héctor immediately bursts into tears, but swallows his wails to avoid crying uncontrollably. The scene cuts to Héctor sitting alone at a bar, and it is clear that he is very inebriated. The audience watches his character dissolve into despair and sexual panic. He finds himself alone in bars yet again.

On his walk back to the hotel, he finally receives a WhatsApp audio message from the photographer, learning that he is no longer needed. Héctor came to Mexico City with his heart set on becoming a sexual icon like Adonis García, and now he finds himself in a city with no purpose. He is fucked. Clearly there are parts of Adonis's life he did not expect to experience. In the final scenes, back at the hotel, Héctor spots an older, muscular man across the airshaft and goes over to his room. Once he enters, Janis slams him against the closet. Héctor submits, moaning in affirmation. "Do you like that?" Janis asks. Héctor softly groans, "Yes, yes." He begins rimming Héctor. He gets a bit louder—"Do you like that?"—"Yes, yes." This is the first and only time we see anyone play with Héctor's ass. The two move to the bed and Janis begins inserting his hard dick into Héctor's ass. He starts whimpering—"Shhhh. Do you like that?"—"Yes, yes." Slowly, and in real time, the audience is confronted with a close-up of Héctor's face as he relaxes, and Janis starts to thrust harder and harder. He is about to push a bit further and asks Héctor, "Do you like it deep?" as he slides his dick directly into Héctor's prostate. As his eyes roll into the back of his head, Héctor loudly screams, "Yes, yes!" The screen fades to black and opens onto the lobby of the hotel. With his duffel over his shoulder and a smile on his face, Héctor walks out, pauses, and chuckles. He takes one last selfie in front of the hotel.

Héctor deviates from Adonis García in a rather curious way, captured in this chuckle as he leaves the hotel, perhaps at the irony that he ended up getting fucked in the end. And that he liked it! The chuckle might also vocalize a need for bottoming. Unlike Adonis García, Héctor does allow himself to submit to the penis's power and let it hit his bottom, by letting Janis go deeper, in full acceptance of the consequences. The out-

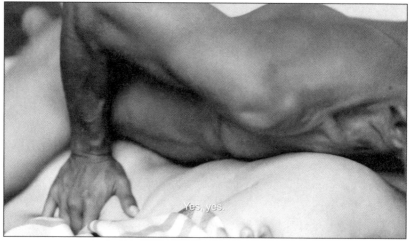

Figures 2.5–2.6. Video stills of Héctor bottoming for Janis. *Siempre Sí*, dir. Alberto Fuguet, 2019. © TLAReleasing. Reproduced with permission.

come was ecstasy—we've seen Bernini's statue; the face is uncanny. Pain and pleasure necessarily confuse themselves with one another through abjective submission, ultimately positioning bottoming as a cure for the negative affects produced by exclusively topping out of something to prove.

The film ultimately reveals the instability and failure of Adonis's lifestyle. In a sense, Fuguet rewrites the ending. The consequence of accepting being fucked is a happier life with his new partner, Natalino, as they celebrate their two-year anniversary. By allowing himself to be bottomed, he discovers how fucked-up Adonis's lifestyle ultimately is. Adonis is not meant to be a role model. Always saying yes comes with consequences. Loneliness haunts Héctor's character and is visually noticeable in ways that it is not in the novel. But perhaps that loneliness and the silence of that loneliness were always already there. The novel is full of gaps. It is quite literally full of nothing. Could the gaps just be dead air? Through film, the camera allows the viewer to see the loneliness in ways that cannot be captured by literature, except perhaps it always was. Drowning that silence are Héctor's Spotify playlists, which give texture to those gaps and silences.

It would appear that the *vampiro* lifestyle met its own end upon the demise of its admirer, who still just ends up fucked in the end. Ultimately, Héctor Vásquez reveals the impossibility of remaining faithful to the novel and the character, because the novel and Adonis were never meant to be fully conceivable, understandable, or (re)presentable. Even in the aesthetic rhetoric of bringing the real to bear on the narrative, the film also highlights the difficulties of how to show "real" sex—in terms of consequences that extend beyond the physical. The film responds from the position of a romanticized idea of what gay Mexico City is. One of the prominent critiques among gay *chilangos* is that they do not see themselves represented in the film. Missing for them are essential cruising sites that would more accurately capture where one might find today's *vampiros*: the last car of the Metro, non-touristy bathhouses, the dark basement of Tom's Leather Bar, maybe cruising in the Bosque de Chapultepec, or paying for the cheap *cabinas* at adult bookstores. There is something unfulfilling about the film through Héctor's fidelity to a Mexico City that does not exist anymore. In the end, he still must leave the capital and return home to Hermosillo. In the end, everything does still come to an end.

Time to Say Goodbye, Cruel World

El vampiro de la colonia Roma is the autobiographical demise of a character so empty and unfulfilled that he imagines a life not just outside Mexico City, but out of this world. In fact, he leaves Mexico City by the time he is done with these tapes and never tells the reader. He has recorded in two locations and over two years apart: October 1975 in Mexico City and December 1977 in Erongarícuaro, Michoacán. It is not clear which tape was recorded when and where, but it is worthwhile taking into account that not even Adonis García is indebted to Mexico City, even though his readers are. Perhaps that denial makes Adonis García desirable.

The protagonist continually alludes to being a misanthrope. He never describes having close friends, or wanting them. Even with love and romantic attachment, the reader is never given access to a vulnerable space in which Adonis is truly open and honest about his emotions. Everything he shares is carefully chosen to portray an image, because the truth is: there is no truth. He does not even know who he is anymore. He has defined his identity as sex. Narrowing in on the passage overlaid upon Héctor in his hotel room in his own depressive state, Adonis García finds himself suffering in solitude and very self-aware of his depression; he even comments that he has been to see someone about it. At length, he tells us at the end of Tape 3,

it's like i was always made of nothing but holes, no?   of nothing but needs that could never be filled   in the end   the depths of sadness, right?   but what really takes me out   what hurts me the most   is that i realized slowly i was losing everyone i loved   first my mother   later my father   then my godmother   because of the escorting, right?   then later my brother   that left the country   and finally rené   or rather   it was like it occurred to me that i've always been alone   that i was always going to be alone and there's nothing you can do about it   you're always alone   you could have company for a second   or for a moment   or forever, no?   but out of everything in life you're going to be alone   i'm sayin   the moment you die there's nobody that's going to be there with you   you're going to die alone, no?   although there could be people with you   there could be someone who loves you   well they wouldn't die for you, right?   and that's it   the weight of being forgotten during a time   i realized that the only person that was going to be with me until the end of my days was myself   and that if i couldn't even do that for me   nobody in the world was going to.[48]

Adonis is keenly aware of his depression and loneliness, which might contribute to his drive toward a sexuality based on negative affects. Sex is approached as a self-annihilating, un-becoming act, a type of passivity reflecting an embrace of the abject contours of a sexual futurity that shapes the nation-building project. The bottom and its performative utterances respond to false universal ideals that emerge from hetero- and homonormativities. The bottom is already earmarked for a "fucked" future, but even in his annihilating embodiment, he represents the back on which modern ideas of Mexicanness are bred. Sex becomes an imperative to express not a resistance to politics, but rather the expression of what the political system has always already enabled through sexuality.

Adonis García exemplifies this through a story full of negativities. Adonis is a character defined by what he is *not*. He does not share an optimistic lens that is often imposed upon or applied on top of him. He does not self-project into the future, other than hoping to leave on a spaceship shaped like a huge penis. He is open and honest about his depression and the unfulfillment of the life of a *vago*, but we have yet to examine that in the larger scholarship on the novel. Adonis's negativity captures a sexual Other who has yet to arrive, because he may never, because he was never intended to. Adonis shows that refusal is a possibility, if even only to die in the depressions of his life until the end comes for him—which, as the reader knows, does, because he leaves Mexico City.

Death serves as the mirror for how many Mexicans see life, in a way that is woven into the cultural fabric of contemporary expressions of Mexicanness. Death and life are inseparable. In *El laberinto de la soledad*, Octavio Paz tells us, "Our death illuminates our life. If our death is meaningless, so was our life."[49] The poet lyrically explains Mexico's intimate relationship with death in our living lives. To understand life, one must understand death, and vice versa. Paz rhetorically asks, "Does the Mexican, obstinately closed off to the world and his fellow man, open himself to death?" To which he answers, "The Mexican does not surrender himself to death, because surrendering requires sacrifice. And sacrifice, in turn, demands that someone give and someone receive. That is, someone must open up and face a reality that transcends them."[50] Thus the position and identity at and from the bottom are death-dealing positions and identities, because the identity is based on a presumed acceptance that the world has fucked you, or even perhaps you have fucked yourself and therefore the world has been able to fuck you as it always already had.

In light of the death of the author, I think through the framework of being positioned after *Vampiro*, best described by what Jacques Derrida coins "autothanatography," in which one attempts to write one's own death, or rather, to narrate an author's multiple deaths: that of the writer and that of the text. Reading *El vampiro de la colonia Roma* necessitates accounting for the autobiographical and how we are led as readers through this paradigm, signing the proverbial "contract" as Derrida and Paul de Man have named it, one that demands of its reader recognition. De Man describes autobiography as a moment that "happens as an alignment between the two subjects involved in the process of reading in which they determine each other by mutual reflexive substitution." Both difference and similarity are implied by this structure, since "both depend on a substitutive exchange that constitutes the subject."[51] As such, de Man argues, "This specular structure is interiorized in a text in which the author declares himself the subject of his own understanding. . . . This amounts to saying that any book with a readable title-page is, to some extent, autobiographical."[52] In this same vein, Derrida also seeks to blur the borders of text and autobiography in literature and philosophy. He proposes that the autobiographical genre is an egotistic affirmation of knowledge about anything and especially about oneself.[53] Derrida explains that this phenomenon occurs in a rounding and cyclical movement from mouth to ear, and moreover, "this necessity requires that we pass by way of the ear—the ear involved in any autobiographical discourse that is still at the stage of hearing oneself speak."[54] The chapters are presented as tapes, and Adonis reminds some "you" in the second person at the very end that they need to turn off the recorder. Whether someone is in the room or not, he does hear himself speak. Throughout the novel he corrects himself or hears himself out loud and makes comments about his words or laughs at his own jokes. He is very self-referential and communicates with himself and a second object. In view of that, *El vampiro de la colonia Roma* echoes what Derrida describes of the autobiographical moment: the self-communicating with the self in harmony and aesthetics. It is egotistic, yes, but also conciliatory. Adonis feels pleased with both his past, current, and future self. Yet his own timeline is ambiguous. He is ambiguous.

Nonetheless, just as we cannot apprehend the moment of encounter, we cannot apprehend fully both knowledge and language. And here is when we veer toward the impossibilities of living. Yet only after dying could we say that we have lived. Again, as in the search for comprehending phenomena, knowledge, or language, we face the dynamic of the impossible. For Derrida, this is in the context of the relations between fiction and autobiographical truth—which is also to say, between literature and death. Adonis García offers a testimony of his time in Mexico City, even though he is a very unreliable witness to whom a lot of credit has been given. Derrida argues, "In essence a testimony is always autobiographical: it tells, in the first person, the shareable and unshareable secret of what happened to me, to me, to me alone, the absolute secret of what I was in a position to live, see, hear, touch, sense, and feel."[55] That secret is, "What runs through this testimony of fiction is thus the singular concept of an 'unexperienced experience.'"[56] One of these experiences, of course, is passion, since "passion always testifies." Moreover, passion also implies "a certain passivity in the heteronomic relation to the law and to the other, because this heteronomy is not simply passive and incompatible with freedom and with autonomy, it is a matter of the passivity of passion before and beyond the opposition between passivity and activity."[57] As a poor sex worker, Adonis shares his sexual autobiographical experiences to reflect on the life of passive decision rooted in the secret of the missing holes of the text. He arrives at these conclusions through the solitude of his passion, which activates the pain and pleasure zones of his senses, making the autobiographical so sensorial, and also still incapable of being fully legible and intelligible.

El vampiro de la colonia Roma teases out the fluidity between sex and death through the penetrative acts that lead readers to anger, frustration, or even panic. Through sex, Adonis narrates an "ends" to class distinctions that have created an elite Mexicanness. He is keenly aware of the ways sex has the potential to subvert social and class division. Describing a sexual orgy, he explains, "something very curious happens   well   there's a lot of cooperation between everyone you see? as if everyone were equal   there   all the social classes fall into sex right?"[58] In the act of the orgy, lines of separation are blurred through the mixing and overlapping of bodies. In the orgiastic event, both the sense of the self and the recognition of an other, or many others, is suspended. The self is opened up to his own otherness in relation to his proximity to the collective: his sense of individualism dies. While Adonis celebrates sex, and has a lot of it, there is a sense of unfulfillment in his life. After his first anal sex experience as a top, Adonis becomes absolute pleasure. Sexual experience defined his being from there on out. He asserts that life is only worth living to experience the pleasures it can provide, which for him is only through sex. For Adonis, life is sex. He is sex. He articulates a sexual culture that has sustained itself pre- and post-AIDS, a culture of those who aspire to pursue sex for the sake of sex alone, in its purest form, without those rudimentary fears of STIs or any of that shit; they don't believe in relationships, they only believe in just fucking. Often this worldview is read as a very cis white gay male perspective, which has been perpetuated by white queer negativists who espouse a theoretical nuance of a barebacking culture without naming the privilege it takes to even name one's claim to an identity formation. We thus have to remember that Adonis is primarily white and white-passing. Rather, a view from the bottom makes this evident because it forces us to actually consider what and which bodies are doing during male-to-male sexual encounters, challenging the doxa of sex as a marital act in the privacy of the bedroom and filling it with the images of deviant sexuality. By employing sexual ideologies dependent on the primacy of being fucked and attempting to perform these acts and ideas in spaces not typically afforded to him, Adonis actively returns to sex as an act of fidelity to his first orgasm. Yet every sexual act thereafter is unfulfilling. The orgasm had already died.

Adonis belongs to a broken Mexico, brought about by a constant interplay of fucking and being fucked. Through the sexual act, Adonis meets his own ends. At the end of his narration he describes abandoning it all and leaving the world behind on a penis-shaped spaceship.[59] As he makes his ascent out of Earth's atmosphere, he describes the monuments that have anchored the mapping of his sexual adventures around Mexico City but have also memorialized the nation-building project. The last images he sees as he departs from Earth are the symbols of a nationalist ideal and figures of a futurity that fail those who remain faithful to its practices. He could also just be describing his plane ride from Mexico

City to Michoacán. Rereading *El vampiro de la colonia Roma* reveals how to open oneself to the event of being fucked. Focusing on passivity enables this current work to consider the significance of sexual acts and gendered and sexualized constitutions of Mexicanness. Gained are a new lexicon and theoretical framework by which to read the disruptive nature of sexual acts in nationalist literature, but also the paradigmatic qualities that posit an ethics of engaging sexual alterity through how one accepts their own by narrating it as an expression of the affective encounter with that otherness that ultimately resides in the self.

3

Bruno Ramri and the Corruption of a Mecos State

What pornography is really about, ultimately, isn't sex but death.
—Susan Sontag, "The Pornographic Imagination"

Bottomness as an aesthetic may be characterized by a bottom through their foundational signifiers, like *pasivo, puñal, joto, vampiro*. But what they are called is not the practice of bottoming itself. There are those forms of bottom performances that are not so easily labeled. Let's adjust positions to more clearly discuss ethico-political orientations of the exposed body. Reconfigured in this way, we might be able to consider how bodies in their exposure from and to the nation-state may be bent over, ass-up, face-down, and fucked over *and over*. This chapter is curious about getting fucked in fucked-up circumstances. Here, submissive positionality differs from the versions of exposure unfolded in the preceding chapters by narrowing in on how bodies in their bottomness bottom toward being fucked into submission that takes the passivity of passive bottoming even deeper. This chapter addresses how bodies in their exposure are fucked into intimate attachments with the nation-state's dominating actors—even when they are abusive. Interfacing with the conceptualization of exposure as a mode of "being fucked," which we have examined as a practice and a cultural paradigm, I change the exposed body's position to explore the full depth of its potential for reading the aesthetics of sex and death. The power of the body in submission charges the structural qualities of a body exposed as a social position within the nation-state. This triptych of practical, cultural, and structural forms of exposure conceptualize "being fucked" as the event: how it is calculated, interpolated, and verified.

Surrounding acts of submission is a question of where pleasure is located, or rather, with whom pleasure is identified. Bottoms can expose various stages of vulnerability that may be raptured or strategically deployed as the result of its positionality. Yet, as a structural positionality constituted by and constitutive of the nation-building project, the politics of pleasure problematizes, even reimagines, how violence (symbolic or otherwise) may be carried out against the body in the public sphere, crossing the boundaries of the private to make knowable the processes through which a bottom is always already positioned for a "power" top to fuck up a bottom.

The line distinguishing between what is fucked up and what is sexually arousing about certain forms of fucking is often very thin and blurry. And if even noticeable, the line's existence is definitely ignorable. Even a body in submission experiences sex and death on the same affective register at the same time. It is that involuntary action forced upon the body, like a sneeze (resist as one may, it finds a way to erupt from the body) or the way a tickle makes someone laugh, even if they are not happy. The abject at the core of the bottom and their performances comes from that orgasm that escapes while getting fucked in fucked-up circumstances. Pleasure structures how specific scenes that are set in the theater of the nation-state cast sex and death as necessary actors that entangle their relationship with one another on stage—or on camera.

For example, six months preceding the unresolved disappearance of the forty-three Ayotzinapa students that caught international attention in the fall of 2014, Mexican president Enrique Peña Nieto, by presidential decree, declared May 17 the "National Day for the Fight against Homophobia":

> This Decree defines homophobia as fear, rejection or dislike toward people because of their orientation, sexual preference, identity, and gender expression, based on stereotypes, prejudices, and stigmas, expressed in attitudes and behaviors that violate the equality, dignity, rights, and freedom of everyone, which can generate various types of violence.[1]

Announcing this proud moment to protect the lives of Mexican gays and lesbians, President Peña Nieto posted the news to Twitter with the hashtag "#MéxicoIncluyente" (#InclusiveMexico), documenting a major step in inclusion and progress for the nation writ large.[2] The distinction over whose lives are worth protecting and those significantly without basic survival resources is fraught with curated images and narratives about contemporary Mexico's social progress and inclusion. State-related violence that may be sexually loaded by nature cannot truly be understood, or made legible, as the result of the nation-state painting its own versions of what inclusivity looks like, while simultaneously refusing to investigate other forms of violence carried out against other bodies.

The interdependent relationship between violence, sexuality, and the state is excessively prevalent and yet remarkably underexamined, because we simply cannot see it. Hidden from the public eye or not, one only has to look through the recent history of cases of violence and death in Mexico to see this relationship. On May 22, 2016, an attack on a gay bar in Xalapa, the capital of the Mexican state of Veracruz, left five dead and fourteen wounded.[3] Security cameras captured multiple suspects, who arrived at Xalapa's Bar Madame on motorcycles around 1:00 a.m. and began opening fire upon entering the club's doorway. Those inside the club sent out pleas for help on social media and text message. However, as in the Zona Rosa cases I recall in the first chapter, authorities largely blamed the Xalapa shooting on narco-violence and drug conflict in the area. The question of homophobia or sex crime was not considered. Moreover, the murderers were never apprehended.[4] In fact, from 2010 to 2016, 154,557 people were murdered in Mexico, and in 94.8 percent of those cases, there is no suspect facing charges. From 2015 to 2018, Mexico experienced a remarkable increase in homicide cases.[5] News about the attack at the Xalapa gay bar did not gain the same international attention as other attacks against sexual minorities in other parts of the globe, like the shooting in Orlando, Florida, three weeks later, at Pulse Nightclub on Latin Night.[6] Yet, over the past decade, Mexico has certainly borne witness to its fair share of aggression toward sexual minorities.[7] The inconsistency between a presidential decree that defines what "homophobia" means and an attack on a gay bar underscores the reality that Mexico does not have issues with homophobia, because it is never documented. What is undocumented simply does not exist within the arena of the nation-state. Rather, the universal narrative that must spin these events is curated for the public: Mexico is a *modern* nation with significant recognition for its inclusive culture, clear protection of LGBTQ+ individuals from homophobia, and advancement in gay and lesbian rights, *and* the country just happens to also have narco-related violence that may have nothing to do with anyone's sexual orientation or desires. The narrative in this regard changes based on who is the victim and who is the perpetrator. The victims of the Pulse shooting are rightfully remembered by a nation that collectively mourned this great loss. The best interest of the victim in some cases can be liberatory to some degree. And yet, in cases like Xalapa, the triangulation in naming a perpetrator also denies who the victims were and what their deaths signify.

This violence relates to notions of spatializing the queerness of those exposures through the lens of performance. Death as a formidable cultural force that propagates violence reflects a radical displacement and dislocation of the sexual body onto competing narratives about sexual violence and inclusivity. As a concept that speaks to the figuration and disfiguration of the body, death orients my discussion of queer performance in hemispheric Latinx American landscapes. I suggest that violence, in particular, is the inadvertent cause of queer form, which can be defined as the affective realization of bodies constructed by their attachment to the political structures of sex. Queer form is best understood by a particularly violent constitution of sexual identities, practices, and hierarchies. Performance perhaps then makes knowable this relation through embodied practices and spatial interventions. Accordingly, queer analysis extends itself to account for the critical spatiality of the nation-state wherein bodies are violent fucked into submission and might find certain entryways to pleasure.

The way that narratives about *diversidad sexual* are complemented by and contrasted with death reveals tensions between pleasure and violence that capture and describe the structural aspects of being the submissive exposed body. The submissive bottom is always already caught in the abyss of the impasse. José Esteban Muñoz presents this as a manner of responsive politics, which he theorizes through the idea of "disidentification" as a strategic queer process that neither assimilates nor opposes but rather reimagines ways of negotiating power. Through his examination of the performance of politics for queers of color, Muñoz reconceptualizes the queer body and critical thought through a radical performance of resistance by how it negotiates power within dominant white heteronormative ideologies. As such, through these modes of thinking, queer of color cultural critique is called upon "to transform a cultural logic from within, always laboring to enact permanent structural change while at the same time valuing the importance of local and everyday struggles of resistance."[8] This paradigm of thinking posits a strategy of existence—of being—and a postcolonial consciousness. As a strategy, this resonates with how non-mainstream queers—those who cannot be defined by the nation-state's neatly packaged narrative about sexual diversity—navigate other queer spaces.

Within dominant narratives about sexual culture, and the institutions that disseminate these narratives about *diversidad sexual*, there has yet to be a pause to address the others who reside outside the boundaries of homonationalism, who do not wish to participate in the normative trajectories of sexual culture as it is (re)produced and determined by the social capital of the state. And yet, even residing outside those lines, sexual others still remain captured by the borders of the nation-state. The displacement, disjuncture, and disfiguration of "accepted" forms of sexual identities and desires constitute a site for the formation of violence. It is the formation of hegemonic and prescriptive narratives about violence that, when filtered through a queer lens of analysis, become unstable and disrupted. In this sense, narratives about "acceptable" ways of naming and studying death—through homophobia, misogyny, and femicide, for example—fetishize the sexual other as a tool that disseminates false universal narratives about progress and victory over adversity: to basically become a rainbow flagbearer for social growth and cultural inclusivity. In other words, this chapter is invested in engaging with queer performances that do not *just* address the different forms of homophobia and toxic masculinity at play in Mexican culture. These performances produce affective encounters that take on political and cultural discourses in sexual terms that necessarily shed light on the overlooked intersectional and interdependent ties between sex, death, and politics.

Let's Make a Porno: Doing Sexual Labor for the State

Central to the artistic methods deployed in this chapter is the role of pornography, opening a space to produce a language through which to talk about sexually violent experiences that not only reside within the body, but also get performed by and onto the sexual bodies themselves. In its earliest definition, "pornograph" referred to an image or a piece of writing about prostitutes. Put another way, a pornograph is the aesthetic representation of sexual labor. The *Oxford English Dictionary* elaborates upon this idea by defining pornography as "intended to stimulate erotic rather than aesthetic feeling."[9] But the works discussed thus far already push back on distinctions made between aesthetic and erotic feelings as mutually exclusive. Linked to art, aesthetics has traditionally referred to the study of beauty and taste that elicits feelings in the spectator upon seeing the artwork. The assumption, then, that scenes of sex cannot produce an erotic feeling that is aestheticizing in nature seems naïve. Surely, these scenes arouse the human body in ways that extend beyond libidinal effects. This distinction inhibits sex—and the body by extension—from poising its ability to produce new forms of knowledge and criticism. I want to consider, then, how the erotic charge of scenes of sexual violence produces a similar affective experience, wherein aesthetics is not limited to the study of art in high culture. Here, thinking pornographically invokes a new and divergent reading gaze through those erotic entanglements with the aesthetic. Braiding this idea with the term's early definition, I am interested in how the body writes about its sexual labor through the exposure of its sexual subjectivity.[10]

Thus, this chapter narrows in on the radical visibility of bodies participating in, or forced into participation in, this pornographic-oriented construction and critique of the idea of the "nation-state" on both explicit and implicit registers. Through a close reading of bodies as always already captured by the pornographic gaze of the nation-state, these texts offer new understandings of abjection and submission as they relate to the actors in question. I begin with performance artist Bruno Ramri's *Revenge Porn: La invasión de la privacidad* (2014) as an exemplary model of the body in submission onto which different and divergent memories of, experiences with, and anxieties about state-related violence are performed and projected onto the exposed body. Ramri combines his traditional formation as a contemporary dancer of primarily Martha Graham technique with experimental uses of space and body work to perform a commentary on the role of state-involved censorship and the public's sexual relationship to it. Ramri uses the genre of "revenge porn" as a guiding parameter for viewing the body through a pornographical gaze, one that may be violated or otherwise exploited in ways that blur the borders of consent. Complementing Ramri's more abstract approach to these themes, I also turn to the porn archive itself as the most appropriate scene partner to shed light on these same dimensions. This chapter takes seriously the aesthetic performance of sex acts in the adult film *Corrupción mexicana* (2010), produced by Mexico City's infamous porn studio Mecos Films. Together, these versions of pornographical display give access to the aesthetics through which the bottom is fucked by those actors dominating within and for the nation-state: literally, by fucking for the state to exercise its sovereign power to make decisions about sex and death.

I take literally and with utmost seriousness the sexual excess at work in the images produced by the bodies fucking in what follows. At stake are reading methods that are imbricated with performance studies and that may make sense of how bodies are sexualized within narratives about state-related violence. Further, how do we handle these sexual bodies? What is our relationship to them? These questions navigate a pornographic reading of the aesthetics, ethics, and politics of sex and death in hemispheric Latinx America.

The space of the erotic in pornography is really about the aesthetics of art: those feelings of pleasure that are produced even when they're deemed problematic. Through pornographical performances, sex just might tell stories about the queerness of politics that rely on that sexual labor. Preoccupied with aesthetics as a driving force that guides our reading of sex and death in and from the bottom, I recognize how aesthetics make the symbolic order of sexual politics not only legible, but tactile, seductive, and intelligible. Etymologically and socio-historically, an aesthetic approach to porn captures the experience—sensational, affective, sensorial, emotional—of encountering the world, thus making sensorial and affective paradigms central contributors to the production of queer knowledges about the hemispheric bottom. Aesthetics, in this sense, necessarily reveals and makes knowable the pleasurable experiences of violence, even as abject as those experiences may be.

Here, abjection describes a positionality achieved by way of, symptomatic of, and constitutive of violence. Violence does not function in the field of agreement, but rather, in those of contested claims about who produces violence and who is the receiver of said violence. Through this ambiguity, we find an idea of abjection that overwrites a contested discursive field. I understand abjection as an act of violent governance that projects power by leaving its mark on the body. My approach to the abject body is indebted to Black studies scholars of sex who have conceptualized the abject through those racialized and postcolonial bodies who cannot and will not wholly function within the normative trajectories of sex. Darieck Scott articulates the possibilities for pleasure while being Black, in which sex is always already the grounds for the aesthetics of imminent violence. He posits, "Though sexuality is used against us, and sexual(ized) domination is in part what makes us black, though sexuality is a mode of conquest and often cannot avoid being deployed in the field of representation without functioning as an introjection of historical defeat, it is in and through that very domination and defeat also a mapping of political potential, an access to freedom."[11] In refusing the aesthetics of death—here read as violence—as inherent in the sexual experience as racialized and postcolonial subjects, Scott articulates the possibility for abjection to be both claimed and refused. In the same vein, Jennifer C. Nash reads this call to politics and evocation of liberation as constitutive not only of Black sexual experience but also, more sharply, of pleasure. That is, "pleasures in blackness are pleasures in abjection, where the wound of blackness is taken up as a site of ecstasy."[12] The racialized constitution of the body determines a violent construction of pleasure when those racialized bodies move toward or even away from violence. Pleasure experienced by racial subjects is felt along the same continuum of trauma that nests in the folds and crevices of the body.

I focus on hemispheric Latinx American sexual subject formation through critical bottom studies that reads and engages with exposed bodies being fucked. The bottom holds sexual memories of the Conquest, corrupt governments, and enforced imaginary borders that when deployed are navigated and negotiated with what Leticia Alvarado describes in Latinx performance as an "irreverent aesthetic strategy" articulated through the tenor of the abject.[13] Exposed in these acts are aesthetic strategies that have been deployed to determine who is ultimately fucked. The bottom is constitutive of and yet a critique of the systemic violence of their subjugation.

The violence fucking the body into submission speaks to a distinct characteristic of the nation-state's affairs that envelop and take hostage the bodies of those for whom the law does not exist and whom the law does not protect. Violence functions both inside and outside the law. As Juana María Rodríguez notes, "A central feature of the law is the way it authorizes its own power, through violence," wherein law is the prerogative of sovereign power, including in the secular democratic guises it dons within

Figure 3.1. Bruno Ramri, *Revenge Porn: La invasión de la privacidad*, 2014, Festival Inter-nacional por la Diversidad Sexual, Museo Universitario del Chopo. Photography by Ulises Escobar.

the social contract of the nation-state. In other words, "sovereign power asserts an unchecked autonomy over the interpretation of the law."[14] Whether we are speaking about the state's complicity in organized crime and corruption, the effects of narco-warfare, or the appropriated borders enforced by imperial powers permitting children to be locked in cages, the hierarchy of abjection locates these producers of violence at the top, tops that necessarily fuck them into submission as a fundamental exercise of sovereignty. Thus, to speak about what I describe as the nation-state's pornograph recognizes and locates the submissive body as a central actor in this violence. The internal/external dichotomy of violence as produced by the work of the "law" (as illusory as this may be) creates the stage, the plot, the soundtrack, and the camera angles through which the collec-tive and public imaginary gets off on seeing this violence played out. My turn, then, toward the structural elements of exposure that create a social positionality out of being fucked interrogates these moments of conquest in which those in power exert their power by fucking certain bodies into their "right place" in society—at the bottom and into submission.

Bruno Ramri's Invasive Body and the Subjects of Bondage

Bruno Ramri's *Revenge Porn: La invasión de la privacidad* was first performed on November 9, 2013, in an adult movie theater in Mexico City.
In concert with Lechedevirgen Trimegisto's repertoire discussed in the
first chapter, this solo performance reflects shared investments in the
exposure of and to the sexual body. In his work, Ramri wears patent
leather stiletto boots and combines body contortion, modern dance,
and BDSM to present his body to the audience in odd and seemingly
uncomfortable positions. Decorated in fetish gear, he binds his genitalia,
creating a large bulge out of his testicles, and places a leather harness
over his head. He is naked, his body glistens with his sweat, and he wears
thick black eyeliner. His body movements are paired with a projection
against the wall of varying images and videos presented in real time,
ranging from sex scenes to Mexican political figures. A year prior to
Lechedevirgen's censored performance of *Inferno Varieté* at the 2014 Festival Internacional por la Diversidad Sexual at the Museo Universitario
del Chopo, I encountered Ramri's *Revenge Porn* in the same venue. The
festival organizers described Ramri's work as an "interdisciplinary spectacle" that breeds together dance and eroticism.[15]

Departing with and from the controversial genre of "revenge porn"
as the nonconsensual distribution of sexual videos or photos of a person
with or without their knowledge, *Revenge Porn: La invasión de la privacidad* creates an interactive experience playing with the notion of a de-
lusional and nationally fictionalized individual privacy in which, under
the influences of eroticism, the image of the Other might be exploited
and disclosed without their consent. For the artist, the performance is
a sensorial experience that reveals an idea that there is nothing more
public than intimacy. Truly, in this performance Ramri is bound and
exposed, as we are up close and personal. On entering the space, spectators are confined to a close proximity with the artist. Ramri moves
freely throughout the space. He is not restricted to a designated stage
area that would require a fourth wall between him and the audience.
The audience is repeatedly instructed to take photos and videos, using
their mobile devices to capture the artist and his body. Likewise, the artist also takes his own photos and videos of his spectators, which he still
possesses in his own personal archive, to perhaps be used in a future

gallery or performance. The act of documentation, possessing images of each other, is central to *Revenge Porn* (both the genre and Ramri's performance). While both the audience and artist are visually documented, the artist also engages in an interview with the spectators using a voice recorder.

Bruno Ramri's performance moves beyond the borders of what might be deemed private or public through varying modes of documentation, which could be also read as surveillance. Within this performance space, no one can "freely" move without being noticed, recorded, uploaded, and embedded into the expansive archive of bodies already documented in Mexico. Both artist and audience are exposed in their bodily presences to one another. Moreover, the audience is placed into a position of unexpected and undefined vulnerability, being put on the spot by Ramri's extremely pointed questions to express their thoughts and opinions. His questions oscillate between the explicitly political and the sexual. To the latter, Ramri asks a question that distinguishes submission and pleasure from one another. Yet one audience member refuses to see any difference between the two:

> RAMRI: Tell me, should we submit to the body or should we indulge it?
> MAN: Both [*chuckles*].
> RAMRI: How do you submit?
> MAN: I submit to its desires; in which they become the same at times.
> RAMRI: And . . . any particular way of indulging the body?
> MAN: Sex.[16]

The young man pauses, as if to wait for a response, but the artist says nothing. The audience member then softly chuckles as if to relieve the pressure of his poignant responses. In his responses, he articulates his point of view with complete confidence and conviction: submission *and* pleasure, the two being not so easily detangled. Perhaps his chuckle after responding that he would choose both is a display of how illogical such a question could be—as if one should be expected to only choose one or the other. His answers center desire and sex at the core of the body's submission and pleasure. The body may submit to its own desires and appetite, but may also become that which is craved and desired in the first place by and through a subjugation. In this respect, the audience member acknowledges the abjection of his own desires and body. Another man chooses indulgence by, as he describes to Ramri, "Listening to it, and . . . taking care of it, and . . . trying to know what it needs." But a young woman's answers were somewhere between the two; she tells Ramri, "I indulge it by allowing it to feel. I submit sometimes by not avoiding what it feels, a bit." Feeling is at the heart of these various responses because it is at the center of the question itself: In what ways does the state allow one to feel? And how might it interfere?

In concert, Ramri narrows in on the public opinion of the current state of affairs by asking audience members about their views of the government and state writ large:

RAMRI: Do you think we are the state?
WOMAN: The state . . . government?
RAMRI: The government.
WOMAN: Yes.
RAMRI: Do you think this government represents you, and how?
WOMAN: Like me personally? No, no it doesn't represent me. But I'm part of a society.
RAMRI: Aha.
WOMAN: So . . . it has to do with, like . . . the idiosyncrasy between my family and the country or society in general. And the current government is part of that.
RAMRI: And how does it represent you?
WOMAN: I don't identify.
RAMRI: Can you write it?
WOMAN: Uh-huh.

[*writing sound*]

RAMRI: Gracias.

This seems to be a consistent answer among audience members, yet most are also confused by what Ramri means by "the state," whereas "government" stands in for a term already fraught with meanings conflicting with an other or many others. In another exchange, a similar interaction:

RAMRI: Do you think we are the state?

MAN: To which state do you refer?

RAMRI: Government.

MAN: Eh . . . no.

RAMRI: Do you think this government represents you?

MAN: Mexico's? [*laughs*]

RAMRI: We could say that. Let's begin there.

MAN: No.

RAMRI: And yours?

MAN: Λ little more but not much.

AUDIENCE: [*laughs*]

RAMRI: Why?

MAN: Life's events.

RAMRI: Tell me, why doesn't it represent you?

MAN: Sometimes, maybe you need help from your state, although bureaucratic or also, I don't know, paperwork, and this makes you realize that it works well for you. Both this and mine.

RAMRI: Okay. Write it.

Complementing these questions and responses, some are asked to write words or phrases that objectify or shame his body, which includes asking others what part of his body they find arousing. Some are simply asked to write out their sexual fantasies or sexual fears onto his body. By the end of the process, most of the artist's body is covered in black marker, complementing the black leather harnesses he has on.

Ramri combines BDSM practices with his training in modern dance to inform his movements within and across the space. One of the signature images of *Revenge Porn: La invasión de la privacidad* is the performance of self-bondage. With a rope, Ramri binds certain parts of his body and fixates himself into submissive positions. However, a clearly defined dominant figure, or master, ordering him into these positions (as traditionally understood in BDSM practices) is not fully present or identifiable—at least not in an obvious way. Rather, the artist performs this act of bondage upon himself throughout the twenty-minute duration of the performance, until his body is completely bound by rope. He submits himself to us to become a "fucking machine" through which pleasure and pain are sexualized, racialized, and projected while it is

Figure 3.2. Bruno Ramri, *Revenge Porn: La invasión de la privacidad*, 2014, Festival Internacional por la Diversidad Sexual, Museo Universitario del Chopo. Photography by Ulises Escobar.

filtered onto and through his body as the "spectacle" of performance. In *The Color of Kink: Black Women, BDSM, and Pornography*, Ariane Cruz offers one of the most elegant theorizations of "fucking machines" from sex toys to robot penetrators in relation to their racialization in the process of functioning as machinery of the industrialized state that fucks at the interstices of race, gender, sexuality, technology, and visuality— indeed, as that which is industrial and automated in ways that turn the bottom into a tool for the machine. Cruz points to how the imbrication of race, gender, sexuality, technology, pleasure, and visuality is at stake in the "new medias" of the body by underscoring how these machines are extensions of whiteness and, more specifically, "not merely extensions of their white inventors and the white male imaginary but . . . embodiments of white masculinity." As such, these moments of performance in pornographic settings function as, according to Cruz, "a technique of racial-sexual alterity nonetheless."[17] By this, I look to how Ramri's body is bound to be an object through and onto which information is uploaded, but also absorbed and filtered in sexual terms. His body is converted into an avatar of the patriarchal gaze that demands his subjugation for these questions to be posed.

Bruno Ramri's self-binding and self-imposed passivity before the spectator are to be gazed at, like a roped creature. These encounters are always already racialized by the construction of the white spectacle of museums and galleries themselves; it is interesting that Ramri insists that this performance take place in the grimiest and most atrocious of places—the bottom. In Bruno Ramri's *Revenge Porn*, audience members do not know how to react to him, engage, or even express their nervousness about being close to the artist. One audience member stated, "I just want to be a happy and content man, and enjoy the performance." In a way, he almost refuses to participate, even if his passive participation is participation enough within this space. Refusal is not something afforded to the body, as one discovers in their encounter with Ramri. Perhaps one of the most salient examples of this encounter with the Other is best captured in an exchange with a non-fluent Spanish speaker:

RAMRI: ¿Te sientes intimidado?
MAN: Un poco.

Figure 3.3. Bruno Ramri, *Revenge Porn: La invasión de la privacidad*, 2014, Festival Internacional por la Diversidad Sexual, Museo Universitario del Chopo. Photography by Ulises Escobar.

RAMRI: ¿Qué te causa miedo?

MAN: Umm . . . las personas me mirando. ¿*mi-oleando*? ¿*O-oleando*?

RAMRI: ¿Mirándote?

MAN: Me mirando. Mirándome.

RAMRI: ¿Por qué?

MAN: Porque es *fijo* and vergoñado. ¿*Vergoñado*?

RAMRI: Avergonzado.

MAN: ¿Cómo?

RAMRI: Avergonzado.

MAN: Avergonzado.

RAMRI: Uh-huh. ¿Cómo te hace sentir eso? ¿Que te observen?

MAN: Ahora estoy como . . . uh uh [*mimicking shaking sound*]

AUDIENCE: [*laughs*].

MAN: ¿Tremoles?

RAMRI: ¿Puedes escribirlo?

MAN: Sí.

The real spectacle in this performance is not Ramri's body or even the act of bondage, which might seem so interesting and enticing; rather, it is our relational proximity to it. While Ramri may be positioned as the performer and the central focal point of the piece, the performance does not transmit or divulge cultural knowledge from the artist. He provides the audience a vehicle within which the body cruises and travels with new technologies to store and download information that is being projected upon it by the audience, once they are triggered by his questioning. We are given access to a body as the receptive vessel for our collective and public political and sexual fantasies. Through its confrontational intervention, *Revenge Porn* reveals a position of privilege without it entirely being visible or necessarily knowable—the power, control, and surveillance that are exerted from the position of invisibility and anonymity. Yet, while the body is presented as aggressively open to the audience, coded in BDSM tropes in which the body is submissive to the spectator, that accessibility is also strictly regulated by the frameworks and questions that are curated by the artist, the duration of the piece, and the space. The performance of *Revenge Porn* actually varies based on location: I have encountered the performance in an abandoned bus, a museum, and the basement of the Teatro de la Ciudad Esperanza Iris in Mexico City. Because the space drastically changes between performances, it is difficult to describe *Revenge Porn* as a wholly structured entity. Ramri's work is best understood as a sexual durational performance through its spontaneous and surprising sexual occupation of space and proximity.

The imposition of censorship and its invasive nature in the collective and national imaginary fetishize violence to the degree of the sexualization of death. Undertaking a queer reading of death and Mexicanness underscores the pornograph in Ramri's work through the displacement of affective responsibility onto the audience: the formation of violence through an inversion of the channels by which memories of state-related violence are transmitted between artist and spectator. Taking into account the orientation of the body and space that foregrounds ideas of shame, resistance, and identity, this performance also reorients and reframes the notion of the "invasion of privacy." Here, invasion is twofold. First, it refers to a breach of an individual citizen's confidentiality—more specifically, the invasion of their private lives, which are and continue to be exploited and exposed by those in power. Second, I refer to the idea of "privacy" itself as that which invades cultural production and violates cultural memories through the body's bondage to the ideas of "privacy" and "protection."

Formed as a well-trained contemporary dancer at the Colegio Nacional de Danza Contemporánea in Querétaro, a former member of the prestigious Ballet Independiente, and the famed gay men's dance company La Cebra in Mexico City, Ramri combines the definitive qualities of Martha Graham technique in modern dance with experimental uses of space and body work to compose a performance that acts as a commentary on the position of the exposed body within political discourses and society's engagement and complacency with the specters of violence that linger in quotidian life as a force blocking the body from moving freely in the theater of the nation-state. Graham technique is designed to present the dancer as overly expressive and dramatic in their movements. The movement vocabulary associated with Graham technique draws connections between the physical and emotional meanings of power, control, and vulnerability. Movement begins from the core of the body and incorporates large back movements and lots of floor work.[18] The motivation behind each movement is that the dancer is making their way through the weighted force of their environment, like a heavy mass that the dancer is slowly pushing through. Yet *Revenge Porn* does not represent overcoming adversity or the obstacles of the world. Rather, a violent gesture is summoned and transformed by the audience's binding proximity to the artist, conjured and recast as an erotic and sadomasochist fantasy. In this respect, the body of the artist is not merely an object of consumption, subsumed by the exploitation of neoliberal markets and pinkwashing social capital campaigns, but instead is manufactured into an object of desire.

Upon approaching Ramri's bound, inquisitive, naked body, we would expect something profoundly dramatic or shocking to happen in that encounter. Yet, surprisingly, the interaction with Ramri is confoundingly anticlimactic. There is often an assumption that while attending a performance, a certain level of intelligibility could and would be attainable through and from the performing artist. In this sense, we attend performances to learn something, to access a particular artefact through some embodied archive that has been momentarily unlocked for us. However, over the duration of the performance, there is nothing overly meaningful to be received or downloaded *from* Ramri—or at least there wasn't for me. On the contrary, it becomes apparent that within the all-encompassing performance space, the audience is not there for the artist, but rather, he is there for *us*. Our intimacy as an audience with Ramri is charged by our solicited active participation in the performance, in which the affective encounter with the sex of the Other becomes intelligible—in the sense that we somewhat understand what is going on—only through our own actions in the space. In other words, *we* are the performance and Ramri's role is not to entertain or to divulge any sense of "truth," but rather, to motivate the audience to access the archive within our *own* embodiments.

This is the opposite of, though complementary to, the work being produced in Lechedevirgen Trimegisto's *Inferno Varieté*, in which the body *is* the event for the production of knowledge—or, more nearly, the body is rhetorically positioned to confront the audience. On the other hand, in *Revenge Porn* it is the audience that confronts the body. This confrontation underscores a failure that cannot be contained: the state strips the image of violence from the public imaginary. Ramri has curated a space in which his alterity as sexually divergent is confronted by the public gaze. The audience assumes its role on top, while Ramri binds himself through their narrative production about the repressed traumatic histories that have been purged and projected onto his exposed body. The performance is visibly sexual, calling attention to painful and uncomfortable forms of sexuality. But the performance's relationship to sexual desire and pleasure is also deformed through the mediation of the audience. The pain and discomfort brought to the foreground through the masochistic practice in *Revenge Porn* become reflective of the audience's own pain and discomfort, thus assuming a role in that relational power dynamic that distributes and redistributes certain formations of pleasure and violence.

Audiences become acquainted with the Other ultimately residing within the self. The performance realigns the question of the ethical relationship to the sexualized and racialized Other. The affective encounter at stake in this piece is Ramri's encounter with *our* alterity, by which he is passively taken hostage: his body is literally bound by a rope. *Revenge Porn* draws on the theme of failure on both explicit and implicit levels.

Plate 1. Lechedevirgen's bloody lip-sync to Agustín Lara's "Como dos puñales." *Inferno Varieté: Devoción*, 2014, Teatro de la Ciudad, Monterrey, Nuevo León. Photography by Herani Enríquez HacHe.

Plate 2. Lechedevirgen painting "JOTO" on their body. *Inferno Varieté: Devoción* (2014). Teatro de la Ciudad, Monterrey, Nuevo León. Photography by Herani Enríquez HacHe.

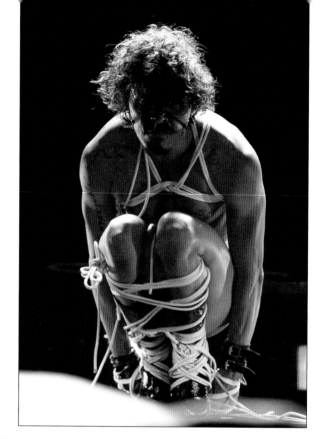

Plate 3. Bruno Ramri, *Revenge Porn: La invasión de la privacidad*, 2014, Festival Internacional por la Diversidad Sexual, Museo Universitario del Chopo. Photography by Ulises Escobar.

Plate 4. Video still from *Todos somos hijos de la Chingada*, performed July 14, 2019, in Mexico City by Yanina Orellana and Vicente. Filmed by author.

Plate 5. Video still from *Todos somos hijos de la Chingada*, performed July 14, 2019, in Mexico City by Yanina Orellana and Vicente. Filmed by author.

Plate 6. Carlos Martiel, *Monumento I*, 2021, Museo del Barrio, New York City. LA/Reinal 20/21.

Plate 7. Carlos Martiel, *Monumento I*, 2021, Museo del Barrio, New York City. LA/Reinal 20/21.

Plate 8. Carlos Martiel, *Insignia III*, 2021.

The performative qualities of the work underscore the state's failure to fully censor or cleanse the images and memories of the daily necropolitical violence that occurs in Mexico. The body remembers. Bodies can disappear, be buried, or remain deserted, but the collective and public imaginary is not amnesiac. The self is held to its own accountability for these experiences. Those cultural and collective traumatic memories remain stored within our own bodies to come out and take shape through our sexual desires, fetishes, and fears, only to be mapped and printed onto Ramri's body when he provokes said memories with a series of interrogations about our own sexual practices in relation to the nation-state.

Moreover, the performance produces a critique of the very constitution of sexual subjectivities: to think of them as the product and effect of numerous practices of power and discourses. Ramri positions himself in a bottoming position in a way that asks to be fucked, passive to what that demand even makes. The displacement of the audience's own traumatic memories is affixed onto a sexualized body and is thereby annihilating to his own sense of self. It is imperative to emphasize that an act of sexual violence is committed in this performance. Ramri's work addresses a latent social violence toward the body that links violence to the defacement of the body through a sexual vocabulary. The demand made from the Other to shame his body is presented to the audience and they oblige, by marking his body in terms that call on shame and objectification. While Ramri may present his body to be used and "abused" by the audience, the hesitancy to participate creates an odd and strange relationship between the artist and the audience. Yet their complacency, complicity, and compliance with the demand to participate, which create an over-comfortable feeling with the access that has been granted so freely, are perhaps the most jarring aspects of the performance.

Corruptive Scenes of the Porn Overlay

The exposition of Bruno Ramri's submissive status as a corporeal canvas onto which sexual memories of violence may be painted or tagged upon a cultural mural of death's defining presence within queer hemispheric Latinx America raises questions about the location of pleasure in all of this. While his interview questions to audience members bring together an erotic charge of submission and pleasure in the body, alongside and against how that body may be represented by the government and state writ large, there is a gap left between these two areas of thought. I may have made a convincing argument that reveals how both lines of questions are actually the same question, yet these inquiries are asked and answered in two different linguistic registers that are performative of the distinctions often made in the public imaginary regarding sex and politics. In other words, it would appear that audience members are prepared to code-switch their social location based on their proximity to either sex or political opinion—always separate, never to be thought of or responded to in the same semantic space. The gap is an aesthetic possibility for imagining how these seemingly disparate or contradictory ideologies might overlay one another. For Ramri, his body literally became bound and tied up in that space, representing the bondage of that impasse that refuses to account for the sexual dimensions of governments and hierarchies of power that fuck bodies into submission.

In that respect, the pornographic stage is set. The lights are on and the camera is rolling. Surely, what exists in the impasse is fantasy itself: getting fucked into submission by actors of the nation-state. Juana María Rodríguez rightfully argues, "Pornography, like other forms of cultural production, emerges in a social context wherein preexisting narratives circulate around available forms of representation, forms that must be legible in order to acquire social meaning."[19] Perhaps no text enacts this confounding of social context and pornography better than *Corrupción mexicana*, produced by Mecos Films. As the title would suggest, the erotica of being fucked by actors of the corruptive state becomes portrayable. The viewer enters into the impasse for whatever arousal might ensue, to satisfy that urge and desire to see how these corrupt interactions might unfold. I treat *Corrupción mexicana* as an aesthetic performance of the relationship between sex and death by reading it as a text revealing, with literal symbolism, how actors of the nation-state fuck others into submission. The Mecos website describes the film as "a daring production that takes us on a journey through the nation by way of its hot and corrupt inhabitants. Four stories [*historias*] reveal the horny reality of Mexico."[20] Doubling down on the translation of *historias* into both "history" and "story," the film is presented as an alternative genealogy through which to understand cultural history. That is, the aesthetic qualities of narrative bear on constructions of the history by injecting it with the same erotic fantasy we come to know as part of the nation-state's pornograph.

In an opening sequence set in Mexico City, with the sound of a helicopter overhead and the constant honking of cars, the camera hovers above a car with a man receiving a blow job while driving. This sets up the first scene, in which the two men are forced to service a policeman who has stopped and frisked them. In the second scene, a young man stops to urinate in an alleyway outside an art gallery when he is caught by a soldier. The soldier pulls out his own dick and begins pissing on the young guy before fucking him, and pisses on him again. The third story is that of a *fresa* (entitled rich kid, read as white) who is kidnapped by two *narcos* and is obliged to undergo a double penetration, while his politician father is forced to listen on the phone and becomes aroused, as does the kid's friend as he later recounts to him what happened in a chat window on the Mecos website. Finally, in a scene entitled "El indio cogido" (the fucked Indian), a *vaquero* fucks an Indian in a wheelbarrow, luring him with the fantasy of a life together in the capital as the camera lingers on a picturesque provincial town resembling the countryside of Northern Mexico—and on a street named "The Sad Indian," ironically and problematically enough.

It would seem appropriate, given Mecos's attempt to convey a consciousness of the social and national contexts of Mexico's historical present in a realist way, to mention that unlike the more commercial (read as Western, white-dominant) gay porn studios of the time—like Corbin Fischer, Randy Blue, Sean Cody, for example—that featured muscular jocks or petite smooth twinks, the performers in *Corrupción mexicana* are physically "average" (or "realistic") in comparison to these problematic sexual beauty standards set by the gay porn industry. Some of the men are balding, one has very untidy dreadlocks, beards are unkempt, sixpack abs are not featured, there are major height discrepancies, and most of the men have fully grown, ungroomed pubic hair. They are not presented in a way that exoticizes the global South's gay male body for Western fetish niches—such as BiLatinMen or LatinBoyz, which are targeted to a white audience with a taste for something spicy. As we bear in mind the relationship between pornography and social context, as Rodríguez reminds us, these bodily features of "everyday" or "average" guys create a sense of plausibility that reels fantasy back into a realist set-ting in which one could conceive of these scenes as entirely possible. In other words, a space is constructed for the viewer to truly identify with the scenes and characters, when they already know them all too well in their quotidian affairs.

Following this trajectory to create a sense of aspirational drag to the production (as observed in Alberto Fuguet's experimental film *Siempre Sí*, discussed in chapter 2, in which the aesthetics of the real are made plausible with casting), and by dropping characters and their audiences into plausibly realistic scenarios, Mecos Films produces a cultural text that fosters and cultivates ideas of a social responsibility to these "real-life" scenes, by foregrounding performers who look and sound like the real actors of the nation-state's pornograph. Other scholars have taken up similar claims about the stakes of *Corrupción mexicana* and the porn house Mecos Films more broadly.[21] These readings are written primarily with a tinge of queer optimism that casts a problematic utopian ideal-istic interpretation on the film. *Corrupción mexicana* is praised in the academic literature for its perceivably ethnically and racially diverse casting, which broke with nonnormative ways of representing mascu-linity. Gustavo Subero, for example, argues, "The work by Mecos Films shows multiculturalism and multi-ethnicity as pivotal elements in the construction of queer national identity."[22] This assertion of a national identity dovetails with his earlier claims that the Mecos oeuvre fosters a notion of a "gay nation"; he posits, "The idea of the gay nation that is promoted in these porn films is not necessarily related to geography, but rather to culture's ideological formations and civil society." That is, "They foster a sense of citizenship amongst national viewers who see the elements that construct their own national gay identity portrayed in the film."[23] However, such attempts to fold homosexuality into the nation-building project are alarming. While I have argued that represen-tations of violence against the bodies of sexual minorities are central to the construction and critique of bottom performance, this is based on a positionality that always already operates outside any project of nation. The submission described is not rescuable to create a sense of a "gay na-tion," as both seem to be overly aspirational.

A nonnormative attachment to constructions of a "gay national iden-tity" reflects a cruel optimism and belief in the promise of sovereignty.[24]

The effects of a "slow death," what Lauren Berlant defines as "the physical wearing out of a population in a way that points to its deterioration as a defining condition of its experience and historical existence," are made visible.[25] This queer aspirational slow death reframes reading the submissive and fucked body in these sexual experiences with—or the fantasy of—the figures of power who constitute a corrupt idea of nation-state. There is no promise of sovereignty, and yet it is part of the national and collective imaginary, deployed as instrumental rhetorical objects within the nation-building project. Berlant even contends, "Sovereignty, after all, is a fantasy misrecognized as an object state: an aspiration position of personal and institutional self-legitimating performativity and an affective sense of control in relation to the fantasy of that position's offer of security and efficacy."[26] In other words, the idea of sovereignty promoted by critics of Mecos Films remains caught up in the expression of control and domination, as it is overly exercised. Rather, I turn my attention to the ways whereby the body wears and tears from the everyday processes of participating in the nation-building project. Everyday pleasures, such as sex, weigh heavily on the body, leaving slow but long-term damaging effects. These pleasures have been converted into the tools of the state to optimize labor production. Yet we still partake in them. Sex might vacillate between violence and the desire for life-fulfilling necessity. In the scene of being fucked into submission by actors of the nation-state, fidelity to the sexual systems of power in place is rightfully called into question.

More broadly, I am less interested in Mecos Films—the company—as a case study or a rescue mission for the gay male body to be redistributed into the workings of the nation-state, than I am in the performance of submission that determines and describes the national myth. I focus on submission in relation to the figures of power that fuck the exposed bodies, and how they determine a structural device that reconfigures and redistributes the bottom as a social position that enables, but is also symptomatic of, the violence performed by these figures. Reading the fucked body in this way shows how the bottom wields the power to exercise what Mireille Miller-Young coins an "erotic sovereignty," that is, "a process, rather than a completely achieved state of being, wherein sexual subjects aspire and move toward self-rule and collective affiliation and intimacy, and against the territorializing power of the disciplining state and social corpus." This does not assume that the fucked body operates outside the nation-state, or somehow constructs its own versions of nation, but rather, as Miller-Young describes, "It is part of an on-going ontological process that uses racialized sexuality to assert complex subjecthood."[27] This complexity always remains in-process, leading me to read this overlay of sex and death as captured by the nation's pornograph. The promise of sovereignty is something that may never be fully realized or may never be attainable, because it was never promised to certain bodies in the first place. Rather, I am interested in how the body bottoms and continues to contribute to constructions of nation and state through the act of being fucked into submission. What happens when we find pleasure in those fucked-up scenes? We are taken back to the impasse wherein sex and death are imagined through the overlaying process that reveals how pleasure and violence are indelibly intertwined. Lingering in this abyss is the visualization that makes legible or possible such an overlay. *Corrupción mexicana*, accordingly, offers a kaleidoscopic view into the complexity of these abject relations.

A Desire for Corrupt Cock

Corrupción mexicana, like Ramri's performance, illustrates the impossibility of moving freely through the world without being seen, noticed, and documented. The body remains under constant surveillance and under the fears of capture or overexposure. Those who operate this surveillance are sexualized through knowable figures within the systems of power that create the power for surveillance. Let's begin with Officer Suárez. A dark-skinned, smooth-shaven, average-bodied policeman in a helmet, Officer Suárez encapsulates and sets up, from the very first scene, the relationship between abusive power and pleasure. The viewer arrives on the scene with two men driving in an old-school white Volkswagen Beetle—emblematic of the streets of Mexico City. The camera comes over the sunroof to reveal that the passenger is giving the driver a blow job. The two arrive at their location, the driver zips up his pants, and they knock on the door of the building of their dealer. Officer Suárez casually catches a glimpse of the exchange. What began as a seemingly routine traffic stop turns into a raunchy public sex act.

This opening scene portrays a seemingly plausible situation in which to find oneself: a policeman watching as a dealer sells items to person,

Figure 3.4. Video still of Officer Suárez. *Corrupción mexicana*, dir. El Diablo, Mecos Films, 2010.

trailing the buyer, searching their vehicle, and presenting an opportunity to be convinced to look the other way—usually by cash. Of course, the interaction with Officer Suárez takes a sexual turn in the moment he pats down the passenger and begins groping his crotch, but it is deescalated with humor as Officer Suárez pulls the passenger's pants down to his ankles and reaches into his underwear to pull out a tube sock. The condensation of sex into this exchange exposes the thinly veiled sexualization of the state's abuse that drapes the relationship between agents of power and civilians. The moment the knees of the passenger hit the ground and Officer Suárez's cock gets hard collapses, or at least makes ambiguous, lines separating the nation-state's hegemony and the erotic violence that fucks the body into submission and subjugation.

The abuse of power—represented by a uniformed policeman—is converted into a pleasurable situation. Yet Officer Suárez takes this one step further: he pulls out his baton and forces the driver to his knees to suck on it, while the passenger continues to fellate him. This image of both men on their knees on each side of the policeman, one with a cock in his mouth and the other with the baton, epitomizes the gap identified earlier that bears questions about the bottom's relationship to the nation-state and whether pleasure may be found in acts of submission. Even further, the tryptic image of pleasure, power, and submission captured in this scene perfectly portrays the aesthetic representation of a hierarchy of abjection—the camera is angled from beneath the men, focusing on Officer Suárez standing tall over the two men on their knees. So why would this be this arousing? Rodríguez reminds us that, in theory, we are not supposed to be aroused by such scenes of subjugation, let alone desire participating in their reenactment. She argues, "When we find perverse pleasure in these moments of submission or domination, we expose our own erotic attachments to power, to other scenes and stages that jumble together desire and disgust."[28]

Perhaps, then, maybe all we can do is reenact these scenes, because these scenes of the state's abuse of power remain looping in the historical present. The sexual conversion of these acts uncovers the queer structural components of power and subjugation. That is, "queer" describes how sexual identities and positionalities are captured and converted into political structures. Someone will be at the bottom, whether they are fucked into that submissive state or not—but most likely, they are fucked. Officer Suárez ejaculates over both of their faces and the two men lick up his cum and begin making out. The policeman zips up his pants and leaves.

To think with the desire to reproduce and become aroused by these scenes underscores how the hypersexualization of the body fucked by hegemonic systems poises its potential to be disruptive of the normative narratives about state's power. Amber Jamilla Musser describes such a disruption through acts of masochism in which "what emerges . . . [is] a continued fascination with the questions of agency, subjectivity, and difference."[29] These approaches to reading death through, from, and against the submissive body pour into queer methods of interrogating violence through their interruption of any state-endorsed narratives about sex and death. Called into question are the processes through which sexual subject formation can be imagined.

If we think back to the set of questions Bruno Ramri asks his audience members, we see that on one level the questions address whether one should submit to their body or indulge it, and on another level,

Figure 3.5. Video still of the soldier's golden shower. *Corrupción mexicana*, dir. El Diablo, Mecos Films, 2010.

whether the current government represents them, whether "we" are the state. *Corrupción mexicana*, though predating the performance of *Revenge Porn* by a few years, could be thought of as an answer to both lines of questioning as captured in the same register. The porn film makes use of more or less obvious representations of state power through uniformed agents of the state. In addition to Officer Suárez, a soldier named Federico, perhaps a member of the national guard, makes an appearance in the second scene. Federico approaches a young guy urinating in an alleyway and then pees on him (a golden shower) to show him how disrespectful it is to piss in public. The scene shifts to the two fucking in a garage, where Federico gives the young man another golden shower. The representation of two uniformed men who are obviously associated with the state and its power brings new light and angles to Ramri's question, "Are we the state?" These figures in *Corrupción mexicana* who force the private citizen into submission are surely constituents of the state. Yet let us not abandon the private citizens on their knees, sucking dick and police batons, and being pissed on. Their submission, their bodies, and their orifices are necessary components for the state's power to be realized. While pleasure is extracted from these situations, these actors of the nation-state necessitate a fucked and exposed body. As such, are these dick-sucking private citizens necessary actors in the theater of the state? Of course. Their sexual labor enables structures of state hegemony.

While a policeman and a soldier may be easily identifiable agents of the nation-state, the angles and dimensions of corruption in hemispheric Latinx America are much more heterogeneous. One of the most compelling scenes in *Corrupción mexicana* involves a *fresa*, kidnapping, *narcos*, and a politician. The scene opens to Canek groping himself while searching through profiles on the Mecos social networking website, when he receives a direct message from "Fresa," who tells him, "I have to tell you what happened to me yesterday leaving your house." Canek quickly responds, "Tell me." In flashback, the *fresa* is leaving Canek's house when he is approached by two men who force him at gunpoint into a car and drive him to an undisclosed location. On the bed, they have the young man blindfolded with his hands tied behind his back with his own belt. The *jefe* walks in and asks for the young man's cell phone. He scrolls through his contacts and calls his father, a politician. The politician asks what they want, to which the boss says, "Nothing your extravagant corrupt lifestyle could ever give." He asks how much money they want. But the boss doesn't want money; instead, he wants him to listen to what happens to his son next. He sets the phone down with a large wad of cash for the kidnappers and leaves the room. The men then start fucking the *fresa* with their toes, before they start double penetrating him with their penises. One kidnapper tells the father over the phone, "It seems like he likes it, *puto!*" They cum all over his face and then start fucking his ass with the gun. His politician father has also become aroused and gropes himself while listening on the other line. The scene ends with Canek shooting his load all over himself and closing his laptop.

This one scene is fraught with the erotically abject details of corruption, desire, and submission. While the uniformed officials in the earlier scenes are obviously more identifiable nods to the state and its strategic use of power, this scene captures the complexity of narco-warfare and how it has equally created a corrupt state that penetrates and seizes the lives of many. As I recall in earlier chapters, since the 1970s organized

Figures 3.6–3.7. Video stills of a *fresa* being sodomized while his father listens. *Corrupción mexicana*, dir. El Diablo, Mecos Films, 2010.

crime led by narco-warfare has gained a monopoly over many current sociopolitical affairs, which has bred a hypermasculine state that abuses power, but also looks to the side when that power is called into question. We see this through the interesting interaction between the boss and the politician, in which the politician is being called out for his corruption. The revenge is in a vigilante system of fucking the politician where it hurts—well, where it hurts his son. And then to get off on it!

This fantasy of being fucked into submission by criminals is not an uncommon trope in narratives of Mexicanness. Crime and violence already occupy all aspects of life. The presence of criminality has been normalized in Mexico. It is a penetrating system, completely masculinized through its dominating effects, that exposes a vulnerability in others, and thus characterizes Mexicanness. Yet there is a sense of yearning and fantasy about these criminal figures. Queer cultural and literary critic Héctor Domínguez-Ruvalcaba describes this phenomenon of figures of crime being routinely folded into national narrative fiction: "The seduction of power passes from this capacity of terror, a seduction that is imposed by rapture. The power that seduces leads to an intrinsic relationship between power and beauty."[30] The normalization of crime in the collective and public imaginary, which is constantly reproduced and actively consumed, is a fascination with the gendered and sexualized tropes of crime itself. It is a sexual relationship that fetishizes images of violence. The criminal actor, almost always male, is an object of desire: heterosexually, men want to be like him, and women want to be seduced by him. By extension, then, what if men also want to be fucked by him, even if it means a radical disintegration of subjecthood in the process?

A Fantasy of Fucking to Kill and Killing to Fuck

It is fair to say that neither Bruno Ramri's *Revenge Porn: La invasión de la privacidad* nor *Corrupción mexicana* by Mecos Films produces a sense of resolution to the violence carried out through, from, and against those who bottom for the actors of the nation-state. These are not optimistic performances. They are, however, a reflection of the impossibility of bearing one's own subjectivity. Further, they reveal the failure to "cleanse" the national and collective imaginary of the residues left behind from the traumatic penetration of the nation-state. The aesthetic framework of Mexicanness put forth is constructed within sexualized systems of power derived from the violence explored throughout this chapter. Domínguez-Ruvalcaba posits, "If violence is a gender mandate, it is in the sense of establishing models of masculinity where the enjoyment of domination provides meaning to violence, whose refinement and progressive intensification are an expression of power."[31] Yet those who enjoy domination are not just the ones inflicting it. Rather, complicated forms of pleasure may be derived from the receiver of that subjugation, characterizing a system of violence nascent to the hierarchies of abjection. Brushing up against this pleasure and exercise of power is a question, then, about death.

Death and the imperative to kill or be killed are always already part of the quotidian performing bottom through Mexicanness. By exercising this power to dominate and distribute death in a sexual pathologization of violence, the killing of sexual minorities and women becomes inevitable because it is necessary for the system to even be effective. Sex produces a system of death that regulates gender and sexual norms in the national and collective imaginary: the nation-state's pornograph. Domínguez-Ruvalcaba remarks, "Gendered violence is not a supplementary aspect of the violence of organized crime, but rather, it is its form and meaning"—that is, "a constitutive part of the characterization of the perpetrator exalted in a sovereignty that is complacent in its capacity to transmute sexuality into violence or to extend the plane of the sexual into the mortal."[32] The bottom in this case, in their submission, is both a symptom and a necessary contribution to the aesthetics of death that paint Mexicanness. Sex and death mutually imbricate and contaminate one another, conceiving ideas of contemporary expressions and feelings of Mexicanness. We just have to sit with the images of these acts.

Bruno Ramri helps to demonstrate in *Revenge Porn: La invasión de la privacidad* that what is out of sight is never truly out of mind. While images may be tampered with, they can never fully be erased. The traces of traumatic pasts and histories remain deeply engraved as an embodied archive. As Ramri and *Corrupción mexicana* playfully draw out, these experiences and images are loaded with our sexual histories and fantasies. We engage in sex acts with these recalled moments of violence, by uploading our own images of sex and violence onto these scenarios—be it porn or the writing on Ramri's body—to be projected, binding, and yet enjoyable. We have an affective experience and feel the fragments and residues that can be transferred sexually.

These sexual traumas, while sought out in abject ways through bodies that figure into the nation-state's system of power and domination, are rememberable. Moreover, they carry legacies that are passed on and have been inherited since the first scenes of hegemonic powers fucking others into submission to advance the labor of the nation-state: the Conquest. These memories and sexual legacies expose themselves to one another, across bodies, borders, geographies, and disciplines.

4

Altars for *los Hijos de la Chingada*

Crossing Sex with Yanina Orellana and Yosimar Reyes

> Bringing me back to life more intimately than any regenera-
> tive nourishment, the other's hands, these palms with which
> he approaches without going through me, give me back the
> borders of my body and call me to the remembrance of the
> most profound intimacy.
> —Luce Irigaray, "The Fecundity of the Caress"

Borders are spaces of confrontation, encounter, and risk. They are also permeable and penetrable. As I have argued throughout these pages, sexually motivated brutalities move between and among material worlds, transcending any national belonging. Rather, performances of the bottom at their bottom point make one feel their place in the world and with others precisely through how their bodies are confronted and criticized with these forms of violence while affected by the other performances of sexual feelings. This analysis leaves me preoccupied with the affective labor that borders do. Sexual encounters loudly echo and reverberate throughout this book, in explicit detail, finding themselves watchfully gesturing toward the horizon and onto borders: geopolitical borders, disciplinary borders, and *body* borders. I have argued that the bodies of sexual minorities are centered in the representation and critique of modern expressions of hemispheric Latinx America, which rely on a primacy of sexual domination, funneling directly into cultures of crime, killing, and mortality. At stake in these associations is an account of the rhetorical presence of queer bodies in the construction and critique of these processes.

Queer Latinx American scholars, artists, and writers have a long history of theorizing and making sense of the relationship between the body, sex, and violence. But as I began pursuing the themes that would fill these chapters, I was confronted by a vanished idea of sex within Mexico's aesthetic imagination of itself. In the case of Mexicanness, the scholarship in Mexican studies often creates its own borders that distinguish itself from hemispheric understandings of sex and death. Crossing these borders, I have anchored queer Mexicanness as a conceptual framework exposing the sexual structures and bodies in place that give way to necropolitical landscapes. This chapter preoccupies itself with how exposure lends itself to reading Mexicanness and hemispheric performance through geographic and sexual histories exposing themselves to an other or many others. In other words, these legacies are carried and disseminated hemispherically, exposing themselves to new forms of Latinidad.

The artists studied in this chapter conceptualize diasporic performances of what Mexicanness does to death through sex in space and practice. In the work of queer undocumented performance poet Yosimar Reyes, we encounter the former. Reyes's video performance of the poem "For Colored Boys Who Speak Softly" situates viewers in a desolate borderland contoured by the inheritance of sexually motivated violence. The second case study, addressing practice, puts audiences up close with feminist performance artist Yanina Orellana. Orellana embodies what she describes as an inherited legacy of Malinche through dance and movement, creating a body language about the complexity of sexuality and Mexicanness vibrating throughout her body. These works shed a necessary light on how Mexicanness extends beyond Mexico and is a moldable category of experience and feelings that is always shifting and moving across borders to create new lexicons on a hemispheric Latinx American level.

One only has to look at the recent co-optation of the x into the vocabulary of diasporic Latinx Americans to recognize a hemispheric and collective attempt to make sense of these structures in relation to identity and community formation beyond the prescriptive gendered binaries of Hispanophone traditions. As with all politics of representation, a queer reading reveals the limits of these social, political, and linguistic categories. A cultural pivot toward the x permits us to not have to confront the penetrative power of masculinist language; moreover, its symbolic sign of elimination comes to violently erase the trace of the feminine. As scholars of queerness, gender, and sexuality, we find that at times in our efforts to affirm and name the nonbinary, queer lexicons breed oversight and neocolonialism. I suggest that it would be more theoretically advantageous to wade into the complicated and messy waters secreted by the unnameability and untranslatability of gender and sexuality when thought alongside Latinx America more broadly. These mixing identities, though at times incompatible with one another, flow into new channels that lead us to new topographies where brown bodies roam.

Reading through, from, and against the bottom performing in Latinx America and its diasporas does not outright reject the *x*. Rather, it calls for the possibility of other critical vocabularies that account for the sexual legacies imprinted upon the hemispheric tongues of Mexican sexual minorities. The condensation of *x* into "Latinx" and "Chicanx" reveals an urgent and timely need to reevaluate the role of gender and sexuality in the construction of national, geographic, and ethnic identities. As such, I am less interested in translating "queer" into the nonbinary than I am in accounting for how the diaspora gestures with the embodiment and inheritance of ancestral sexual histories. In this sense, we can think more productively through the *x*'s chiasmic shape of two epistemological nerves crossing each other to redirect our focal point to different disciplinary borders. *X* invites us to read lines of inquiry that overlap, cross, and realign borders of thinking so that we may account for the sexual histories that the *x* symbolizes.

In its Anglophile roots, "queer" describes and engenders a history of sexual trauma and loss. I advocate for thinking with and through border crossing as a passage to other lands. But the old adage "We didn't cross the border, the border crossed us," made popular by early immigration rights activists, speaks to a belief that bodies born in and of the diaspora, too, have been violated. Border crossing raptures, penetrates, and ruptures geographical and corporeal bodies in their state of belonging and movement. Queer Mexicanness, as an aesthetics, exemplifies an interpolation of racialized and geopolitical histories of sex in those other lands. These are histories of sexual violence that reflect a sexual inheritance of the cultural fabric of the nation-state. To understand these inherited sexual histories that paint a hemispheric bottomist approach, we may find it generative to think with sexual history by returning to the historical figure of Malinche, or *la Chingada* (the fucked woman), a figure whose entire identity is grounded in her being fucked. And that fuck has haunted many resentful generations.

Fucking Malinche's Borders

Malinche—Malintzín—was born in the region of the River Coatzacoal-cos, which empties into the Gulf of Mexico (today the southern Veracruz coast).[1] Her family, as historians have purported, more than likely comprised a lineage of conquerors and rulers from an earlier era.[2] At the time, Nahuatl was the language of the minority elite. At a young age, Malintzín was kidnapped by long-distance slave traders and rowed 150 miles down the coast, where she was sold to the Chontal Maya.[3] When the conquistadors arrived in 1519, intending to explore the mainland from their base in Cuba, the natives didn't stand a chance against the Spanish artillery. The Chontal Maya lost over two hundred men within a matter of hours against the conquistadors. Following their defeat, the Chontal gave the Spaniards "gifts" of submission: food, gold, and twenty women, including Malintzín. Hernán Cortés, in turn, gave Malintzín to the most prominent of his men, Alfonso Hernández Puertocarrero, a relative of a Spanish count.[4]

Though she was bilingual in her native Nahuatl and the Popoluca spoken by the lower-class majority where she was raised, and trilingual in Maya since her capture and sale to the Chontal, Malintzín's linguistic skills were not initially utilized by the Spanish, since they already had a translator who spoke Maya. But some weeks later, when the conquistadors sailed north to the present site of Veracruz, they were met by the Aztec soldiers sent by Moctezuma to surveil the coast. The Aztecs spoke in their native Nahuatl, which was an unfamiliar language to the Spanish translator. And it is so that Malintzín made the bold choice to step forward and translate from Nahuatl into Maya, which converted her into her infamous role as *la Chingada*: Mexico's historical traitor.[5] Walking alongside Cortés while he rode horseback, she traveled 263 miles from the coast, where the Spanish had erected the town of Veracruz, up and over the Sierra Madre Oriental, passing near Mexico's highest peak, to Moctezuma's empire at Tenochtitlán (modern-day Mexico City).

Moctezuma's grand empire would shortly fall and Mexico as a new colonial enterprise would begin to take shape, but Malintzín's role in shaping Mexican history did not stop there. Within months after the defeat of Tenochtitlán, as Cortés's concubine she bore him a son, whom he named Martín, after his father. She traveled in 1523 with Cortés to

Honduras and married the Spaniard Juan Jaramillo in 1524, with whom she had a daughter. By January 1529, Cortés returned to Spain, having taken with him their six-year-old son. Shortly thereafter, Malintzín died of unknown causes.[6]

Malinche becomes a sexual landmark—albeit with all the complexities that lie therein—that signposts a significant historical moment in the Mexican national and collective consciousness. If I may briefly turn back to Octavio Paz's reading of *la Chingada* in relation to Mexicanness, he remarks that Malinche "has been converted into a figure that represents the Indian woman, fascinated, violated and seduced by the Spaniards."[7] Paz's preoccupation with Malinche's sexual activity narrows in on what he perceives to be a willingness to accept the passivity of being fucked by the oppressor. She is historically converted into a promiscuous figure who is to always be juxtaposed with the purity of the Virgin Mary, whose passivity is venerable because she was *chosen*. Yet performing as a bottom reconceptualizes and restructures the *chingado* positionality as a necessary desire to be fucked—that is, a willingness for one's subjectivity to become undone and submitting oneself to a form of fucking that fucks back. We can think, however, about the difficult choice made by Malinche to come forward and speak in Nahuatl with full knowledge of the potential implications and consequences of how she would be perceived by her indigenous counterparts.

I contend that it was indeed a choice. Let us restore to this brave brown woman some of the agency that has been violently ripped away from her by both Spaniards and Mexicans alike. Yet even in that "passive" act of being converted into the role of interlocutor for Cortés, she is still restored a sense of agency through her willingness and acceptance of the foreseeable risks. Through their sexual relationship, Malinche's birth of a *mestizo* nation breeds a new culture that is all too familiar within Mexicanness: *los hijos de la Chingada* (the children of the fucked woman). For Paz, "Everyone else is the *hijos de la chingada*: the foreigners, the bad Mexicans, our enemies, our rivals. In any case, the 'others.'"[8] At the risk of giving Paz too much credit, considering he means this derogatively, this description couldn't be more apt when thinking through and alongside the radicality of bottom performance. The exposure of those bodies who cannot and will never form part of the nation-building project, when describing *los hijos de la Chingada*, are always already othered.

We learn from Malinche's courageous journey and her difficult choices that she is, above all else, a border-crossing figure—even when those borders were forced upon her. Being captured, sold, and exploited may describe one aspect of her history that necessitated a life of movement across Mexico with the colonizers. Yet these experiences also speak to how her borders, her body borders, were crossed. At times, she had to cross her own borders too. As she traversed these corporeal geographies, the borders of Mexico and the Aztec empire became sexualized as they moved, formed, mixed, and straddled each other. From these crossings, a beautiful brown race emerged from her womb. In her always already penetrated status as the *Chingada* and a Mother, Malinche represents a lineage of displacement: a sexual diaspora created for the "others." It is understandable, then, why her sexual legacy is necessarily inherited by her children of the diaspora, even when it's forced: the border-crossers, the undocumented, Chicanxs, or the otherwise Other.

The crossing of the *x* raises the question of a queer motherhood to those lost children at the bottom, never to be desired at the top. If Mexico is born out of Malinche's fucking sins, then what does it mean to carry the legacy of the body borders being crossed? Examining those passive figures who are always already marked for disposal at the bottom leads to more sustained readings of the racialized and sexualized caste systems that are not unique to national boundaries, but rather a condition of the sexual ecology.

While there are differing and divergent accounts of what—or who— historically constitutes the diaspora, especially when thinking about Mexico and the United States, this chapter is invested in intimately thinking in bodily terms about diaspora through the idea that "we didn't cross the border, the border crossed us." This idea expresses something that has happened to and is experienced by their bodies in their state of being, movement, and mere existence. These are the borders of the body—those lines and limits that expose the body in its bare sexual form and passivity—that become crossing points and converted into political landscapes. These sexual topographies are rich with the inheritance of Malinche's own border crossing, thus enacting the idea of a contemporary diasporic Mexicanness. It is obviously fitting, then, that these body histories were taken up by queer Chicana feminists in the latter half of the twentieth century. The late Gloria Anzaldúa famously describes the US-Mexican border as a living entity that bleeds and hemorrhages, a borderland defined as "a vague and undetermined place created by the emotional residue of an unnatural boundary." It is a space inhabited by those who must cross borders of the "normal" in their daily lives.[9] The borderlands, in this regard, form a space of acquired transgenerational sexual histories that characterize the nonnormative, the queer, and the "others." For Anzaldúa, the event of *mestiza* consciousness and the radical identification with *jotería*—Chicanx queerness—performs a dialectical legacy by bringing the sexual past to bear on the historical present precisely through being *los hijos de la Chingada*. This "mixed breed," the *mestiza*, "undergoes a struggle of flesh, a struggle of borders, an inner war" that converts her into a figure who always already negotiates with the ambivalence of sexual power relations.[10] Grazing the same philosophical plains, Cherríe Moraga writes, "Chicanos are an occupied nation within a nation" where the bodies of "those men and women who transgress their gender roles have been historically regarded as territories to be conquered."[11] That is, she posits, "Chicano Nation is a mestizo nation conceived in a double-rape: first, by the Spanish and then by the Gringo."[12] Anzaldúa and Moraga center the fleshly body as the physical landscape of the Mexican diaspora. This body is not merely a symbolic enterprise for queer Chicana feminist rhetoric; rather, we are positioned to look at bodies as spatial categories. The relationship between the body and land is inseparable: both feel, react to, and gestate a shared sexual history. Moraga elongates this duality, writing, "Like woman, Madre Tierra has been raped, exploited for her resources, rendered inert, passive, and speechless."[13] She continues, "For women, lesbians, and gay men, land is that physical mass called our bodies."[14] This mutual imbrication of bodies and land speaks to one of the central struggles of diasporic Mexicanness: the sovereign right to wholly inhabit oneself—that is, the right to one's own territory and borders, even when those borders are crossed.

Certainly, the queer hemispheric Latinx American performance I conceptualize in my own work is significantly indebted to Anzaldúa and Moraga. Thinking about Mexicanness in the diaspora involves a sexual labor that reads the body as occupied territory. While histories of sexual trauma and violation inform and shape how we read these bodies, I am more interested in the trace that has been left behind to be imprinted on these corporeal landscapes: those specters of passivity that whisper in our ears when we are bent over. Perhaps *jouissance* could be better understood when we remember that the borders of our bodies are always crossed. In this sense, I depart from Anzaldúa and Moraga to think further with violation and rape as affectively constitutive of the diasporic sexual experience, but not static. If modern expressions of Mexicanness are defined by the centrality of penetration—or rather, being penetrated—then a turn toward diasporic Mexicanness involves accounting for a double penetration. More succinctly, it is to be fucked, then fucked again. We should not hastily move too far beyond the idea of pleasure when thinking through this double-fucked occupation of the body. Rather, the issue of power as it oscillates between domination and submission as part of the diasporic experience of racialized sexual minorities needs to be read against the grain.

Understanding the sexual embodiments of the queer diaspora is never truly subversive of or directly dissident to histories of oppression and colonialism. Rather, the performances of different accounts of those histories that contribute to an idea of diasporic Mexicanness are indelibly intertwined with sexual genealogies that are politically charged, asking, How do Mexicans in the diaspora wield these forms of sex as means of telling stories about their own Mexicanness? Complementing the double-penetrated status of diasporic Mexicanness is the difficulty of parsing what is pleasurable and what is that traumatic residue that remains sticky after we've crossed certain body borders. Those blurred lines are the borderlands.

My approach to the "diasporic" within the frameworks of queer Mexicanness bears witness to the affective experiences of those sexual bodies that roam on the other side, outside, and beyond the borders of what we call "Mexico." While in its historical usage in cultural studies "diaspora" has referred to the exile and refugee, both of which can certainly be apt to describe those people studied here, I veer toward an idea of "diaspora" that describes those lands where inherited sexual histories have displaced borders. In this regard, I lean on how "diasporic," as Ricardo L. Ortíz describes, is a category that "retains an entirely informal, unofficial, ambiguous, even improvisatory, undocumentable" quality. That is, "No one can ever ask for, and no one could ever produce, official 'papers' or documentation proving 'diasporic' status."[15] The language of a queer of color diaspora, Gayatri Gopinath tells us, is a "visual record of the past" that rethinks the archive by underscoring how the convergence of history and visuality conceptualizes a diasporic way of approaching the aesthetic.[16] By studying the "everyday" of the queerness of the archive, we see how these visual relics are associated their past in a reading of their present form. For Gopinath, this is a visuality that "instantiates alternative cartographies and spatial logics that allow for other histories of global affiliation and affinity to emerge."[17] This gesture thus exposes a theory or modality of new queer cultural analytic practices, which directs an "unruly" gaze backwards to regional archives and the past.[18] This would also refer to the overlapping ways in which diasporas and regions expose themselves to one another.

Centering the body, with its sexual feelings, acts, and desires, presses up against these points of debate that comprise the history of gender and sexuality studies in Latin Americanism writ large. The aesthetic practices of diaspora—or the hemispheric Latinx Americas in this case—are a means through which a "queer restaging of the region" occurs.[19] These aesthetic practices provide a locus and necessary point of entry from which to conceptualize a counter logic of gender, race, and sexuality. The queer regional imaginary and its aesthetics, Gopinath emphasizes, "suggest different forms of relationality" that move beyond liberal narratives of queer despair.[20] These aesthetic practices effectively challenge conventional configurations of global/local area studies and instead propose interrelated, region-to-region cartographies that convincingly produce new mappings of space and sexuality.

I center, then, on those shared experiences of sexual hegemony that penetrate bodies and redefine where the borders of Mexicanness begin, or perhaps will never exist. These experiences could never produce sufficient ideas of what is documentable and what is not. Diasporic Mexicanness is always already an idea of translating, or making intelligible, those inherited sexual histories that reside in the depths of the body. Accordingly, I lean into the works of undocumented performance poet Yosimar Reyes and transnational Mexican artist Yanina Orellana to bring substance and texture to these ideas.

Yosimar Reyes Speaks Softly at the Altar

The spatiality and verbosity of the queer diaspora are conjured and manifested by the eloquent vocal vibrations of undocumented performance
poet Yosimar Reyes. His spoken word engages in an act of queer world-
making: a sacred diasporic geography. The flicks and cuts of his tongue,
the urgency of his tone, and his own embodied reality as a queer brown
undocumented person carve out spaces where the spirits of brown bodies roam and are memorialized. Walking through the fields of his poetic
vocal register, we find ourselves in the terrain of those whose borders
have been, and every day continue to be, violently crossed.

A fire blazes out of focus, shifting to candles flickering in the daylight,
and the camera pans to a photo above the candles: Gwen Araujo, a Latina transwoman who was brutally murdered in Newark, California, in
October 2002. The distorted sounds of a bass echo as the camera shifts
to more candles and another photo comes into focus: Michael Sandy,
a Black gay man from Brooklyn who was struck dead by a car while
escaping his bashers in 2006. We hear a voice out of the frame say, "For
colored boys who speak softly," as the camera continues to wander, revealing photo by photo: Rawshawn Brazell (the Black nineteen-year-old
found dismembered in Brooklyn in February 2005), Latisha King (the
fifteen-year-old Black transgender student from Oxnard, California,
murdered in February 2008), Sakia Gunn (the fifteen-year-old Black
lesbian murdered in Newark in May 2003), Ruby Rodriguez (the twenty-
four-year-old Nicaraguan transwoman murdered in March 2007), Ryan
Keith Skipper (found dead on the highway in March 2007 in Wahneta,
Florida), Sean William Kennedy (beaten to death in May 2007 in Green-
ville, South Carolina), and Nireah Johnson (a Black transgender lesbian
murdered in July 2003 in Indianapolis).

The video performance of Yosimar Reyes's poem "For Colored Boys
Who Speak Softly" (2009) places us in an unidentified wasteland. Yet,
as each photo is revealed, it becomes clear that we are not just in a scrapyard with photographs and open flames: we are at an altar anointed
with white and red devotional candles traditional to Latinx American
altars. The spectator is brought to their knees in an amorous ritual of
mourning and remembrance. Altars are all too familiar in Mexico, and
hemispheric Latinx America more broadly. Symbolizing piety, altars

Figure 4.1. Video still from Yosimar Reyes's performance of "For Colored Boys Who Speak Softly," dir. Carl Brown, 2009. Courtesy of Corduroy Media and Yosimar Reyes.

occupy a prominent place in the theological legacy of the Americas. In Christianity, an altar is prepared to enshrine and consecrate the blood and body of Jesus Christ into the Eucharist ritual. It is a focal point in church sanctuaries where one is able to "come to the table" and receive the blessings that the altar symbolizes. In theological practices indigenous to Latinx America, altars are spaces of offering, sacrifice, and atonement to the divine, the goddesses and gods for whom they are prepared. They serve as sites of both loss and life. Moreover, Blackness surrounds this altar. We are at the gravesite of the social death of a trans Blackness.

Across religious traditions, an altar is a space intimately tied to the idea of a physical body. The altar in the video performance of "For Colored Boys Who Speak Softly" certainly points to bodies; moreover, it represents a sacred queer space. The burning of white and red candles links this queer altar to Latinx American spiritual practices: white symbolizing healing and protection, and red grounding the altar in the physical world to put one in touch with the power and temporal pleasures of the flesh. I take these symbols further and describe this altar as not only queer, but sexual. The spectator is not positioned to worship Christ or any of the Christian saints; rather, it is a face-to-face encounter with those who have sexual stories to share.

My reading of the aesthetics strategies employed in Reyes's video performance of "For Colored Boys Who Speak Softly" is informed by Christina Sharpe's attention to Blackness and being through what she terms "wake work." Sharpe describes wake work as "a mode of inhabiting *and* rupturing this episteme with our known lived and un/imaginable lives. With that analytic we might imagine otherwise from what we know *now* in the wake of slavery."[21] This framework denotes the difficult task of world-making anew, without stepping outside it and all its terrors therein that haunt and repeat themselves. In other words, this type of work—an aesthetic, ethical, and political labor—happens when one occupies the present's imbrication with the past that is not past, the continuously unfolding event of the disasters of the past—for Sharpe, slavery—and imagines an otherwise future. This harmonizes with what Sandra Ruiz describes as "eternal looping" in the colonial project of the United States, "whereby actions to redress the past lead us into the future and back again to something prior." It is a temporal positioning that reveals "an active state in the here and now, looping forward and back into itself as if time never started or stopped ticking."[22] While Sharpe, Ruiz, and I differ in case studies and geographies, they both gesture toward thinking about the temporal qualities of death that, I argue, construct a more accurate reading of the racialization and violence of queer diasporic Mexicanness.

In this respect, the altar in Reyes's video performance exposes bodies at the center of a new theology that attends to death when it makes its mark on the sexual diaspora. Here, "theology" speaks to a study of the divine that captures how people understand, interpret, and make meaning out of the world around them through ritual and storytelling. As such, the rituality of erecting an altar in "For Colored Boys Who Speak Softly" does not represent just a memorial project: it is a new form of theological production capturing the sexually violent crossings of queer body borders that constitute an idea of the diasporic. Acts of homophobia and transphobia are vicious crimes grounded in an idea of sex that violates the body in its bareness of mere existence. As such, this altar's relationship to the body is grounded in the stories of the sexual minorities and transgender individuals for whom it was built. This line of thinking invokes the late queer Argentine theologian Marcella Althaus-Reid, who contends, "Sexual theologies are the opposite of ide-

alistic processes. They are materialist theologies which have their starting points in people's actions, or sexual acts without polarising the social
from the symbolic. It is from human sexuality that theology starts to
search and understand the sacred, not vice versa."[23] The violent killings
of these individuals tell a story about the sexual experiences of queer
and transgender folk, even when those experiences include brutality.

We return to the materiality of the body from this altar, examining
borders of the normative that had to be crossed, and how their own
borders were seized from them. The body becomes a defining factor in
helping us understand the erotic entanglements of sex and death that
constitute queer Mexicanness, and the diaspora by extension. Within
this space of renewed meaning-making—learning from those queer
and transgender lives we've lost—Reyes's poetry thus takes on new
qualities that harmonize with the inherited sexual histories of diasporic
Mexicanness.

Wearing a tight, olive-green, button-down military-style shirt opened
to expose a black undershirt and gold chain, and dark denim skinny
jeans extending down to his black and white sneakers, Yosimar Reyes
walks toward the camera. The grassy path he traverses, accented by
small wood fires, cuts through piles of rocks and scrap metal, with the
sight of luscious foliage on the horizon beyond the rubble. His entire
body fills the frame and he recites,

> For colored boys who speak softly,
> I would build a stage on top of the world
> Give them a microphone and let them free flow
> Because they too have something to say
> And this is more than rainbow coloring our face
>
> This is broken spirits speaking for a better day
> So in the tenderness of our words we carry blades
> To cut ourselves free from gender roles
> Build a life free from social norms
> Redefine humanity and sexuality through our own terms.[24]

Reyes speaks to and from the position of the colored boys who speak
softly: those queer and trans children who grew up not sounding

masculine or straight enough. The imagery of giving a stage and micro-phone to them "because they too have something to say" is realized through the preparation of an altar for those who carry their stories of sex and death to the grave and beyond. *They too have something to say* problematizes and extends the archive of narratives that attempt to account for the history of how the Americas were brought into existence and continue to exist. What is at stake in subverting these genealogies goes beyond the curiosity of coming out of the closet, visibility, and Gay Pride festivals, because the privilege of "pride" is only an experi-ence of the First World—read as white, normative, and passing. Rather, these are the stories of the "broken spirits" who imagine at least one day more of survival. These counter histories are spoken in the words of those who cannot and will never "pass" in mainstream straight or gay societies, because their voices and their differences are determined as marginal. Resonating with Lechedevirgen Trimegisto's turn to the *puñal* as a sexual politics, Reyes's line "So in the tenderness of our words we carry blades" streams into the same queer ethico-political channel. As we have learned, the *puñal*—these blades—straddles that live wire crossing political activation and the precarity of impending violence. This effectively positions sexual and gender minorities to readily appear more as a threat and targeted for death, rather than being able to poise their politically transgressive qualities. The individuals in these photos, the colored boys who speak softly, embody and expose the vulnerability and lethal penetrability of the borders of bottom performance.

The Prophetical Mouths That Taste Cum

The camera moves behind Reyes and focuses as he stands before the altar, gesturing with his hands to the photos as he continues:

> For colored boys who speak softly
> I would sacrifice my tongue
> Make an offering to the Gods
> Pray to them to wash my mouth clean
> 'Cause boys like us
> Should never taste cum
> And men should never lie with men

Because this is a crime punishable by death
And it is in this very same dark silence that many of us
rest Left bruised and dead[25]

As I describe above, this is a sacred sexual space that bears on the symbolism of altars recognizable to Latinx American and Latinx religious and theological traditions. If theology has remained resistant to sex and sexuality as forms of knowledge production, queer theory has revealed its own resistance to theological and religious discourses as vital frameworks to read the spatiality and temporality of sexual bodies. Both Reyes's vocal poetic register and the consecration of an altar for the fallen queer and transgender center this space as a site for sacrifice and atonement. Through the sacrificial act of giving his own tongue, that organ that enables Reyes to speak softly, the poet brings our attention to the queerness of orality: the mouth being used for storytelling, but also for tasting cum. This intimate lingual duality situates queer bodies at the center of a theological imaginary. In other words, those mouths that taste cum also speak prophetically. He shifts his position to stand chest outward toward the camera with the altar behind him and continues:

For those who speak softly
I would crucify myself like Christ
Let my blood purify and sanctify these words
Create a doctrine and go knocking door to door
Letting the people know
That the messiahs are here
That we are all messengers
Although, we embody the word queer[26]

These queer bodies who speak softly interpret and speak of a cosmovision that thinks beyond the cisgender heteronormativity of mainstream Christian theologies that contribute to their fatality. The camera zooms in on the photographs at the altar as Reyes likens queer bodies to "messiahs" and "messengers." Even in his self-portrayal, with his arms extended outward, as the crucified Jesus of Nazareth, Reyes's language brings us into this semantic space of the prophetic. Etymologically, the word "prophecy" comes from the Greek *propheteia*, meaning "gift of interpreting the will of the gods."[27] This gift is not one taken lightly. That is, the soft voices of colored queers, spoken from the mouths that also taste cum, get to speak about their own histories and imagine their own ideas of world-making and ceremonial centers. Moreover, in this prophetic vision, those bodies deemed too dangerous or a threat become sacred entities through which to understand the experiences of a diasporic Mexicanness.

To say, "Let my blood purify and sanctify these words" rejects the idea we explored in chapter 1, in which the blood of queers is too toxic and threatening to be life-giving. These words get to be their own and not forced upon them. As Reyes states later in the poem,

> Because not all of us were taken into consideration
> When they developed our identity
> Telling us we should act like this
> Exploit our sexuality
> Rather than embrace our divinity[28]

Reyes points to those who have a long history of being part of Latinx American and Latinx understandings of divinity, even when they have been overlooked and eliminated from the dominant narratives. He disrupts the normative trajectories of how the history of sexuality is read and accounted for in the Americas, while intricately weaving the threads of a queer of color theological poetics into the cultural fabric of diasporic Mexicanness.

I would thus like to pause and think more closely about the spatiality brought forth in the video performance alongside and against Reyes's theologically provoking verses. A grassy scrapyard converted into a racialized space for an altar/gravesite, which I have named as a form of sacred sexual geography, takes on a particularly new form of spatial poetics from the rich vocal ambience produced by Reyes's religiously tinged vocabulary. The photographs, fires, and candles and the artist's movements between the large mounds of debris transform and designate a sense of specificity to this area. It is obvious, then, that this space bears meaning and utility that extend beyond just being a dumping ground. Rather, it is precisely the presence of fresh green grass and the sight of lush foliage beyond the mess that reminds us that while we may be mourning at the altar, this space is still full of the possibility of a life to come—a new creation sprouting through the soil. This grassy clearing, marked by the "messiahs" and "messengers" named by Reyes, resonates with the imagery of the Garden of Eden. Yet its inhabitants are not Adam and Eve, nor Steve (as Christian fundamentalists have often decried). Rather, this "garden" is filled with the spirits and presence of the boys who taste cum, the colored boys who speak softly. That is, the queer and transgender people who are brutally killed, the undocumented, the border-crossers: this is *their* garden.

The theological space conjured in this video performance encultures those sexualities excluded from the Garden of Eden—namely, sexualities of color, which is why outside Steve remains. Their exclusion designates them as always already foreigners to spaces of power that find their genesis in the Garden of Eden. The foreignness of their bodies creates diasporic spaces, narratives, and histories. As Althaus-Reid argues, "At the bottom line of Queer theologies, there are biographies of sexual migrants, testimonies of real lives in rebellions made of love, pleasure, and suffering." As a result, queer theology is "diasporic, self-disclosing, autobiographical and responsible for its own words."[29] In other words, these theological trajectories, in their diasporic state, exist beyond the borders of the normal, acceptable, or passable. By pointing to those who bear divinity in their own embodiments, Reyes subverts and rejects the normativity of theologies that make way for the killings of queer and transgender folks of color. We are called to rethink theology from the position of those on their knees tasting cum. That is, reimagining what could be considered sacred geography through other forms of sexual praxis.

The idea of queerness I am conceptualizing is a diasporic one. José Esteban Muñoz reminds us, "Queerness is that thing that lets us feel that this world is not enough, that indeed something is missing."[30] Queerness for people of color is the daily reminder that most spaces, including gay and lesbian ones, are not created for them. Their insufficiency, or rather their inability to assimilate or pass, positions their being and movements on the outside and beyond the borders of the hegemonic mainstream. This flows from the same waters of Muñoz's attention to the feelings of brownness, wherein "Brownness is a mode of attentiveness to the self for others that is cognizant of the way in which it is not and can never be whiteness."[31] This affective consciousness brings into focus an idea of the diasporic that speaks to the conditions of those figures who live and move in spaces that are impervious to their existence and movement. The scrapyard altar in Reyes's video performance evokes the spatial dimensions of the diasporic as indelibly queer *and* brown. This symbiotic relationship that paints the imagery of a diasporic space necessarily makes knowable other traditions and histories that may account for other or new forms of belonging, even as unintelligible and untranslatable as they may appear. Reyes taps into this vein, recalling

> That
> Centuries ago
> We were
> Shamans and Healers Gifted
> warriors
> Two-Spirited People
> Highly respected by villagers
>
> And now we've become
> Nothing more than FAGS and QUEERS
> Making ourselves believe
> That capitalism will solve our issues[32]

This theologically rich, queer, brown altar gives sound to the voices of individuals who may have wielded their sexuality and gender variance as a survival strategy and healing—truly enveloping the inherited legacy of *los hijos de la Chingada*. Yet their historical embodiments of the sacred have been converted into labels and identities—fags and queers—that could never truly clench the complexity of their diasporic being. The structures of power giving way to the privilege of "to be" (in its imprecise multipronged infinitive verb form) cannot and would never fully describe them. This line of thinking leans against the Spanish infinitive *ser* (to be) that doubles up in a noun form signifying a "being"—such as *un ser humano* (a human being). Yet the materiality of the consciousness to come into a being, that is one with the power "to be" is never promised in any prior meta-moment for the Black bodies commemorated here. In other words, they will never possess or be able to furnish the appropriate documentation that could label them as here, or there;

rather, they are always moving as the traversing diasporic other. These diasporic figures are excluded from dominant forms of social and libidinal economies that benefit from the neoliberal promises of capitalism. The diaspora of queer Mexicanness is marked by the vulnerability of its borders, which may render it passive, yet still remaining politically charged and contentious.

A vital turn in Reyes's verses occurs when he reminds us that these embodied memories of trauma and loss are not exclusive to one territory or another, nor are they exclusive to one form of violence or another:

> For those who speak softly
> I will recognize
> That there is more than one wound to heal
> More than one struggle that we feel
> But this ignorance
> Blocks us from seeing the bigger picture
> The greater evil

Reyes narrows in on the intersectional qualities of struggle, which must always be taken into consideration and thought alongside of, never against, the construction of ideas of the diasporic. These issues include not just race, gender, and sexuality, but also economic class, ability, and transnational mobility, among others, all bringing different textures to the diasporic landscape that expose the precarity and vulnerability of those most affected. Reyes, then, walks toward the camera, making eye contact with the spectator as he says,

> And these same issues
> Transcend borders
> Because
> Brothers and sisters
> In Oaxaca
> In Chiapas
> In the Philippines
> In Iraq
> Are resisting
> This very same system

Reyes places us outside the boundaries of the United States back into Mexico's indigenous lands, but then takes an even broader transnational reach to include the Pacific and Middle East. These "issues" he describes are the violent disenfranchisement of brown bodies by "bad governments," issues that know no borders, because violence and traumatic histories do not discriminate.[33] Rather, they rapture global populations into the otherwise never here, nor there, only to then be found at an altar memorialized by other Others. The spatiality of the diasporic is widened by a transcontinental epidemic of killing sexual and gender minorities, with each body being fatally crossed over and over.

We find ourselves dwelling in a space constituted by mourning and memorial. Yet, by considering the stakes of these deaths to be remembered, through our gentle strides, we are also vigorously stroking the surface of an aesthetics of the political. That is, the structures of power in place that underpin the stake of these deaths are visually magnified to such a large degree that they envelop the spectator into an affective encounter with the abuse of said power. As Reyes walks the grassy clearing marked by the photographs of fallen queer and trans folk, reciting his words that conjure a violently sexual and sexually violent imagery, like a spell calling up the spirits of the past, present, and future, these verses are not just a poem, they are a eulogy. Eulogies recall the past to linger in our perspective of the present, so that it may offer us something to remember in the future. These are delicate words, chosen with carefulness to decorate our memories of those who have passed on. Reyes's "For Colored Boys Who Speak Softly," however, functions as a eulogy beyond the traditional form of fondly sharing anecdotes of youth and laughter. Rather, he recalls stories of loss, pain, and suffering, only to be resolved by more loss, pain, and suffering. The memories of the past that weigh on the present and future, those histories of sexualities of color, are the embodied scores of traumas that remain perpetually cyclical. As a eulogy practice, then, these words keep the spectator accountable in their memories: one cannot remember without suffering again.

In this regard, for Reyes, the most appropriate way for him to tend to the dead, or perhaps the only way, is to bring the past to bear on the present and reveal how aesthetic practices of remembering death in the diaspora can only be through the never-ending, always-already-repeating reminder that *our dead keep dying*. This captures an idea brought forth by Sharpe and Ruiz that the past is always already violently penetrating the present and will continue to repeat itself in a vicious cycle of life and death. I find in their works a language to discuss the temporal nature of violence as it is systematically carried out against bodies of color.

I have foregrounded the altar throughout this chapter as a politicized gravesite and geographical entity capturing the sexuality of death, as a microcosmic representation of diasporic space, and as a queer constitution of the aesthetics of sex, death, and Mexicanness. By thinking through the temporal qualities of the traumatic past as a force that haunts the present, I return to our image of the altar as a locus for the condensation of temporality into spatiality. This altar represents life and death in the same image. Looking into the eyes of queer and trans folk who are brutally murdered, we look death in the face while remembering that that violence repeats itself precisely through the act of memory, as it continues to repeat itself on the streets. The altar, thus, represents and is constituted by a form of violence that can never be undone. If altars represent sacrifices that are to give new life, we remain trapped in the loop that Ruiz describes. The altar is the spatialization of those temporal cycles that can only bring trauma back to the foreground to do more harm to the bodies and corpses of those we are called to memorialize. Ruiz explains that "eternal looping exposes what is done in the material, national, and discursive body in the name of historical expansionism."[34] If the altar captures the parameters and borders of what we call diasporic, it certainly functions as an aesthetic representation of this historical expansionism—colonialism—that Ruiz recalls. This decorated altar is a space where we see this cycle of *our dead keep dying*. The dead being memorialized still do work. The deaths still do a labor to name the brutal terrors of our historical present. As such, being at the altar is much like being at a wake—a term obviously central to Sharpe's meditation. Sharpe invites us to be in the wake, "to live in those no's to live in the no-space that the law is not bound to respect, to live in no citizenship, to live in the long time of Dred and Harriet Scott. . . . To be in the wake is also to recognize the ways that we are constituted through and by continued vulnerability to overwhelming force though not *only* known to ourselves and to each other *by* that force."[35] This video places the viewer into that space to do the work of tending to our dead who keep dying.

The spatiality of diasporic Mexicanness is brought to the fore when we are forced to face realities of sex and death that permeate and leak into other geographies. It highlights a necrotic quality of Mexicanness that describes the landscape of violence that sets the backdrop wherein to cruise the incessant bond between sex and death. The image of a necrotic Mexicanness, as a characteristic of the diaspora, forces us to think about death in bodily terms. Biologically, "necrosis" refers to a toxic chemical or physical injury to a cell that results in premature death. It is messy and causes an immunological response that forces the cell to aggressively explode and affect surrounding cells and corresponding tissue, systematically imposing even more trauma.

Yanina Orellana's Sexual Histories

If Yosimar Reyes's "For Colored Boys Who Speak Softly" situates us within a spatiality of the other as imagined through an altar, then Yanina Orellana's erotically charged performance art as a dancer brings us into close proximity with the embodied practices that occur at the altar. Her use of dance conjures the temporal trespassing of the past into the present. These practices that originate in and are translated through the body further portray how critiques of these pleasurable gestures might contribute to the constitution of a diasporic understanding of the body within the construction of bottom performance.

We find ourselves at another altar: decorated with flamboyant glitter sponges, limes, and colorful fabrics, while the soundtrack of a vibrant *cumbia* fills the room. As maracas continue to shake in the background music, the artist in an ankle-length red dress and floral veil draped over her head enters with a *vitrolero* in her arms, harmonizing with the *cumbia* signature two-count beat with the melody of liquid sloshing and the ladle tapping against the glass.[36] She places the *vitrolero* at the center of the altar, waving her hands and arms around over the opening, as if to cast a spell over a witch's cauldron, while a distorted electronic deep voice says, ¡*Vamos nena! ¡vamos chica! ¡baila la cumbia! ¡baila la cumbia! ¡que chingón!* Orellana stands in the frame of the altar with the *vitrolero* at her feet, as she brings her hands together in a prayer gesture. "¡CHICAAAS!" she exclaims loudly, breaking into the *cumbia* score, as she moves her body from the hips and pelvis upward in a long body roll.

"Have you asked yourself how I can move like this?" she asks. Kneeling at the *vitrolero*, she continues, and I retain the Spanish cited for its rhetorical gestures:

> Pues hoy es el gran día, en el que les daré mi receta secreta.
> Esta receta, me la pasó la mamá, de mi mamá, de mi mamá, de mi
> mamá.
> Así es que presta mucha atención, porque hoy, ¡es para ti!
> Los ingredientes son:
> Limones, agua, azúcar, y . . .[37]

The soundtrack cuts in with a distorted voice, preventing her from sharing the last ingredient, which will always remain a mystery. By directly addressing the audience, this opening monologue interpolates the public into this altar space with her, as she offers to share a secret recipe that has been passed down for several matriarchal generations. This recipe, then, carries with it the extracts of a historical lineage that becomes a corpus of inheritance to which the audience is given special exclusive access; the audience members will also become inheritors, or tasters and consumers, of these histories.[38]

Yanina Orellana's *Todos somos hijos de la Chingada* is a performance, at its core, responding to the exceedingly common Mexican expression, *¡hijo de la chingada!* As explored throughout the preceding chapters, this phrase and the implications of the verb *chingar* (to fuck) participate in the construction and critique of modern expressions of Mexicanness through the bottom performing its bottomness. Accordingly, I closely engage with Orellana's final live performance of *Todos somos hijos de la Chingada* in Mexico City in the summer of 2019, to which I was invited as a Chicana performer to collaborate and participate. At the time, I was known by the name Vicente, which I retain in this chapter.[39] My proximity to the piece and Orellana's identity as a genderqueer and gay artist uncover a lineage that can be observed as embodied, that carries through the ways a body performs the bottom through the different versions in which the self may manifest—as was the case then, with Vicente, and now. My relationship with the work changed drastically; the choreography and movement strategies with other bodies within the piece complicate and reveal new textures to a critical trajectory that situates the feminine and queer body at the center of these discourses about how bodies give access to those sexual genealogies through its trauma and sacrifice.

As the *cumbia* resumes in the live performance, Orellana further explains her secret inherited recipe from the matriarchs of her family. Grabbing one of the limes placed at the altar, she explains,

> Primero, escoge tu limón con mucho cuidado.
> Ya que tengas tu limón, raya la cáscara con un pulso constante
> Después, exprime el jugo del limón hasta humedecer.
> Repite hasta conseguir la consistencia deseada.[40]

With lime in hand, Orellana begins to squeeze the lime carefully and slowly between her hands, allowing the juices to find their way down her body and into the *vitrolero*. She grabs another lime. This time, she places the lime between her breasts and begins squeezing the juices into her *limonada*. Body part by body part, the juices drip off her body into a sacred citric elixir. Finally, she places a lime in her mouth and looks upward while the lime juice glistens down her chin and neck, over her chest, seeping into her breasts, as it makes its way into the *vitrolero*. It's time for the final step: Mix. Orellana then hikes up her dress, revealing black panties, and carefully inserts her foot into the *vitrolero*. She starts vigorously mixing the *limonada* with her foot, while the sound of liquid splashing harmonizes with the *cumbia* music in the background. The force of her shaking foot travels up her body and through her chest, as she braces herself against the pillars of the altar while her eyes roll into the back of her head.

The artist carefully removes her foot from the *vitrolero*, readjusts her skirt, and stares directly at the audience as a red light is cast over the altar. After a long pause, she yells,

> Estoy lista para que me comas, como un puto pedazo de carne
> Devórame con la mirada, arráncame un pedazo
> Y saboréame con tu piropo, pendejo
> Pero cuidado, porque si te quedas chupando mucho tiempo,
> Te va a arder, ¡cabrón![41]

Figure 4.2. Video still from *Todos somos hijos de la Chingada*, performed July 14, 2019, in Mexico City by Yanina Orellana and Vicente. Filmed by author.

A sharp piercing tone rings loudly three times and the stage goes black. This transgenerational *limonada* she prepares becomes more than just a refreshing beverage. Rather, by interpellating the male gaze in her final words, whether directed at the audience or at hegemonic masculinity more broadly, she names how her body as a microcosm of feminine bottoms is exploited while simultaneously being desired, used while enjoyed, and yet—it comes with a warning. This *limonada* represents a history of inheritance extending beyond its ingredients, reflecting a lineage of lessons and stories about what it means to be a woman, and moreover, to be a sexual woman. These are inherited sexual histories being stirred together in the *vitrolero* that have been passed down from the women in her family. The *limonada* is thus converted into a bodily fluid. Orellana literally uses her body to prepare it: from her mouth, to her breasts, to her feet. The traces of her body, with all its sexual memories, are poured into this sacred mixture that she has now prepared for the public.

My affective relationship to this piece drastically changed from my first encounter with it in Santa Monica, to its final performance in Mexico City. Orellana expressed wanting to have a final chapter to *Todos somos de la Chingada*: a collaborative performance with a diasporic queer Mexicanness. Through Vicente's active participation *within* the performance itself as a queer Mexican American artist, the elements of sex and encounter began taking on new meaning. My initial reading of the performance had linked everything to pleasure and sex—admittedly, in a very superficial way—from the ways she had treated the limes, to the choreography (which I will discuss in more depth).

Her body movements had told me a story about sexuality, especially when considering the figure of *la Chingada*, from whom the title is de-rived. Yet, in the process of scoring the movements and choreography for the collaborative performance at the time, Vicente was asked to think about two things: first, words that describe an event, time, or experi-ence in which they felt pleasure and expressive of their sexuality; and second, words that describe when they felt their body or sexuality being repressed, denied, or violated. The former seemed obvious and in line with my earlier readings of the performance—she is telling a story about pleasure and sex. However, it was the second request that complicated,

Figure 4.3. Video still from *Todos somos hijos de la Chingada*, performed July 14, 2019, in Mexico City by Yanina Orellana and Vicente. Filmed by author.

Figure 4.4. Video still from *Todos somos hijos de la Chingada*, performed July 14, 2019, in Mexico City by Yanina Orellana and Vicente. Filmed by author.

problematized, and extended my relationship to the piece altogether. Both pleasure and violation were to be part of how the performance would be scored and perhaps performed.

On the night of July 14, 2019, at the Foro Tecuicanime in Mexico City, the stage goes black and Vicente rises and proceeds to Orellana's feet. The lights come up. Arriving at the altar, disrobing, and kneeling before Orellana, Vicente's body is presented at the altar as the music quietly resumes with the same *cumbia*. Orellana picks up a lime. She gently caresses and glides the lime across the curves and folds of Vicente's body. With a sponge she soaks up her *limonada*, wringing those fresh juices out over their chest. Mexicanness. Slowly, the sponge grazes over arms and torso. After, she gently lays their head back over the *vitrolero*, pouring the *limonada* through the raspy curls of their mixed-race hair in baptismal-like ritual, anointed with this mixture of bodily fluids carrying the sexual charge from Orellana's body. Only now, perhaps that final missing ingredient may be those combined residues and embodied histories of pleasure and pain of the diaspora now dripping into this transgenerational sexual *agua fresca*. Finally, the *limonada* is served. And we drink.

The music has stopped and Vicente faces the audience in silence. Behind, Orellana removes her dress and veil, wrapping the veil around her waist, and without music she begins to move. Standing in the frame of the altar, with a strongly fixed pelvis, she begins to vibrate, percolate, as if a ball of energy is about to expel itself from the inside out. Her arms stiffly positioned in front of her body, centered in front of her pelvis, she moves in a violent vibration. The light taps of a *cumbia* rhythm begin to play as she begins swinging and activating her hips in isolation. The music builds upon its light rhythm with layers of deeper bass, more treble, a vibrant two-count beat, until finally becoming a fully solidified *techno-cumbia* sound with the same deep, distorted electronic voice imploring the artist to *¡Vamos nena, vamos chica!* Vicente rises to their feet, as the audience watches the rhythm creep up their body and begin to move in unison with Orellana.

Chingada Choreographies: Fucking with Pleasure

The choreography extends the opening scene into a narrative about the centrality of the body's capacity to tell stories about cultural memories.[42] Thinking back to the two lines of thought introduced by Orellana to influence and shape how the performance would be scored, we see that the body is centered to reveal stories about pleasure and trauma that are carried over time and through their inheritance. The choreography, or scoring, of *Todos somos hijos de la Chingada* becomes a central narrative to the performance. As André Lepecki argues, "Choreography, once enacted, displays disciplined bodies negotiating their participation within a regime of obedience for the sake of bringing an art piece into the world. Thus, it becomes a site for investigating agency, compliance, the forces of imperatives, and the capacity to collectively surrender oneself, as dancer, to an outside force."[43] Orellana opens her body in a vulnerable way, to share stories of its pleasure and violation. That is, she reveals the borders of her body and shares a divergent narrative about sex and Mexicanness that can only be read through how her body moves. She reveals how her body has been forced by external forces to move in certain ways over the course of her life and in different contexts. More pressingly, she also exposes how those forces have also violated the female body she has inherited.

While the music attached to *Todos somos hijos de la Chingada* projects the familiar sound of a *techno-cumbia* that rouses certain affects and movements in the performance of one's Mexicanness, Orellana does not

Figure 4.5. Video still from *Todos somos hijos de la Chingada*, performed July 14, 2019, in Mexico City by Yanina Orellana and Vicente. Filmed by author.

dance a "traditional" Mexican *cumbia* in this performance. Rather, as a dancer, she brings ballet, contemporary technique, Afro-Latinx American dance, and movement art to problematize and extend the Mexican genre of the *cumbia* as it is processed through her body. The composition of her choreography is diasporic, and actively calls on the diaspora, to reimagine and reinscribe Mexicanness with new borders of belonging and expression. The result is the exposure of disparate narratives about the performance of sex and sexuality through gestures and movements. Her steps are precise and structured, but also possess a rich wildness to them. Her arms elongate and sweep across the space. Her legs lift and swiftly move across the frames. She whips her hair around, covering her face, while her body gyrates and moves in sync. This wildness, particularly female wildness, is an essential contour of the masculinist gaze as it views *la Chingada*. The *Chingada* (Malinche, the fucked woman), as we described earlier in this chapter, represents a wild and unconfined sexuality that cannot be tamed. She is a woman who gives in to her sexual instincts without recourse. By extension, this wildness is always already attached to hemispheric Latina sexuality as an exotic point of desire and allure. Popular culture and mainstream media construct an image of the wild and exotic Latina as a sex symbol available for export to quench the thirst of the American consumer who has a taste for something spicy. Yet if it is considered integral to scoring the performance, the body shares stories of this sexuality by embodying figures of sexual inheritance that are always caught by borders, or have their borders crossed. The body remains at the center as a territory. As Lepecki argues, "A dancer's labor is nothing else than to constantly embody, disembody, and re-embody, to incorporate as well as to excorporate, thus permanently refiguring corporeality as therefore proposing improbable subjectivities, modes of living, moving, affecting, being affected."[44] In her intentionally imprecise choreography, Orellana captures and converts a wildness into a new form of body politics and lexicon that recognizes and affirms, rather than rejects, the inherited sexual legacy of the *Chingada* that is central to many Latina forms of subject formation. She imagines a corporeality that will always be diasporic—that is, always outside the boundaries of anything that can be contained within a confined space or embodiment.

As a young girl in Guadalajara, Orellana shared with her mother that she wanted to become a dancer. Her mother enthusiastically suggested enrolling her in *ballet folklórico* (Mexican folkloric dance). Yet the young Orellana had her aspirations set on becoming a ballerina. With this focus, she began her training in Mexico at a young age, until moving to Los Angeles to further her studies with a degree in dance. Her end goal was to become "the perfect ballerina."[45] She trained in the traditional techniques of ballet and contemporary dance, each teaching her to structure and discipline her body and her movements. It was not until the end of her training that she broke from the ballet tradition, into other forms of dance. She became acquainted with African and Afro-Latinx American dance techniques, which, according to her discipline, were considered a form of "worldly" dancing. However, it was through those techniques that Orellana discovered that her body could *move* differently—that movements could originate *in* her body.

Yanina Orellana's movements in *Todos somos hijos de la Chingada* are eclectic and transnational in their technique and composition, finding their energy and origin in her pelvis. In the opening movement, we see the artist isolate her hips and begin to vibrate; slowly gyrating, then rapidly, this movement moves upward from the pelvic frame, through her core, across her chest, until finally reaching her head as she whips her hair around. For Orellana, in this one movement, she responds to, complicates, extends, and even rejects the traditional techniques of placement and alignment imprinted on her body through ballet. The disciplining of the body in ballet in controlling the narrative through which the choreography and thereby the body communicates and conveys narratives about passion and desire is not new. However, as Susan Leigh Foster argues, "The body, parsed into tiniest increments, each capable of registering distinct kinds of movement, pronounce[s] its state of distress." This is most notable in the control Orellana has over her isolations in the choreography. These tiny gestures, from the curl of a lip to the flipping of her hair, "all distinguish[] the subject's state of suffering from adjacent feelings of melancholy and pity."[46] Orellana tells a transgenerational, transnational sexual story through her *limonada* as much as she does through her choreography. Ballet is never abandoned in this piece; rather, it is problematized by its inability to contain the trauma of female sexualities. These trauma narratives of melancholy become visualized through the staging of the sexual body as something to be choreographed, as something that, in abjective response, will reveal its narratives about sex and desire.

This is a performance about liberating her pelvis: those sexual zones asked not to move or have power. In our conversations, she shared that it was only through turning to the movements of Afro-Latinx American dance, deviating from the formalism of ballet and contemporary dance, that she began thinking about the scoring of *Todos somos hijos de la Chingada*. In her words, "I wanted to do a piece that pointed me toward a physical practice that honored all the cultural influences that were in my identity and in my body."[47] Surely, we see the tension between the technically disciplined movement of contemporary dance and ballet and the postcolonial wildness of African diaspora dance movement, wherein the latter complicates and rejects the moral strictures of the former. In her choreography, we can witness the articulation of her spine between *enveloppé* and *développé*, formed by the electronic drum of the *cumbia*. She takes up space with an *arabesque attitude* to the back that does not need to go back into full *relevé*. These movements are a process of liberating the fixed pelvis and shoulders that ballet had trained her body into. Her body comes undone in this process of leaning into diasporic and postcolonial dance movements.

The convergence of these techniques reveals how the Latina body moves across different landscapes and crosses borders: she crosses her own borders. It also reveals the juxtaposition between meeting social expectations (mediated through a masculinist gaze—here, codified in ballet's disciplinary structure—to keep her sexuality contained, confined, and proper) and rejecting these norms in favor of the raw, pleasurable, and wild performance of a sexuality grounded in her brownness.

Her body tells a story: it is literary. Describing the relationship between dance and literature, Karmen MacKendrick explains, "Dance is of all the arts perhaps the least amenable to discursive or any linguistic description, just as literature seems of all the arts most disincarnate."[48] As a result, "Dance intensifies ordinary movement as literature intensifies ordinary language, thus, paradoxically, bringing into it that which opposes it."[49] Susan Leigh Foster reminds us, "Insofar as choreographers and aestheticians conceived of the action ballet as the visual and moving representation of a story, they relied heavily on the analogy between dance and painting in order to elucidate the visual impact of dance."[50] In her use of gestures, diasporic dance techniques, and her embodied history of sexuality, Orellana creates new literary conventions out of the movements that produce a language that is, at times, untranslatable yet fraught with competing and colliding narratives of sexual embodiment.

For Orellana, the figure of Malinche most appropriately captures the visceral tensions, confusions, and resistance practices of sex and womanhood anchored in her body. Through the very name of the performance, *Todos somos hijos de la Chingada*, Orellana leans into a history that resonates within the body and outwardly flows in her choreography. She explains,

> I felt like I was embodying Malinche, because I spent so much time and energy trying to become a ballerina and a model of a good American dancer, that I forgot how I used to move before dancing. I forgot how my mom speaks with gestures. I forgot the way, just in general, how in my culture there are ways of approaching movement that I was not including in my art. And I felt very Malinche. I don't even know how to dance Mexican folklore![51]

Figures 4.6–4.7. Video stills from *Todos somos hijos de la Chingada*, performed July 14, 2019, in Mexico City by Yanina Orellana and Vicente. Filmed by author.

Malinche, then, symbolizes what lost memories look like when we try to make sense of the practices we call Mexicanness. She is the Mother who is fucked twice, from two cultures that make up the borders of her body; her betrayal of her people is a betrayal of her own embodiment. Orellana speaks to how she once let her body be contained, for those borders to be regulated. The tensions that build up in her body are those repressed memories, movements, gestures, and body language that express who she is as she moves across varying landscapes.

This traveling movement performs a special labor in this piece: doing the work of building narratives about the everyday performances of Latina and Mexican womanhood. The movement in *Todos somos hijos de la Chingada* merges into a sensibility grounded in the quotidian alongside an unmistakably postcolonial body framework. One of the gifts of Orellana's performance is its framing of pleasure as both painfully desirable and deliciously bitter—that is, the spectacularization of the multifaceted dimensions of sex and death as they are embodied by and projected onto Latina and Mexican women.

In that final performance, Orellana's choreography is coupled with movements expressing the embodied legacies of a diasporic queer Mexican body through Vicente. Susan Leigh Foster argues that in these moments of exchange, when passion and desire are at stake, choreography becomes a "new conception of individuality as contained within and supported by individual bodies."[52] This is very obvious in their interaction with one another, allowing the mouth, pelvis, and hips to move in ways revealing tensions with the material worlds surrounding both of their Mexicanness. The movements exchanged between both bodies come to a point. Very precisely, as if in slow motion, they cross each other and go into an expressive state of ecstasy. Both faces portray a climactic experience resembling orgasmic release. But slowly, that orgasm turns into disgust, pain, and repulsion—nausea, even. In this very slow and elongated movement, the poles of sex as pleasure and trauma collide with one another. This performance calls upon the Latinx abjective register. Lingering behind our desire to experience histories of sex with our bodies are the traumatic experiences that cannot be left behind or in the dark. As Leticia Alvarado explains, "Abjection, as an aesthetically based political strategy, can serve as the basis for addressing political injustice, invoking broader collectivities beyond conventional identity categories even as we remain attuned to the particularities that create the abject realm."[53] What is uncovered and made public through our movements and this climactic movement between pleasure and pain is how we as sexual minorities are positioned into restrictive and imposing categories by systems of power. Foster would also argue, "Each body could undergo, just as it could faithfully depict, self-generating sequences of passion. Each body could be compelled into reactive responses to other bodies according to the causal logic of emotional syntax."[54] As such, the political nature of the choreography underscores how resistance to those systems—political, social, and cultural—is always met with pain, which we are willing to embrace and exhibit.

The tempo increases. Faster, faster, and faster the music plays. Bodies on the stage are incapable of keeping up with the tempo. Orellana is on the ground, rolling around, pulsating and extending her chest and pelvis upward in sync with the tempo until she can no longer keep up. She moves to the stage, returning to the altar and kneeling with the *vitrolero* between the exhausted legs of a diasporic subject who in that encounter crossed a multiplicity of borders—perhaps too many to list—risking exposure. In English, the words "Hail Mary, full of grace" loudly echo in the room. "Holy Mary, Mother of God, pray for us—" Orellana begins shoving lime halves into this queer mouth reciting the Virgin's Prayer. With the lime in her mouth, she emits moaning sounds that cannot be distinguished between pain and pleasure. Juice trickles down the queer diasporic chest. Finally, with the utterance of the words "Now and at the hour of death. Amen," the music comes to an end. The lights go down.

While scoring the performance, Orellana and Vicente imagined an ending that united itself with the altar at the beginning of the performance, and assumed that this moment captured an act of devotion and reverence, while bringing the narrative full circle. Yet, in our conversations with the audience following the performance, there was a resounding consensus among them that the last scene was about death and violence. Perhaps the audience knew better than we did. Two bodies occupied that stage—one a Mexican woman, the other a diasporic queer Mexican. With both sharing stories and histories of sexual pleasure and trauma, the performance space became a contact zone. These bodies exposed their borders to one another in ways that became so infinite that the body could no longer keep in motion because sound and time move faster than the body ever could. The performance forces exhaustion by trying to access the tugging and pulling between trauma and pleasure. In those crossings, the body could only share stories of death. As a diasporic body performing within the Mexican state, with a Mexican woman, I found that the lines that once determined diasporic experiences were quickly removed as I became subject to the parameters of the context in which I was participating. Conversely, Orellana had opened her body, filled a diasporic subject with her secret *limonada*—a potion and substance of bodily memories—and allowed her own Mexican subjectivity to become undone in that exchange of bodily fluids.

Death was always already in our vocabulary while scoring, just under a different disguise: repression, denial, and violation—in other words, a language of pleasure's unruly relationship with death. We had told a story about how our body borders had been crossed in ways that are pleasurable, while equally traumatic and unforgiving. Perhaps the diaspora—diasporic Mexicanness, at least—can only be death.

5

Stuck on Carlos Martiel

The Blackness of Hemispheric Latinx American Performance

Blacks do not function as political subjects; instead, our flesh and energies are instrumentalized for postcolonial, immigrant, feminist, LGBTQ, transgender, and workers' agendas. These so-called allies are never *authorized* by Black agendas predicated on Black ethical dilemmas. A Black radical agenda is terrifying to most people on the Left—think Bernie Sanders—because it emanates from a condition of suffering for which there is no imaginable strategy for redress—no narrative of social, political, or national redemption.
—Frank B. Wilderson III, *Afropessimism*

"That looks sticky," I muttered to myself as I was visually confronted with images on my phone of a nude Black man, painted from his collarbone down to his toes in what I had correctly assumed to be blood. He stood firmly still and tall on a white pedestal in a large empty white gallery. Such was my first encounter with the Cuban artist Carlos Martiel's *Monumento I* (2021), a body installation performance of a temporary monument commissioned and produced by LA TREINAL 20/21 and curated by El Museo del Barrio in New York City in the midst of the global COVID-19 pandemic.

While my first encounter appeared to be a bit anti-climactic, my underwhelming reaction was definitely not the result of perceiving the photos of the ensanguined Martiel to be devoid of meaning or profundity—quite the opposite—rather, my apathetic response was toward what I initially perceived to be a lack of novelty to the nuance of the aesthetic representation itself that the blood does in performance art, particularly in hemispheric Latinx America. Blood often feels like just another visualized "thing" folded into the national and collective imaginary. Perhaps, then, my initial indifference toward the aesthetic representation of violence through blood and nudity collides with larger stakes of a political aesthetics of a violence that has not yet passed. Rather, it is captured and looped by the structures of power that set it into motion in the first place. In other words, perhaps the blood never actually dries. If blood as a signifier for systemic violence and death is just another "thing" in life, then Martiel arguably situates his body through a sensual thinghood that performs a disturbance in a seemingly quiet and still space.

Carlos Martiel stands still and tall, with his bare, dark-skinned body perfectly painted by a thick, dried, oxidized, blackened red layer of human substance so precisely, evenly neat and sharp on his muscular body. Only four photos were released of the performance. As these photos followed me across social media, it became apparent how not even the slightest sheen of light bounces off the dried blood. The blood is almost matte and opaque. I began thinking about how the stickiness still affected me, as if the blood were still drying, as if, under the oxidized layer, the blood was still wet. Or rather, perhaps the blood could never *fully* dry even if it is captured to appear as such. The artist describes the performance thus: "This work proposes a temporary monument to bodies that have historically been and continue to be discriminated, oppressed, and excluded by Eurocentric and patriarchal hegemonic discourses."[1] The form, practice, and technique of the artist's visually minimalist yet aesthetically and affectively complex performance are indeed a clear representation of a hemispheric Latinx bottom performance. It captures the minoritarian aesthetics of Mexicanness's hemispheric span as collective abjective experiences in which the past makes itself violently knowable in the present. This formative theoretical praxis, which brings into concert aesthetic practices, cultural production, and the critical analysis of body politics, enables an engagement with aesthetic embodiments of sex and death through an affective encounter with the alterity of minoritarian subjects.

"Minoritarian," as an aesthetic strategy, articulates less of an identity than a commons contoured by the exigencies of an identity-in-difference operating at a sociopolitical level.[2] Alexandra T. Vazquez reminds us that Muñozian framing of minoritarian performance refers to a "relationship to the majoritarian public sphere in the United States. The public sphere

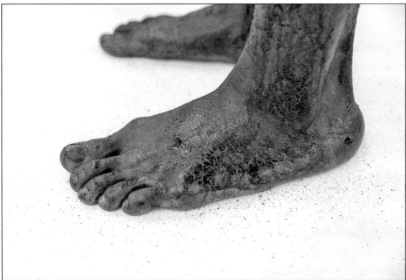

Figures 5.1–5.2. Carlos Martiel, *Monumento I*, 2021, Museo del Barrio, New York City. LA/TREINAL 20/21.

in this sense is one that privileges whiteness, the masculine, the 'native born.' And the heterosexual."³ I would define this as a negative relationality by the negations of who or what is a subject through a process of formation or undoing. Negativity, here, describes that endless deferral of difference rooted in processes of becoming and unbecoming. Joshua Chambers-Letson extends this definition with attention to how "minoritarian" also "describes a place of (often uncomfortable) gathering, a cover, umbrella expanse, or refuge under and in which subjects marked by racial, sexual, gender, class, and national minority might choose to come together in tactical struggle, both because of what we share (often domination in some form by the major, or dominant culture) and because of what makes us different."⁴ These highlight a proximity to minoritarian bodies exposed in their social, cultural, and political loci at the bottom. Performances at the bottom are uncomfortable across queer aesthetic formations, producing new epistemological trajectories through which to read sexual subject formation as a necessary articulation of new ways of understanding the affective registers of the Latinx American hemispheric body, in so far as the negative relationship is always already hemispheric through Latinx's endless deferral of difference.

Martiel presents his body through a minoritarian aesthetic that does not deny the cliché of blood spill, but rather stands firmly in its discourse, which resists in an uncomfortable way. Yet the discomfort is remarkably pleasing to some degree in the bottom, in ways that know how to convert that trauma into pleasure. That mutual affective bond results from the frottage of the imagined and idealized tropes of heteronormativity through which Blackness and diasporic trauma can be accessible. Keguro Macharia teaches us that thinking through and with frottage "keep[s] the body seeking sexual pleasure in view" and can sensualize the discomfort available.⁵ Macharia offers the notion of frottage as that sensual and mutual rubbing that one can feel, in ways less intense than fucking. Rather, the mutual feelings of rubbing of two bodies "privilege conceptual and affective proximity." In this case, the rubbing of Blackness against its discourse reflects "rubbing produced by and as blackness, which assembles into one frame multiple histories and geographies."⁶ In this sense, allowing the cliché to be a cliché that becomes a type of "thing" can give renewed meaning to the way diaspora can be conceived through what Macharia describes as "a multiplicity of sense-

Figure 5.3. Carlos Martiel, *Monumento I*, 2021, Museo del Barrio, New York City.
LA TREINAL 20/21.

apprehensions" that grasps the quotidian performances of "intra-racial experience" into a moment in which "blackness coalesces through pleasure and play and also by resistance to antiblackness."[7] Martiel shares an unruly performance that produces a discourse about Blackness while also being a critique of the process through which it occurs. That movement is felt, even in a still frame. In other words, there is an aesthetic strategy to his exposure that has broader stakes for hemispheric Latinx American sexual cultures of death.

Bottoming Stands Up and Stands In

Aside from the photographer, there is no one else in the large gallery with the artist. The melancholy of its emptiness is palpable in a wide shot of Martiel. The gallery is a pristine white, immaculately clean, and as bare as the artist. Even the blood is tidy. The blood lies neatly encrusted upon Martiel's flexed, stiff, erect body as he sternly looks forward. Nothing appears to be out of place. The frames of Martiel's performance visually articulate and enunciate an ethical and political aesthetic of being both in and yet out of place by the juxtaposition of his melanated skin, the blackening oxidized blood, and the brightly lit blank gallery background surrounding him. The artist allows for the condensation of spatiality and temporality invoked by *Monumento I* in its conceptualization and performance.

Carlos Martiel's performance is provocatively and distractingly minimalist. Yet *Monumento I* captures the aesthetic of being interpellated by one's Blackness, with racial difference being treated as his most meaningful feature. This harks back to the intentionality of Lechedevirgen Trimegisto's use of a video of a Black Ugandan man being brutally killed as a means to visually translate sex-related death. A Black body in its suffering becomes a rhetorical prop that signifies an always already recognizable form of violence. Blood on a Black body "must" mean death because we are already familiar with images of Black bodies dead. Harvey Young describes this as a "phenomenal blackness" in performance, in which "projections of the black body across recognizable African American bodies create similar embodied experiences."[8] The sight of a Black body carries signifying power, and as a familiar rhetorical prop, is often deployed to stand in for other individuals, thus overshadowing questions about who the artist is. As Martiel stands with muscles fully flexed, veins bulging in his temples, his expression and posture capture the exhaustion and persistence of the postcolonial condition of being trapped by the hegemony of the blood spilled by those minoritarian subjects whom this monument commemorates, as the artist declares:

> I stand naked on top of a pedestal in the center of the space with my body covered in blood drawn from migrant, Latinx, African-American, feminized, Native American, Muslim, Jewish, Queer, and Transsexual bodies considered as "minority" or marginalized groups in the United States by Eurocentric supremacist discourses.[9]

A continuity of relentless oppression and disruptive exclusion is captured by this proposal to monumentalize victims of systemic abuse and its systematic deployment. The title of the performance describes a series dedicated to the concept of monuments at the national and international register of being installed and truncated in the public sphere.

With monuments, these installations celebrate a futurist promise of a corporeal sovereignty that repeats itself and serve as a reminder of just who fucks whom. They are public entities that physically take up space and thus structure movement and order to surrounding areas; in some cities they are even a main focal structure. Carlos Martiel's *Monumento I* turns toward a different lens that underscores how the invisible blood dripping off those statues—or in some cases materially represented through fake blood or red paint that desecrates the national sanctity of these figures—is not so representative that those violent histories can be encased in bronze. The artist manipulates the materials used to monumentalize trauma by changing the materiality of *monumentos*, by deploying his own queer Black body as a political canvas on which to paint the blood of those fucked over by the fucked-up situations of the modern state. Perhaps, then, he monumentalizes those at the bottom whose blood loss is just another part of quotidian life. *Monumento I*, however, taps into the necessary affective mixing of traumatic mediums of actual human blood against the artist's Black body in a pristine white gallery, on a pedestal in a confrontation with death that also reminds us just who is fucked by whom. The artist describes this as "traumatic inheritance," provoking a reading of the temporal gestures made by the performance.[10] Moreover, he makes intelligible bodies of color and those signifiers associated with the blood in which he is painted. These signifiers thus become realized by bodily matter made present, extending beyond the representative and into the aesthetic blending of performance and body art.

The labor produced by Martiel's performance in its use of a Black body to do the work of sex and death narratives resonates with domestic dramas in which Black characters gather to share something about the events of daily life. Koritha Mitchell describes these as "lynching plays," wherein a spectrality of the dramatic world of Blackness affects the conversations that are produced by something as complexly simple as a Black man posing in an empty gallery. For Mitchell, these dramas "capture the community's understanding of the spiritual, financial, and psychological damage done" by social lynching.[11] In other words, the audience is able to have access to the solitude of the labor Black bodies do in aestheticizing violence. Martiel catastrophizes a bottom that is exposed, yet possibly ignorable because it is already too familiar. His bloody body is just otherwise hung out to dry.

Figure 5.4. Carlos Martiel, *Monumento I*, 2021, Museo del Barrio, New York City. LA TREINAL 20/21.

Eight of Martiel's friends and friends of friends of friends piled into his New York City apartment to donate their blood for the performance. With the assistance of a nurse and adhering to COVID-19 safety protocols, the nine of them had their blood drawn into a large container. He told me, "How could I not do it? I fit like five of the categories!" His body opens as a canvas to be painted with mixed blood. The mobility and layers of these signifiers are seemingly palpable through how they are about to be signified or conceptualized and projected onto a bare body as a canvas in its basic nudity, as a script for those social and cultural narratives and subtexts of racialized and sexualized hegemonic strategies of the state. At the museum, the artist emphasized that it was important to him that the blood dried and became opaque, with neatly detailed and precise edges. After each layer of blood dried, another was painted atop. After the third layer dried and set, the artist stood upon the white pedestal. Not a drop of blood was to seem out of place or falling. In describing this detail of the dried layers of blood encapsulating his body, he stated, "In that aspect, they also are linked to bronze sculptures, like, to simulate the aspect of ferrous metal."[12] During a forty-five-minute shoot with the photographer, Martiel just stands tall, still, hard, fixed, his eyes looking forward. Yet all that emerged from this performance for the public eye are four photographs. Afterwards, Martiel got off the pedestal and showered. And that was that.

Eccentric Stillness of a Black Diaspora

The pedestrian way that the performance ends, according to the artist— that is, in which he just resumes his day as usual—captures a spirit of my initial encounter with the images of a body encrusted in blood. The image and sites of violence become something from which to walk away. The spectator might pause and take in the sights, but the day can and does go on, only to be repeated in an indefinite loop of the postcolonial condition. The concept of a monument is to remember lives lost for the growth of a nation by converting their embodied natures through the permanence of materials that withstand time and replace the body and its matter. Employing layers of blood that have oxidized onto his body changes the materiality of monuments and changes our frame of thinking from the symbolic or representative body to the performative body: a body marked and racialized by its disposability and temporariness. While ignorable, the stickiness, even in a sensation, can ask questions of the remanences that stick behind.

Rebecca Schneider contends, "Performance does remain, does leave 'residue.' Indeed, the place of residue is arguably *flesh* in a network of body-to-body transmission of affect and enactment—evidence, across generations, of impact."[13] Performance is ephemeral, and leaves behind its residues creating their own experiences and thus performances of the political consequences of encounter with the Other. Schneider describes how performance functions "as both the *act* of remaining and a means of re-appearance and 're-participation' (though not a metaphysic of presence) we are almost immediately forced to admit that remains do not have to be isolated to the document, to the object, to bone versus flesh."[14] Disappearance and remains are seemingly antithetical. Schneider explains that disappearance is that which marks all documents, records, and materials as "remains." Accordingly, she rightfully contends, "Death appears to result in the paradoxical production of both disappearance *and* remains." Performance thus engages in a practice of playing the "spectral meanings that haunt material in constant collective interaction, in constellation, in transmutation."[15] Thinking with and from this reading of death and performance, I would argue that death is a structuring device that produces performances out of the disappearances and remains by turning to the figure of the gay male bottom as a paradigm to read these types of performances in terms of their larger impact, which extends beyond the ephemerality of the single event itself. Bottom performances give access to think beyond the cisness of the bottom, while underscoring why the project of bottoming might still need to be spoken about in response to men fucking each other.

The distracting stillness of *Monumento I* engages with the aesthetic violent history of Black performance and takes new meaning when going further with the outstanding Blackness in question. Harvey Young describes "standing still" as an act of "phenomenal blackness" that problematizes and extends "conceptualizations of Black Diaspora as pure movement."[16] He reminds his readers that captive bodies were held for months in the bellies of ships in which movement of the body was heavily restricted; later they had to stand still on auction blocks. In other words, the Black subjects of these performances and their images do not just simply sit or stand; rather, they redirect the gaze and perform an idealized image of themselves.[17] In effect, these forms of body art rightfully need to be reread through the demanding shift of gaze and thus recognizable as a locus for the biographical. In these moments, Young argues, the subject resists being "the black body exhibited for others" and instead becomes "a black body that has chosen to perform itself as an exhibit for itself."[18] Martiel displays a bottom so entirely exposed that it is used to expose those other ways of being a bottom that are not necessarily visible, but are representable through those channels already demanded in death.

The stillness of the performance as both a photograph and a man standing still and silent is paradoxically disruptive. It is too still; there is an uncomfortableness to the way the artist has elected to expose his body. In my own expectation that the body should move and do something, I had unknowingly ventured into postcolonial (namely, white) expectations formed during the interwar era, that demands that Black performers eccentrically move their bodies. Analyzing dance, Jasmine Johnson explains that these eccentric performances "made visible the sonic conventions of the time" in which performers "scouted the body's choreographic reservoir to render new embodied lexicons."[19] As such, missing from a reading of Martiel was a way to think with how the stillness is eccentric, one that dovetails with the spectacle of being still that Young describes. There is movement that is chaotic behind or rather to the bottom of the performance. Johnson argues, "This simultaneity of stillness and flight, of physical lull and spectral getaway, describes both the temporal register . . . and the embodied technique of eccentric movement."[20] The eccentrism desired of Martiel's performance was already there, but under the guise of what is only read as cliché to the postcolonizer.

If the image of Black bodies covered in blood is a clichéd motif that still effectively does the sexual labor of capturing generations and cross-cultural traumas, then one of the most profound aspects of its still aesthetic is that it becomes eccentric to have that much access to the Other. While their signified labor may be demanded, it is a perpetual demand that has movement because it carries over generations. The artist, however, slows down the demand to expose himself. It is now an overwhelming encounter with the Other that faces the subject with their own alterity out of the surprise of stillness. Martiel's performance announces a sexual materiality of passivity that is unique to the bottom's Other but also becomes that material object that bears new meanings when thought through, from, and against the relationship between the role of Blackness as a bottom performance and relational exposure to racialized sexual subjectivities.

Monumento I is striking. Martiel describes the work as a performance, even though we have only four images of this "performance." What then does *he* refer to as performance? For Martiel, the performance began once everyone gathered in his apartment. When asked when it ended or whether the performance continues, he responds, "No, at the moment I got off the pedestal and bathed, it ended. I think it's the same, that's as far as it goes. But yeah, that's when it ended."[21] His answer surprised me, and yet the more I sat with it, I began to think how apt it is. The finitude invoked by his performance, the permanence of only four photographs as "proof" or documentation, is the essence of the performative gestures of the piece itself: that the basic nudity onto which other traumas are projected and performed is finite.

Amelia Jones contends, "Body art practices solicit rather than distance the spectator, drawing her or him into the work of the art as an intersubjective exchange; these practices also elicit pleasure."[22] The performative aspects of *Monumento I* and the performance itself brush hard again this tension between body art and performance. I read this insistence as not a defense of or aspiration to creative futurities in the name of those signified by body art, but rather as the urgency behind how these identities and subjectivities are performed, while other anxieties are also projected upon the body. Accordingly, I found myself thinking alongside the four photographs that perhaps we might need to reconsider the larger context and parameters of the interpellative qualities nascent in body art's performance.[23] The genre of performance is problematized and extended by Martiel's work, like the blood, as multiple layers and registers. As such, I concur with Jones's reading of the photograph as that thing that is "both the visible proof of the self and its endless deferral,"[24] or rather, an endless deferral of the indeterminateness of performance rooted into the body's flesh and matter for a reconceptualization of how time functions and how performance is read queerly through critical race theory, deconstruction, and queer theory.

Hemispheric Performance in a Wake

Thinking with *Monumento I* in relation to the larger themes of *Bottoms Up* is sedimented into the multiplicity of blood layers from minoritarian subjects. That the blood dries, only to be repainted upon the artist's body as signified canvas for alterity, raises two larger stakes within hemispheric bottom performance. First, Martiel's body is deployed as a rhetorical prop for an unstable signifier of a signified other who remains trapped in the oscillatory nature of gender, race, and sexuality. Here, Martiel's body is that fleshly surface onto which writings about Black bodies are configured and imagined, while also being not only penetrable but violently destroyable and disposable. In Carlos Martiel's performance, exposing his body converses with the bare sexualization of the flesh, or what Hortense Spillers describes as the sensual spectacularization of suffering that converts a body into flesh. Martiel's body announces a racialized and sexualized materiality of passivity that is unique to the queer body of color and becomes that material object bearing new meanings when thought through sexual and body matter.

The temporariness of Blackness is an erasure of the body's scripts that would ever attempt to record a history of Blackness's aesthetic and intellectual production. Those in power systematically seek to erase and eradicate—many times more violently than with a shower—the existence of Blackness and its alterities, most especially at their convergence into something as defiling as a naked Black man covered in blood in an art gallery. Martiel tenses, pushing his body, making expression, producing affect, but for whom, if no one else is present? The photos left behind document the hieroglyphics that tell stories of the violence of power before it is washed over and made white and clean all over again. I argue that hemispheric bottom performance in this moment is revealed "as a category of 'otherness,'" in which, Hortense Spillers explains, "the captive body translates into a potential for a pornotroping and embodies sheer physical powerlessness that slides into a more general 'powerlessness,' resonating through various centers of human and social meaning."[25] The ability to declare aliveness is often not afforded to Blackness, and we need no record of it to prove otherwise. Racialized and sexualized xenophobia is ignorable and therefore cannot "exist" if there is no record of its existence within the national and collective imaginary. Suffering signals sensual encounter with otherness, in which the Other is reconstructed through exotic rumination and fantasy—making suffering digestible and empathetically operable. This reading of the body as script calls into question how embodied loci of knowledge production, those "hieroglyphics of the flesh," can be washed away. In this moment, a racialized and sexualized other announces the inevitable destruction of histories and stories of survival, when that survival is always already haunting.

Second, there is a question of temporality and time in relation to the performance and the photos, the durationality of the Other in *Monumento I* as the artist stands still in the blood of others that gets painted onto his body until it dries, only to be painted over again with a fresh new layer of blood. Dry. Paint. Repeat. This perpetual motion is set into action by the temporal gestures of Martiel's performance, insofar as endurance is central to this looping sensation integral to anticolonial Latinx performance.[26] The dried layers of blood dramatize the multiple and sedimented layers of generational traumas of the mixed Americas painted upon the body of the Other in their own alterity, each with another layer of trauma to be added on—not because the traumas beneath healed, but simply because the blood dried up. Once the blood dries up it becomes easier to just paint upon it, as if the original layer of blood were not even there to begin with. We can elucidate this trajectory by thinking of this layering through what Judith Butler describes as "sedimented acts" as a way of reconceiving the gendered, and I would add racialized, body as not a "predetermined or foreclosed structure, essence or fact, whether natural, cultural, or linguistic."[27] The temporal condition of sedimentation in Butler's early thoughts on gender is problematized and extended by queer theory and performance studies through the ways in which time can move in ways not restricted to the normativity of performative speech acts alone. This question has been described by many names, including Elizabeth Freeman's "temporal drag," Rebecca Schneider's "temporal tangle," and Jack Halberstam's "queer time," each in its own way pointing to the perpetual invocation and imbrication of the past into the present and thus affecting narratives created about the future.[28]

As material form, the Blackness performed by Martiel captures looping social death, which describes the negation of a prior meta-moment of plenitude or social life for Black bodies or their livelihood in the hemispheric Latinx Americas. Blackness, then, as a critical paradigmatic cannot be so easily disimbricated or uncontaminated from the trace of the captive body. I thus argue that Blackness is a constitutive part of violent landscapes as both a symptom and supplement of that violence; and conversely, perhaps the most appropriate locus from which to critique that violence.

Carlos Martiel argues that the performance ends the moment he steps off the pedestal and showers. While wildly true in perhaps a material sense, the answer to this question of a performance's end seems insufficient. Yet again, I expected more. I wanted a big finish. Or rather, perhaps as Rebecca Schneider articulates, I found myself responding to the theatricality of time itself, the transivity of time.[29] The finitude invoked by this statement speaks to the temporality of the racialized and sexuality body as something that can be washed away and disappear without a trace. I argue that Martiel's *Monumento I* engenders the disposability of

Blackness by erasing the body's scripts that could or would ever attempt to record its history. Martiel's positioning in the museum as a soiled and "dirty" Black body in a pristine white, clean gallery evokes a tension between sanitation and the public health of the national and collective imaginary. In this regard, Martiel's body is "trapped" or "captured" by the gaze of whiteness of a museum's colonial history that still fucks with the present.

The conceptualization of hemispheric performance, canonically defined by Diana Taylor as that which "stretches the spatial and temporal framework to recognize the interconnectedness of seemingly separate geographical and political areas, and the degree to which our past continues to haunt our present," is thus conceived from and through a political act of "remapping." This remapping shifts from centering a "*US America* to [centering] a hemispheric *Americas*" that, Taylor claims, "would also show histories and trajectories omitted from earlier maps; we include the routes made through specific migrations by exploring embodied performance."[30] However, I would contend that to do the political labor implied by a hemispheric approach to decenter the United States in the study of the Americas does not begin by centering the United States in its own decentering. Moreover, the legacy of the fucked-up past and its documentation through mapping—already a historically imperialistic and Master illustrated manuscript about the movement and trafficking of Black bodies in the Americas—become situated in these crossings to re-fuck those who were always already exposed, that is, to recolonize, reenslave, retraumatize through an attempt to remap the routes and migrations of these traumatic pasts that are never truly past. But the bottom cannot be mapped.

Missing from this vocabulary surrounding hemispheric performance is Blackness. Taylor deploys a forceful and ultimately rough entry into the bottom through a lack of a fulfilling account of the role of performing racialized ontologies in hemispheric aesthetics. A hemispheric approach to performance is an audacious one, yet one that is not evasive of critical race theory. Hemispheric performance studies rightfully points to how race moves in the Americas *through* and *from* bodies, once we determine who or what is determined as a body, which cannot be determined with any determinateness a priori. Accounting for race in the study of a hemispheric Americas—namely, Blackness—opens the space to access new lexicons to discuss the slippage of time Taylor describes as an aspiration for hemispheric performance. Yet we cannot achieve or realize this by redeploying the past and present as a binary opposition, bordered and distinctive of one another even when they are purported to be rescued of such, as opposed to something more betwixt and between or disjointed out of a linear concept of time that, as she says, "continues to haunt." She claims, "The reassuring slash between past/present cannot, in fact, keep these distinct. Talk of tragedy, like references to limit cases, gives these events anesthetic, wholeness, and a political insularity that obfuscates our understanding of them."[31] Not considering the larger stakes of a misunderstanding of finitude, as it relates to the racialized body, cannot be accounted for through the remapping of lost memories and routes. Instead, that slash is converted into the new boundary lines that are socially conceived and thus imprinted upon, or rather, included in addendum or revision to the original colonial project. This critical practice risks imposing the haunting effects of the past's abuse to not only be ever present, but a repetitive practice. In effect, because trauma is racialized and sexualized, it is thus susceptible to its own ontological terrors that are necessarily at the center of any project of hemispheric performance, and becomes one of the most generative, albeit difficult, starting points.

Diana Taylor conceptualizes hemispheric performance as that which displays the interface of archives and repertoires as embodied aesthetic gestures with an urge to account for the postcolonial conditions that continue to mobilize harm. While problematic, it is clear that there is a desire to know how to be with these trauma histories, knowing that they can never be erased or rewritten. Rather than engage with the repetitious project of documenting where death occurs, Martiel performs a way of being with death through his race and sexuality. Christina Sharpe theorizes this affective bond as living "in the wake"—conditions shaped by

living the history and present of terror, from slavery to the present, as the ground of our everyday Black existence; living the historically and geographically dis/continuous but always present and endlessly reinvigorated brutality in, and on, our bodies while even as that terror is visiting on our bodies the realities of that terror are erased.[32]

Accordingly, to live "in the wake" conceptualizes acknowledging that one lives perpetually alongside death. Thinking through "the wake," I argue that Martiel offers bottom performance and additional ways to be in the world through a practice of "care-full" engagement with the history of antiblackness.[33] Zakiyyah Iman Jackson defines antiblackness as an "ecology of violence."[34] Both Sharpe and Jackson give an analytical language to think through, from, and against race as an aesthetic of performance that interfaces with deadly forms of spatial (auto)biography.

Martiel's performance of a blood-encrusted Black nude man is employed to stand still, only long enough, to see what the diaspora looks like when it is hailed and interpellated to teach its spectators about being with violence in the world. Martiel is with others in their material sense, but also in a symbolic sense, in which bloodshed is used as an aesthetic strategy. *Monumento I* does not need a live audience because perhaps this violence often occurs when no one is looking or around to witness its event. Or perhaps Martiel avoids the spectacle of suffering to be something gawked at in public, and rather, allows their absence and his stillness to be just as spectacular. In both regards, it is a performance that captures how the bottom is exposed spatially as a way to be with other bottoms in a fucked-up world.

Carlos Martiel's *Monumento I* employs the eccentricity of his stillness to negotiate Blackness living the wake as a landmark for a literal wake. He stands still as an emblematic and exemplary congealment of the themes of bottom performance through the sedimented layers of the repeated cycle of the dried blood of the many Others being repainted again and again, those layers are ultimately washed away. Those layers of trauma and the bloodshed are meant to be just temporary. It is always just temporary. It is all washed off and all-clean in the end, as if it never even happened. In the case of *Monumento I*, this washing away marks the end of the performance, according to the artist.

The Crimes for National Performance

Monumento I brings into sharp focus a performance of race and sexuality that illustrates the struggle, or rather the instability and indeterminateness, of the categories of "queer" and "Mexicanness" to be performed nowhere else but from the bottom and not Mexico exclusively. Rather, the bottom expands its depths to the hemispheric Latinx Americas that is recognizable because they are indelibly intertwined. Effectively, these acts push further toward how we might characterize or approach hemispheric performance. In my interview with Carlos Martiel, he explains how he planned to perform one of the *monumentos* while in Mexico City only three weeks prior. He had already found a very public location in which he wanted the performance to occur, except for one small complication: it is a rather police-heavy area. As such, Martiel would increase his risk of arrest not only for public nudity, but also for desecration of the Mexican flag.[35] He refers to the January 2008 amendment to Mexico's Decree on the Coat of Arms, the Flag, and the National Anthem, which states that under no circumstances may a reproduction of the national coat of arms (which is imprinted upon the national flag) be altered or changed.[36] While the coat of arms may be used on vehicles of the president of the republic and on official stationery of federal, state, and municipal agencies, its reproduction otherwise must be strictly kept within the law. The risk imposed by the situation was fraught. As the artist tells me, "And there were, like, too many risks. I said, 'Well, I'm here as a tourist. To set up the camera where I wanted to do it, I would have to break the law,' because I have to jump over this place that says you can't be there, and it's fenced off so that people do not enter. So there was a lot, there was definitely a lot [of risk]."[37]

He never shared details of the planned performance or why a flag was necessary, nor did I ask. Rather, his time in Mexico City soon came to an end since he needed to return to New York to prepare for the performance that would become *Monumento I*. Accordingly, I argue that the specters of Mexicanness always haunted the stages of the *Monumento* series. Mexico and its aesthetic risks were always at stake in the performance of *Monumento I* and come to light when we carefully sit with what was left behind after those sedimented layers are attempted to be washed away. Some narratives simply just do not go away, but nonetheless are often ignorable or otherwise chosen to be unseen or unrecognized by the structural politics of the nation-building project. Yet Mexico continued to be a place where he felt that an intervention needed to be performed that called into question other forms of monuments or national icons that could also be "modified" or reimagined through a different medium becoming "a monument to those invisible populations."[38]

The body's inability to inhabit and act on the libidinal infrastructures undergirding acts of political domination and demands for subjugation is at stake in the aesthetics of the bottom and bottom performance in question. Queerness, in this sense, describes the occluded and masked by visual and textual renderings of the human aesthetic. The stake of these conceptualizations is best captured by Robert F. Reid-Pharr's meditation on the concept of "boundary," in which he argues that "the black gay stands in for the border crossings and boundarylessness that has so preoccupied contemporary Black intellectuals."[39] This becomes central to the sexuality of nonnormative ways of bottoming produced into being to form these boundaryless borders. Sexual violence operates within the sphere of Black masculinity on two dialectic levels. The first appears as a direct abrasion with what Reid-Pharr describes as "the presumption of black boundarylessness, or we might say the assumption of black subhumanity and black irrationality that has its roots deep in the history of slavery and the concomitant will to produce Africans as 'Other.'"[40] By effect this enables the creation of boundaries around Blackness that, I would argue, become prescriptive for defining the less-than-human as a central part of racialization in the Americas that enables questions about how boundaries form around who or what is captured by the bottom. Second, this violence enables a reattachment "to the very figure of boundarylessness that the assailant is presumably attempting to escape." As a result, a Black subject may be able to "escape," if only temporarily, "the very strictures of normality and rationality that have been defined in contradistinction to a necessarily amorphous blackness."[41] The (un)containability of the Other is at stake in what configures the boundarylessness of the borders imposed upon the bottom as I perceive it from following this trajectory. Yet a violence always already is proscribed onto and symptomatic of these borders that thus set parameters around the definition of the boundaries in the first place and that make assumptions about its boundarylessness or otherwise.

I strive for a reading of shared violence and the abject performance of race and sexuality in hemispheric Latinx performance studies by examining the nonnormative ethical intimacies with the necropower of the structures of violence that are at stake in these frameworks. A framework of bottoming and the bottom becomes invested in the instability of these racialized and sexualized false universals. Profoundly, the ethical project at stake thinks through the question of denying Latinxs their Blackness at an intersection of coming to the effacement of how the transgender body is sexualized differently and is thus racialized differently.

On an aesthetic level, Carlos Martiel's *Monumento I* effectively actualizes and aestheticizes how this current work defines bottom performance from a hemispheric Latinx performance lens. The diaspora conceived by the layering of bordered bodies whose boundarylessness is at times forced is beautifully and immaculately displayed on a pedestal. Martiel's body and performance capture my understanding of the diaspora from a queer hemispheric lens that departs with and from a reading of Blackness and the boundaryless borders that offers new ways of approaching, extending, and problematizing projects of national consciousness.

Indelible Mexicanness

The spectrality of Mexicanness that haunted Carlos Martiel's aesthetic oeuvre later exposed itself in a new series he began in 2020. With the support of the Lux Art Institute in San Diego and the New York Public Library, the artist presents two visual pieces: two American flags dyed in human blood. The first, *Insignia I*, acquired by and hung at the New York Public Library, is ensanguined with the blood of multiple African American people. *Insignia II* features a flag soaked in the blood of an Afro-Latino immigrant at the Lux Art Institute. The two formed part of a solo exhibit, *Two Insignias*, at OCDChinatown in New York City, from February 17 to March 17, 2021, curated by Pau Llapur. In yet another pristine white gallery, each flag is displayed vertically. Between the flags on an adjacent wall is a small LCD monitor with a video looping of *Insignia I* being activated at a 2020 protest in New York City by Carlos Martiel, outfitted in a black sweatshirt from the Maricón Collective—a Los Angeles-based Chicano and Latino DJ and artist collective—with "Maricón" (faggot) in white Old English typography screen-printed on the front. The influence and impact of limitations on the modification of national insignia appear to have lingered with the artist.

Figure 5.5. Carlos Martiel at New York City protest march with *Insignia I*, 2020. Reproduced with permission.

Figures 5.6–5.7. *Two Insignias*, OCDChinatown, New York City, 2021, curated by Pau Llapur. Reproduced with permission.

The *Insignia* series becomes personal because it is a commentary on how the body is expected to interact appropriately with national iconography. Yet, like *Monumento I*, not seen is the bloodshed that those symbols begin to obscure in the name of protecting the fictionality of the national imaginary, until it can no longer be entirely contained—yet that tension never goes away, as seen through the context of the soiled body and the clean white gallery. Sure enough, though, *Insignia III* (2021) is a Mexican flag that has been dyed in the blood of a queer Afro-Mexican person, displayed by Carlos Martiel holding it over the side of a building in Mexico City. He also appears to be hiding, perhaps reminding of us of the risk he takes activating the Mexican flag in this way, in which he could be charged with a treasonous offense.

C. Riley Snorton's theorization of the correlative relation between "fungibility" and "fugitivity," presenting the appearance of a site of possibility rather than one that solely encapsulates what Hortense Spillers describes as a reduction to the spectacle of Slaveness or the "captive" body's "seared, divided, ripped-apartness," gives way to ready treasons of race.[42] As Saidiya Hartman reminds us, the quotidian violence of these scenes of subjection radically signals attention to the everydayness of violence in the lives of the Black enslaved, while *also* posing a heuristic

Figure 5.8. Carlos Martiel, *Insignia III*, 2021.

that questions what can be committed against a captive body (per Spillers).[43] For Snorton, that fungibility proposes the potentiality of being transformative through this nexus of gender and race—that is, what occurs when fugitivity and fungibility encounter one another vis-à-vis the performance of gender. The fungibility of gender "engender[s] a way of seeing fungible flesh as a mode for fugitive action."[44] What Snorton offers us is a theorization of Black transness as a "critical modality of political and cultural maneuvering within figurations of blackness."[45] At this juncture, one is faced with one's fungibility by their appearance to the Self in their own basic nudity, which they cannot forget. I argue that this revelatory moment of consciousness would yield an ethical moment of encounter with the alterity of the Other's otherness (the other within the Self), here prescriptively and descriptively the captured body.

It is striking that Mexicanness was always already at the center of the questions influencing Martiel's performance. Moreover, one of the relational aesthetics between *Monumento I* and *Insignia III* is a turn toward Mexico—specifically objects of Mexicanness—as a necessary backdrop to ask broader questions about the constellation of hegemony, history, and power present within the landscape of the bottom. This broadening of the breadth of Mexicanness is to think about how one *feels* Mexican through the ways their body moves sexually across landscapes marked by death. Such a critical turn bears significance for cases across the hemispheric Americas. As Carlos Martiel explains, "Basically they are monuments to Latinx bodies, to indigenous bodies, to feminized bodies, to Black bodies. All that would be considered to be the other. That's the majority of us. They say it's a minority, that we're minorities, but really, we're a majority at the end of it all."[46] While this project does not attempt to take on the entire hemisphere, I conceptualize an understanding of hemispheric performance that stems from the affective exposure to race that also lingers in the same ways that Mexicanness has always lingered. What emerges are alterative and divergent understandings of hemispheric performance predicated on the primacy of fucking the Other.

The hemispheric Latinx Americas can never forget the Blackness of their own history. They can only produce an abjective shame triggering overcompensation to still participate within the national and collective imaginary that was never imagined with the queer of color body. Accordingly, thinking through, from, and against the queer body of

Figure 5.9. Carlos Martiel activating *Insignia III* in Mexico City, 2021. Reproduced with permission.

color becomes an ethical event that demands attention to the violence of their Blackness. Encountering the queer body of color becomes an ethical event demanding attention to the violence of their Blackness. I follow a trajectory of negativity in my approach to how I read the racialized body as articulated by Martiel's profound performance, which exposes structural violence that is always already as sexualized as it is racialized. It is an ethics of negativity, one structured by negative relationality to and from the trans of color body.

This bottomness is a hemispheric project that makes space for the convergence of these themes beyond the centering of Mexico and the US/Mexico border as prescriptive loci in the theorization of a failed project of Mexicanness that makes its violence available in an adjacent register as we think about how the transgender body of color advances the work of queer of color cultural theory in the hemispheric Latinx Americas.

Coda

The Trans Pasiva

I inherited a manuscript. Seemingly unbeknown to me, this was never planned, yet, surely, it was of my own creation. I had inherited an idea about the figure of the *pasivo*: Spanish for "passive" and slang for the gay bottom—that is, he who is always already penetrated by just his name alone. The passive bottoming of the *pasivo* has opened hemispheric performance studies to the radical comparativist practices of being with both meanings in the bottom. This idea came from a former gay manifestation of myself that remains spectral in this book and even later named. Encountering "Vicente" engage with bottoming alongside the artists and theoretical stakes in these pages produced a sense of dysphoria within the work that made itself knowable to the writing process. Studying "the past" brought forth different feelings about my relationship to history that did not think directionally—neither backwards nor sideways, nor even liminally. Rather, a dysphoric way of writing uncovers how I had inherited an idea about a figure in cisgender time. The passivity of passive bottoming destabilizes, or deplanes, the binary oppositions of past/present by challenging how one feels when the past makes itself known in the present in and through the bottom.

To refer to a "different version" of my body that is temporal also describes time in ways that suggest something seemingly nonlinear about the body's evolutionary function. There is perhaps a bottom to the bottom that throws a wrench into the nexus of the body's temporal relationships with itself to entirely destroy the system. The language available to describe these phenomena is an endless deferral of difference. The bottom's passivity to being in the world exposes one to the possibility that the past may make itself known in the present in ways that may possess traumatic affects. Queer theory has aided in the critique of the linearity of a heterosexist time that follows capitalist models of privileging prognostication and the construction of a nuclear household—that is, a lifeline dependent upon multiple lifelines being necessarily drawn. By a "cisgender time," I refer to the limits of a binary to time and the body. To the former, I have often treated the past and present as separate but mutually imbricated, yet there was still a separating distinction between the two. In that sense, an uncomfortable timeliness with the experiences of trans of color lives in the face of death by those institutions and actors of power is broadly at stake in these pages. To the latter point, bodies have a capacity to challenge regimes of power and social norms by being positioned at the center of aesthetic practices as a locus for ethico-political discourse. And they do this while ass-up, face-down. And moreover, the binary between alive-dead may no longer be sufficient ways of describing how bodies experience life.

Bottom performances regulate racialized gendered and sexualized systems in places that demand a subjugation of divergent actors and thinkers in the bottom. As an artist and theorist, thinking after a body I once called Vicente exacerbated feelings that there are limits to how some bodies may be defined or even named anything at all. The bottom reveals a difficulty in the task of naming certain embodied realities whose bottom overextends bottomness. What I was eager to see in the bottom was a way to talk about being otherwise embodied. Passivity to the *pasivo* in question is extended through bottoms of trans experience that experience dissociative episodes of being fucked into the bottom that fucks a body of life, perhaps out of full existence. A trans passivity points to the infinite impossibility of a bottom ever being fully alive, except not dead, and perhaps not even fully human. Rather, both the bottom and transness complicate even the most basic sexual evolutionary instincts and traits of a body.

If there exists a primary biological and evolutionary mandate for all living humans, it would likely be that all have to die. The only requirement to life is death. This presumption, then, that everybody comes with a death date, would imply there being a timeline that is embodied in a direct path toward death, because it is inevitably built into the biological politics of nature. We are naturally demanded to die. But what, if anything, is a body called after it has been exposed to death but is not yet dead itself? Does it become a corpse? Does it become anything "else" at all? These types of questions create rhizomatic relationships that link biological timelines of different bodies in ways that risk questioning whether one could ever be regarded as fully human after they have been exposed to death. The bottom to this experience is grounded in a realization that there is a bottom to the bottom in a finite sense. As much as the deep dwellings could appear infinite, the artists and authors discussed in this book have each shown what to do with knowing that there is a finite determination for bodies of the bottom. They do not hide from their own shortcomings, but rather, make space to think beyond the inadvertent use of a binary oppositional logic to address queer and trans experiences of color.

The signified bottom has been performatively captured in the different signifiers that have been hailed by names like *joto*, *puñal*, *pasivo*, *vampiro*, and *hijo de la chingada*, which bear an aesthetics of risk and violence that carves paths toward understandings of a sexual subject formation that are abjectively attained. Each problematizes and critiques the primacy of the cisgender gay male bent over at the center of bottom studies. By hailing the bottom by their names in Spanish, the bottom's performances have given access to a multiplicity of sexual systems that operate within the assemblage of the bottom in a cisgender time. As such, I dare to add just one more name to the list: *travesti*, a bottom that requires the instabilities of sex and death as they are gendered within a bottom that challenges embodied temporal belongings that share abject bonds with each of these signifiers.

Travesti is often insufficiently translated as "transvestite" in English. Even Latin Americanist gay and lesbian studies often reads the *travesti* as a cross-dresser or a queer man engaging in effeminacy or transvestitism as a gendered political expression or identity. The failures of translation discussed apply again in the case of the *travesti*. In Spanish, the rainbow acronym "LGBTQ+" is often reflected as "LGBTTTI," wherein there are distinctions between intersex, transgender, transsexual, and *travesti*. While "transgender" and "transsexual" have the mobility of LGBTQ+ globalization that much of the field is accustomed to, *travesti* is that category for transness that is legible and more knowable as queer in ways that "transgender" simply cannot convey. While transvestitism is included in this umbrella term, transvestites are not pathologized or deemed perverse in their practices and performance of their bottomness with the term's labor in Spanish. Rather, *travesti* describes those forms of femme embodiments that go beyond the limits of the binary opposition of transgender. The fluidity and queerness of trans femmes are accounted for in ways that reject the global North's colonial ways of explaining why one gender may shift to another, whereas *travestis* may pose the potential to think with the ways categories have already existed to describe these parts of the bottom that are visibly ignorable. Each of these identifiers is its own code system, in which gender is understood as an assemblage of algorithmic systems. As micha cárdenas rightfully argues, one of the primary shortcomings of US ideas of transgender are grounded in the "Western notions of the self as unified, unchanging, and separate," or "systems of knowledge that imagine an individual subject with a discrete gender, who crosses a line to another discrete gender."[1] The *travesti* exposes herself to the set of risks waiting for the bottom when she engages in her practices because they remain untranslatable but also confusing to the hegemonic structures in place.[2]

Travesti thus poses its ability to function as an analytical lens for the bottom. cárdenas advocates that we read *travesti* through how it "becomes a verb," in which it is a trans of color methodology and epistemology that reveals how the codes for gender are functioning in the bottom or behind the scenes. In other words, thinking through the alterity of the otherness of transness gives the bottom in their passivity access to the ways the *travesti* creates on her body a way of coming to know the world sexually through the ways in which she is racialized and gendered.

What I am describing is a relational abjective ethical event of bottoming that is activated by exchanges with the Other, triggered by the other. The relationality between trans bodies of color asks questions about why race is sexualized in ways that show other methods of being in the world. Latinidad, José Esteban Muñoz contends, is "an anti-identitarian concept that nonetheless permits us to talk about Latinas/os as having a group identity, which is necessary for social activism." That is, "Thinking of latinidad as antinormative affect offers a model of group identity that is coherent without being exclusionary." This is articulated, for Muñoz, through "a deployment of rehearsed and theatricalized Latino affect."[3] He thus offers the field a way of thinking with "brownness" as an abject strategy of being in the world. In this regard, thinking with and through the trans body of color as a passive entity sheds a bright light on how bottoms are not afforded access to their race through their sexualization and vice versa. I posit that identity is not a real thing, as such identities *of color* are always already created by whiteness's primacy. To riff off of lived experiences is reductive construction work. Yet what a trans intervention offers is access to reading how both trajectories reveal their own forms of violence at the same time, thus exposing an abjective encounter with the ultimate Other within the self as transgender folx of color.

Accordingly, as Francisco Galarte argues, "Transness and brownness are frames that reveal processes of materialization, specifically mattering that is moving." In that process of revealing a materialization, even as cárdenas and I propose of the *travesti*, Galarte concurs: "Transness can often disrupt or cut through the material affective registers of brownness with its own kind of force that is similarly underpinned by excess, potentiality, vitality, and becoming."[4] Useful to this way of thinking with brownness is through Muñoz's meditation on "feeling brown" as a way of "feeling down" that positions bodies into the depressive position. The bottom is invested in these downward positions, which are felt through the way one feels the aporia of their race in its disturbing affects. Feeling brown "chronicles a certain ethics of the self that is utilized and deployed by people of color and other minoritarian subjects who don't feel quite right within the protocols of normative affect and comportment."[5] Feeling the downward positions of brownness is "a modality of recognizing the racial performativity generated by an affective particularity that is coded to be specific historical subjects who can provisionally be recognized by the term Latina."[6] Brownness points to the ways it is neither Black nor white. Neither can it be neatly said to be in the "middle." Rather, in a Muñozian sense, brownness is a self-understanding of the achievability of whiteness. Whiteness is the primacy of the cisgender bottom that seems to hold all of the negativity for queerness. Feeling down is "meant to be a translation of the idea of a depressive position. Thus, down is a way to link position with feeling."[7] The bottom indelibly is tied to transness, a racialized transness that is essential to fully engage with the bottom as an aesthetic, ethical, political, and queer way of being in the world and with others.

The bottom confronts what is actually conflictual to the power apparatuses that keep queer and trans of color bodies separate and trapped, confronted by the violence of their race or an effacement with social death. Trans of color bodily objects can always fuck and be fucked because they have all the right parts to the bottom they need to be "shape-shifters" that go "both ways." She is every woman. But she is also a manifestation of the fantasy of the cis gay male gaze's own obsession with fucking and cock worship—the phallic authority of that penis power described throughout these pages. It is the revelation of a passivity prior to the always prior passivity that is *a priori* in its relation to the Other that loops back to the ultimate other that resides within the self. The gendered racialization of transness and its aesthetic of bottom performance allow *travesti* epistemology to exist as the aporetic bottom that signifies a negativity to bottoming and passivity that engages in the endless deferral of difference, the infinity of the finite to the bottom.

The event of an affective encounter becomes an effacement of the violence of race that problematizes sexuality and gender in their aporetic states. A relational abjective ethical event of becoming is activated by an exchange with, exposure to, and triggering by the Other, thinking with and *after* the bottom. In this regard, thinking with and through the body of color as a passive entity, hemispheric performance brings into focus how Blackness and brownness, as proposed by Muñoz, even in queer spaces, are not afforded access to their own racialization or exposure to one another—namely, the precarities of violence it hails. As voyeurs of the Other, at times the subjects are also conditioned not to see the alterity of the Other even when they are called to. Broader stakes about the labor of an identity as opposed to shared lived abject experiences become central to the framing of a "trans *pasiva* ethics."

The trans bottom engaged in the passivity of bottoming gives a body through which to access an aesthetic practice not unknown to gender outside the global North. Here, then, we can necessarily begin thinking beyond the cisness of the bottom, yet not forgetting that this book necessarily needed to discuss queer masculinities, reading the gay male bottom against the grain with which we retain an abject relationship. Yet this book still extends beyond cisness. As such, I ask to what extent this book was not always already a project *in* hemispheric trans studies. I retain the trace of the masculinization/feminization of the *pasivo* needed to guide this work. The disgust for anal sex must not neglect the masculine, for it reminds us of its origins: those cum stains from men being fucked by the phallic power that prefers them ass-up, face-down. That's it, though: the ass, the most threatening thing to the fragility of the cis-patriarchy of gay cismen, yet one at the center of a relational abjective ethics.

I imagine a trans *pasiva* ethics that accounts for the queer femme erotics that led me to this manuscript, but also have guided our discussion of passivity and the *pasivo* thus far. A queer project of ethics must account for how the passivity of the feminine as Other haunts and leaves the trace of her melanated erasure. This image is rooted in an antinormative ethics of relationality toward to an other. In that regard, Leticia Alvarado tells us that at the site of this shared violence is an aesthetic strategy of abject performance. She contends, "They show us how performances can beckon communities attentive to shared violence but also insist on recognizing violence originating within us, in our specifically marked bodies, altered and transformed by time and location."[8] I concur and go a step further, then, to show what this looks like at the convergence of these sites of shared violence located within the transitional theatricality of the transgender of color body, one that dramatizes the disturbing qualities of not being able to conform to the normative logics of sex, death, and life.

Bottom performance's role in ethical encounters complicates and extends the themes redefining the conditions for how we talk about life within political landscapes that use death as an aesthetic mirror of life, one that makes its presence from the past known in the present to describe uncertain political futures. In this regard, the sustainment of life is an effect of sustaining death. While I chart more negative paths to performance, I read through, from, and against critical notes on survival and spatiality, informing how we might think about minoritarian aesthetic practices and how they are performed at the bottom of hemispheric Latinx performance. I describe the aesthetic through affective experience, almost exclusively using "affective" in adjective form to distinguish from psychoanalytic approaches to affect theory. Yet I also do not want to disregard how "affective" also denotes being "disorderly" or "disturbing," such as in the framework of "affective disorders" referring to the episodic disturbance of moods, feelings, and emotions. I am interested in performances that produce an effect upon someone or something insofar as I am more invested in the effects themselves and how they act on an other or many others in ways that are disorderly and disturbing.

The aesthetics of the bottom is an affective state of the tension and teetering back and forth between arousal and action. The former is objectively measurable and thus constructed subjectively, whereas the latter implies an impulse to act by moving toward or away from stimuli and a decision whether or not to interact. Performance thus follows to interface with those interactions and engagements, or even the performances that emerge through their avoidance. By conceptualizing performance as an act of ethical encounter, I refer to an affective relationship in which the spectator is exposed to the body in ways that disturb or disorder either—or at times both—the subject or the environment in which the subject finds themself. The feelings, impulsive reactions, sensations, and "political consequences" are affectively charged by being affected by the exposure to the performance. Performance, as such, is a method of affective encounter. The relationship between the aesthetic and performance reflects a relationship between ethics and politics associated with aesthetics, a political haunting that asks, Who has the power to affect, and who is affected? The latter part of this question carries us into the ethical register of a nonnormative intimacy to the Other once the subject has been affected.

Bottoms Up: Queer Mexicanness and Latinx Performance is an amorous gesture of the exhumation of those bodies that capture and constitute an idea of queerness from the bottoms of Mexico, Latinx America, their diasporas, and the United States. It brings those bodies out of their clandestine graves and breathes new theoretical possibilities into their own aesthetic narratives of sexual being. Such an act is a form of ethical and political undertaking that reveals a stake in the affective responsibility to account for those stories of trauma and sexuality that gloss over our landscapes in academe. I seek to invoke the names of those exhumed bodies to expose the affectively abject and sexual dimensions of systems of power. While much of queer discourse is belabored by and committed to naming the identity politics linked to particular sexual cultures, my own engagement with queer extends beyond identity politics in favor of exploring how the affective qualities of queerness and transness lend themselves to the production of new logics of representation and the renunciation of power dynamics. Through this reading method, we might be able to explore things like temporality, space, state violence, brutality, and ethics. I do not believe that sexuality is the be-all and end-all of queerness. Rather, I contend that sexuality is informed by other communities and structures of identity that produce a queer abject known to the body of color. An invocation of queer—and later trans—becomes the only necessary vocabulary to be deployed as a reading method: how the body is read, how writing is read, how performance is read, how reading is read. By placing the analysis of sexuality at the center of the study of national belonging, I have raised issues regarding the rhetorical representation of bodies in national narratives. Through the continued practice of queer reading, we can look upon these bodies to understand deeper anxieties about difference in Mexico, Latinx America, and the United States, including not just sexuality, but Blackness, indigeneity, migration, disease, and economic inequality. Surely, these sexual encounters will carry us toward queer futures insofar as we articulate where new lexicons and practices may be rehearsed and spoken.

ACKNOWLEDGMENTS

With the generosity of love, spirit, and support from colleagues, friends, and family during the highs and lows of this work, if this book carries any merit, much of it is due to that relentless care and never-ending encouragement. Earlier excerpts of this book have appeared in different versions published in peer-reviewed journals: "Lechedevirgen Trimegisto's *Inferno Varieté*, Queer Mexicanness, and the Aesthetics of Risk," *ASAP/Journal* 6, no. 1 (2021): 95–122; and "Paz's *Pasivo*: Thinking Mexicanness from the Bottom," *Journal of Latin American Cultural Studies* 29, no. 3 (2020): 333–47. These works are reproduced with permission of the journals' publishers.

I am grateful for the support I have received in my time as a faculty member at the University of Illinois at Urbana-Champaign, where I have been surrounded by students and colleagues whose curiosity and intelligence have offered me intellectual support. I thank the graduate students from my seminar "The Politics of Pleasure: Latin America Affected, Exposed, and Queered," who generously and patiently allowed me to rehearse some of the earlier concepts in this book. I am thankful for my colleagues of literatures and cultures in the Department of Spanish and Portuguese, each of whom has impacted, in some way, how I think about this work: Elena Delgado, Javier Irigoyen-García, Eduardo Ledesma, Mariselle Meléndez, Joyce Tolliver, Anna Torres-Cacoullos, and the late Dara Goldman. A huge debt of gratitude is owed to my extraordinary graduate research assistant Eunyoung Yang, who was able to take to this project in a very appreciated productive way that helped lead this book to completion. Through building relationships with colleagues in the Center for Latin American and Caribbean Studies, Department of Gender and Women's Studies, Program in Jewish Studies, Department of Latina/Latino Studies, and the Unit for Criticism and Interpretive Theory, I created an intellectual community that has sustained and provoked substantive growth for scholarship: Brett Kaplan, Susan Koshy,

Gisabel Leonardo, Sergio Mora Moreno, Chantal Nadeau, Fiona Ngô, Rolando Romero, Sandra Ruiz, Michael Silvers, Siobhan Sommerville. This work was supported by campus fellowships awarded by the Campus Research Board and the Unit for Criticism and Interpretive Theory.

At these earlier stages, I benefitted tremendously from the manuscript workshop facilitated by the Unit for Criticism and Interpretive Theory. To those invited readers: Mi querida Laura Gutiérrez, thank you for years of collegiality, friendship, and support as both a reader and mentor of this work. C. Riley Snorton, I am grateful that you have continued to think with me and my work, and to be a mentor and colleague whom I am privileged to have as an interlocutor. "Generous" would be an understatement to describe Fiona Ngô's incisive attention to detail, which challenged the theory in this book to remain accountable to its queer stakes, and how it empowered my writing. This work gratefully benefitted from the research support gained as an Andrew W. Mellon Career Enhancement Fellow with the Institute of Citizens & Scholars, which came at a crucial moment in the writing process and not only afforded time to write, but also introduced me to an irreplaceable cohort of colleagues with whom I am privileged to continue building our own collegial and collaborative relationships. Earlier versions influenced by this work received the editorial support of Ideas on Fire, Tara Mendola, and Isis Sadek, which motivated my writing to make its most impactful contributions to the field.

The editorial prowess of New York University Press is due so much credit for bringing this book into the world. I am grateful to Eric Zinner, Furqan Sayeed, and their team for the critical roles they played in the production of this book. Just as much appreciation is due to the editors of the Sexual Cultures series (Ann Pellegrini, Tavia Nyong'o, and Joshua Chambers-Letson) for inviting this book to be in conversation with a series that continues to deeply and meaningfully impact my research. To Joshua Chambers-Letson, thank you for welcoming the opportunity to think with and challenge my work, for gifting me with your knowledge as a colleague and writer, and for inspiring and motivating me to bring forth my strengths to share with readers.

The research questions guiding this book were developed and influenced during my time as a doctoral student in Comparative Studies in Literature and Cultures at the University of Southern California. I am grateful to the faculty, now colleagues, in the Department of Comparative Literature and Department of Latin American and Iberian Cultures for welcoming these thoughts in seminars and happy hours: Roberto Díaz, Julián Gutiérrez-Albilla, Peggy Kamuf, Ronald Mendoza-de Jesús, Panivong Norindr, Samuel Steinberg, Karen Tongson, Sherry Velasco, and Veli Yashin. And to Erin Graff Zivin, to whom I owe a significant amount of admiration and gratitude, thank you for continuing to think with me well after my graduate studies, by continuing to challenge me to read against the grain to find more or renewed meaning to this work.

My years at Harvard as a graduate student in theological studies and later as a predoctoral research fellow in Spanish were a formative time for me, as my writing and interests took shape and gained texture. I have gained truly a beautiful community of people who had an impact in these experiences: Susan Abraham, Robin Bernstein, Sergio Delgado Moya, Brad Epps, Mark Jordan, Siobhan Kelly, Laura Pérez Muñoz, Christofer Rodelo, Adri Rodríguez, Mayra Rivera Rivera, and Mariano Siskind.

I was privileged to rehearse various excerpts of this research at the annual meetings of the American Comparative Literature Association, the American Studies Association, the Association for the Study of Art in the Present, and the Latin American Studies Association, and participation at symposia and invited talks. Through each I gained a cohort of colleagues across academia who conversed with this work and continue to be my audience with whom I am grateful to be in community: Iván Aguirre, Kadji Amin, Gabriela Basterra, Natalie Belisle, Mario Bellatin, Mayra Bottaro, Judith Butler, Miguel Caballero, Jeffrey Coleman, Manuel Cuellar, Héctor Domínguez-Ruvalcaba, Jennifer Doyle, Julio Enríquez-Ornelas, Carl Fischer, Zakiyyah Iman Jackson, Juan Ariel Gómez, Antía Gómez-Núñez, Liliana C. González, Joshua Javier Guzmán, Jairo Antonio Hoyos, Jennifer Scheper Hughes, Kareem Khubchandani, Ali Kulez, Christina León, Jacques Lezra, Thomas Matusiak, Uri McMillan, Diego Millan, Mireille Miller-Young, Sylvia Molloy, Nguyen Tan Hoang, Vanessa Ovalle-Pérez, César Pérez, Joseph Pierce, José Quiroga, Guillermo Rodríguez, Juana María Rodríguez, Jorge Sánchez Cruz, Ignacio Sánchez Prado, Jackie Sheean, Sarah Skillen, Ben Sifuentes-Jáuregui, Susan Stryker, David Tenorio, Zeb Tortorici, Jennifer Tyburczy, Sayak Valencia, Miguel Valerio, Abraham Weil, and I'm sure so many more that I am missing. To Adrián Emmanuel Hernández-Acosta, thank you for the tremendous amount of intellectual and emotional labor you have shown me; you have been my trudging buddy in academia from the start, and my steadfast partner in intellectual curiosity, happy hours, darker hours, endless discussions, very long journeys, laughter, tears, and camaraderie. Carolyn Fornoff is a meaningful friend and colleague in this profession that I am very privileged to have grown close to in the cornfields, and whose support throughout this journey thus far has been irreplaceable. Sony Coráñez Bolton's beautiful spirit and incisive wit as a friend and colleague have strengthened me in the most needed of times. I am so grateful for Rodrigo Delgado, who has been one of my closest confidants and always finds ways to bring out the best versions of me. Mi querido Armando García, gratitude does not even begin to fully describe how much love and care I have for our friendship and peer mentorship; your honesty and selflessness are something I could never replace in this journey.

None of this would have been possible without the irreplaceable support and immense generosity of the artists in this book, who shared their space, time, and work with me for years and will always have an impact on my work going forward. Gracias mil a Herani Enríquez HacHe, Carlos Martiel, Yanina Orellana, Bruno Ramri, Yosimar Reyes, and Lechedevirgen Trimegisto.

I am appreciative of the support I am privileged to have from my family; thank you, Mom, Vince Pancucci, Grandma, sisters, *mijas y mijos* for always being there when I needed you to be and for your love, patience, and laughter. And to my beloved cat Charly, whose orange tabby sass always keeps me comforted.

NOTES

All translations are the author's, unless cited or indicated otherwise.

INTRODUCTION

1 This includes major titles that inform the advancement of the critique of bottom theory in this book, including, but not limited to Bersani, "Is the Rectum a Grave?"; Edelman, *No Future*; Dean, *Unlimited Intimacy*; Halperin and Traub, *Gay Shame*; Nguyen, *A View from the Bottom*; Lim, *Brown Boys and Rice Queens*; and Scott, *Extravagant Abjection*.

2 Here I think of work that has inverted Leo Bersani against the grain, as in Lynn Huffer's *Are the Lips a Grave?* Scholarship by women of color in bottom studies pushes back at the antirelationality and whiteness of death drive literature surrounding bottomness. I find this work useful, but it remains hegemonically cisgender, even if not by intent. See, for example, Cruz, *The Color of Kink*; Huffer, *Are the Lips a Grave?*; Miller-Young, *A Taste for Brown Sugar*; and Rodríguez, *Queer Latinidad*.

3 Trimegisto, "El día que no me dejaron sangrar en el foro."

4 Athey, *Four Scenes in a Harsh Life*.

5 The term would be the same for all the Romance languages: *passif, passivo, passiu,* and so on.

6 By "hemispheric Latinx Americas," I refer to the decentering of one country or specific region (e.g., Central America, Southern Cone, etc.) in favor of capturing diasporic traits of these areas; this term at any given time could include and refer collectively to the United States, Mexico, Central America, the Caribbean, and South America. The study of Latinx Americans and diaspora in Canada extends beyond the scope of this current project, but studies exist.

7 Scott, *Extravagant Abjection*, 163–64.

8 Laura G. Gutiérrez, *Performing Mexicanidad*, 7.

9 "The Nobel Prize in Literature 1990."

10 José Quiroga offers a very substantial literary and cultural analysis of these phenomena across each of Paz's canonical works. See *Understanding Octavio Paz*.

11 Paz, *El laberinto*, 86.

12 Paz, *El laberinto*, 85.

13 In French, it would follow suit as *actif/passif*. However, the Anglicism of "top" and "bottom" with a Spanish pronunciation has begun to circulate in metropolitan areas.

14 Paz, *El laberinto*, 38.

15 It is significant, on the other hand, that Paz considers male homosexuality a certain kind of indulgence, as it relates to the *activo*. The *pasivo*, contrarily, is an abject and degraded being. This ambiguous conception is made very clear through the game of *albures*—that is, a verbal battle made up of obscene allusions and double entendre that they practice in Mexico City. Through verbal traps and ingenious linguistic combinations, each of the men tries to stump his adversary; the loser is the one who cannot come up with a comeback, who will have to swallow his enemy's words. And those words are full of sexually aggressive allusions; the loser is possessed and violated by the other. He falls victim to the jokes and ridicule of the spectators. As such, masculine homosexuality is tolerated, on the condition that it consists in violating the *pasivo*. As is the case with heterosexual relationships, the important thing is to not "open oneself up" and, simultaneously, being cut open and ripped apart by the other. Paz, *El laberinto*, 43.

16 The Mexican concept of the *albur* recognizes an erotic act of linguistic negotiation through the ways this term is as uniquely Mexican as it is queer, in a manner that transgresses not only the doxa of masculinity, but also normative conventions of syntax, which are called into question and recodified by language loaded with sexual content. This exchange may result in a sexual encounter between men, or not. But as an exchange, this is a deliberate engagement between *both* men. But for Paz, the bottom is obviously the one who "loses" the game of exchanging *albures*, which otherwise could just be called flirting.

17 Virility is traditionally a primary trope of modern Mexican masculinity, in which the Mexican is defined by his drive to want to fuck everyone and everything. Héctor Domínguez-Ruvalcaba offers a closer analysis of virility as a central trope of Mexican masculinity in *Modernity and the Nation*.

18 Paz, *El laberinto*, 43.

19 This is in line with historical understandings of homosexuality in Latinx America as being based on sexual objectivity and positionality, in which only the bottom is considered homosexual because to be penetrated is to be woman-like.

20 Paz writes, "The Mexican can bow, humble himself, 'bend down,' but not 'split it open' [*rajarse*], this would let the outside world penetrate his privates [*intimidad*]" (33). The terminology used in Spanish is so sophisticatedly articulate of double entendre that Paz's "sensuous intelligence" becomes much more salient. The verb *rajarse* denotes a violent ripping open of the anus, a literal "slicing" open, as if the penis becomes something sharp enough to stab and cut the ass in half, leaving the bottom wounded. Moreover, the word *intimidad* as the location of this penetration translates to both "privacy" and "intimacy." In these moments we can note the literary play of the poet's lyrical rhetoric as it raises questions about which forms of pleasure are considered intimate and which are too invasive with this literary arousal.

21 Alvarado, *Abject Performances*, 27.

22 Alvarado, *Abject Performances*, 59.

23 Alvarado, *Abject Performances*, 58.

24 Alvarado, *Abject Performances*, 163–65. Alvarado opts for a "heuristic of affect" instead of nihilism or negativity explicitly. Nonetheless, she advocates for an abjection "aware of potential disappointment." However, the following Latinx American performances push back on Alvarado's language of the heuristic. A heuristic is about sufficiency, not utopic longing. It is about what is good enough now that thus leads one to their own self-consciousness or self-discovery. I shed light on a heuristic tendency across this book about how emotions and actions mutually influence one another. I do not want to forget about the question of sufficiency or enoughness, because this enables a reading of bodies that are not yet fully dead, but also not fully living.

25 Muñoz, *The Sense of Brown*, 63.

26 Here, Juana María Rodríguez responds directly the queer political project proposed by Halberstam's *Queer Art of Failure* and Edelman's *No Future*. Rodríguez, *Sexual Futures*, 12.

27 Rivera-Servera, *Performing Queer Latinidad*, 37.

28 Laura G. Gutiérrez, *Performing Mexicanidad*, 17.

29 Mbembe, "Necropolitics," 12.

30 Mbembe, "Necropolitics," 14.

31 Foucault, *The History of Sexuality*, 1:137.

32 Foucault, *The History of Sexuality*, 1:138.

33 Mbembe, "Necropolitics," 14, emphasis in original.

34 Foucault, *The History of Sexuality*, 1:145.

35 Foucault, *The History of Sexuality*, 1:146.

36 Foucault, *The History of Sexuality*, 1:147. He argues, "We, on the other hand, are in a society of 'sex,' or rather a society 'with a sexuality': the mechanisms of power are addressed to the body, to life, to what causes it to proliferate, to what reinforces the species, its stamina, its ability to dominate, or its capacity for being used."

37 Foucault, *The History of Sexuality*, 1:147.

38 Foucault, *The History of Sexuality*, 1:148, emphasis in original.

39 Foucault, *The History of Sexuality*, 1:150.

40 For Bataille, sex is an urgent desire to remember to maybe perpetuate a sense of totality. Through the rubric of eroticism as practice and praxis, we as humans desperately attempt to overcome our condition as isolated beings, to overcome our discontinuous reality, no matter if it is just for that very temporary moment of the sexual encounter. However, Bataille argues, the change from discontinuity to continuity that underlies eroticism cannot happen without violence. Accordingly, he argues, "Only violence can bring everything to a state of flux in this way, only violence and the nameless disquiet bound up with it. We cannot imagine the transition from one state to another one basically unlike it without picturing the violence done to the being called into existence through discontinuity." See Bataille, *Erotism*.

41 Bataille argues that the intimation of death, the recovery of continuity to which eroticism adheres, involves the death of social conventions. He posits that sexual desire triggers "a breaking down of established patterns," meaning those patterns of "the regulated social order basic to our discontinuous mode of existence as defined and separate individuals." Bataille, *Erotism*, 16–18.

42 Mbembe, "Necropolitics," 15.

43 Judith Butler writes, "As Althusser himself insists, this performative effort of naming can only *attempt* to bring its addressee into being: there is always the risk of *misrecognition*. If one misrecognizes that effort to produce the subject, the production itself falters. The one who is hailed may fail to hear, misread the call, turn the other way, answer to another name, insist on not being addressed in that way. Indeed, the domain of the imaginary is demarcated by Althusser as precisely the domain that makes *misrecognition* possible." *The Psychic Life of Power*, 95, emphasis in original.

44 Butler, *The Psychic Life of Power*, 96.

45 Butler, *The Psychic Life of Power*, 96.

46 I see this work extending Nguyen Tan Hoang's concept of "bottomhood," which captures these dialectics as "a novel model for coalition politics by affirming an ethical mode of relationality." *A View from the Bottom*, 2.

47 Halberstam, *The Queer Art of Failure*, 139–40.

48 Levinas, *Otherwise Than Being*, 114–16.

49 Levinas, *Otherwise Than Being*, 49.

50 Halberstam, *The Queer Art of Failure*, 144.

51 Here I am thinking alongside Emmanuel Levinas's conceptualization of "shame" as the inability to forget one's basic nudity. See *On Escape/De l'évasion*, which, I would argue, dovetails with my own thoughts about the exposed left behind by the Other through performance, even when that Other is ultimately discovered to be within the Self.

52 *OED Online*, s.v. "expose, v.," accessed January 3, 2022, www.oed.com.

53 Guzmán and León, "Cuts and Impressions," 271.

54 Scott, *Extravagant Abjection*, 163–64.

55 Bersani, "Is the Rectum a Grave?," 222.

56 Bersani, "Is the Rectum a Grave?," 222.

CHAPTER 1. LIKE A DAGGER

1 Laura G. Gutiérrez, *Performing Mexicanidad*, 87.

2 Laura G. Gutiérrez, *Performing Mexicanidad*, 101.

3 Diana Taylor argues, "Every performance enacts a theory, and every theory performs in the public sphere." For Taylor, this is dependent upon a repertoire that incites "embodied memory" and thus "both keeps and transforms choreographies of meaning." However, this does not account for an encounter with an other that would otherwise not be anticipated prior to an event of the performance, even those performative gestures and utterances that occur surrounding

how theories move in the public sphere a priori to an encounter. See *The Archive and the Repertoire*.

4 Some of the more prominent readings of violence and trauma in queer studies have included Ann Cvetkovich, *An Archive of Feelings: Trauma, Sexuality, and Lesbian Public Cultures* (Durham, NC: Duke University Press, 2003); and Heather Love, *Feeling Backwards: Loss and the Politics of Queer History* (Cambridge: Harvard University Press, 2007).

5 Trimegisto, "Cantos Xenobinarixs."

6 My use of "they/them/their" pronouns in English are per the artist's request to be gendered accordingly.

7 Laura G. Gutiérrez, *Performing Mexicanidad*, 72.

8 Laura G. Gutiérrez, *Performing Mexicanidad*, 73.

9 Trimegisto, "Concepto."

10 One of the new tendencies that has emerged in Mexican art since the 1990s is that, according to Rubén Gallo, these artistic interventions "do not merely portray recent history but they stage events that aspire to become historical in their own right and alter the course of politics or the economy." Gallo, *New Tendencies in Mexican Art*, 1.

11 Giménez Gatto, "Pospornografía," 102.

12 Giménez Gatto, "Pospornografía," 102.

13 Gómez-Peña, "In Defense of Performance Art."

14 Gómez-Peña, "In Defense of Performance Art."

15 See Taylor, *The Archive and the Repertoire*.

16 Doyle, *Hold It against Me*, 20.

17 Trimegisto, "Pensamiento puñal."

18 Lechedevirgen Trimegisto, interview with author, July 12, 2019.

19 Trimegisto, "Cantos Xenobinarixs."

20 Trimegisto, "Pensamiento Puñal."

21 Trimegisto, "Pensamiento puñal."

22 Valencia, "Necropolitics," 189fn1, emphasis added.

23 Valencia, "Necropolitics," 190fn1.

24 Valencia, "Necropolitics," 182.

25 Doyle, *Hold It against Me*, 19.

26 Doyle, *Hold It against Me*, 51–52.

27 Trimegisto, "Pensamiento puñal."

28 Bolaños, "Presumen narco tras crimen."

29 These are government agencies located in Mexico City: the Secretariat for Public Security of the Federal District, the Public Ministry for Sexual Crimes, and the Decentralized Organ for Prevention and Social Readaptation.

30 Most media coverage regarding these attacks, especially the 2012 attack, has been redacted by newspapers. What is left of that archive is made available through blogs. However, the Bolaños article does make a reference to that attack.

31 See Valencia, *Capitalismo gore*, 34–35.

32 Valencia, *Capitalismo gore*, 86.

33 Spillers, "Mama's Baby, Papa's Maybe," 67.

34 Weheliye, *Habeas Viscus*, 97.

35 Here, I think from and through Héctor Domínguez-Ruvalcaba's argument in *Translating the Queer* that at stake is not so much the linguistic translation of a term; rather, he seeks to center how queer theory allows us to translate feelings, experiences, and traumas, to share in them, though not to claim them as our own. See Domínguez-Ruvalcaba, *Translating the Queer*.

36 In addition to the prevalence of redacted news stories by journalists reporting on the violence of narco-warfare, presumably due to intimidation and corruption between the media and the narcos.

37 Cited in Wilderson, *Red, White & Black*, 7.

38 Wilderson, *Red, White & Black*, 7.

39 Wilderson, *Red, White & Black*, 11.

40 Musser, *Sensual Excess*, 9.

41 Dreamers Adrift, *Behind the Image*.

42 Levinas, *Basic Philosophical Writings*, 53.

43 Butler, *The Psychic Life of Power*, 96.

44 Muñoz, *Disidentifications*, 11–12.

45 Trimegisto, "El día que no me dejaron sangrar."

46 Trimegisto, "El día que no me dejaron sangrar."

47 Derrida, *Dissemination*, 70.

48 Derrida, *Dissemination*, 100.

49 See Chen, *Animacies*.

50 Chen, *Animacies*, 211.

51 Ryan Long has described this within literary studies as the prevalence of "fictions of totality." See Long, *Fictions of Totality*.

52 Mbembe, "Necropolitics," 11–12.

53 Mbembe, "Necropolitics," 14.

54 Schneider, *The Explicit Body in Performance*, 1.

55 Alvarado, *Abject Performances*, 163.

56 For a close reading and study of the afterimages and the politics surrounding the Tlatelolco massacre, see Steinberg, *Photopoetics at Tlatelolco*.

CHAPTER 2. AFTER *VAMPIRO*

1 Secretaría de Cultura, "Fallece el escritor Luis Zapata."

2 One of the main arguments supporting this reading can be found in Ben Sifuentes-Jáuregui's chapter "Adonis's Silence: Textual Queerness in Zapata's *El vampiro de la colonia Roma*," in *The Avowal of Difference*, wherein he offers a sustained close reading of Octavio Paz's reading of homosexuality as a lens to approach the novel. In this chapter, I begin by positioning Paz to be read as a theoretical paradigm that can be problematized by literature. I follow with and after Sifuentes-Jáuregui but resulting in different readings of both texts. For other

similar arguments, see Irwin, *Mexican Masculinities*; Irwin, "Solitude," in Day, *Modern Mexican Culture*; Schulenburg, "El Vampiro de La Colonia Roma"; and Sifuentes-Jáuregui, *The Avowal of Difference*.

3 Magaloni, *Voting for Autocracy*, 5.

4 See Long, *Fictions of Totality*.

5 Téllez-Pon, *La síntesis rara*, 16.

6 For more comprehensive accounts and study of the 1968 Tlatelolco massacre, see Poniatowska, *La noche de Tlatelolco*; and Steinberg, *Photopoetics at Tlatelolco*.

7 Téllez-Pon, *La síntesis rara*, 65.

8 Téllez-Pon, *La síntesis rara*, 75–76.

9 See Sommer, *Foundational Fictions*.

10 Moreiras, *The Exhaustion of Difference*, 139.

11 Moreiras, *The Exhaustion of Difference*, 136. "The point is not that Latin Americanism should wish itself powerless," Moreiras explains. "It is rather that its force should be to serve against the obliteration of its object" (161).

12 Zapata, *El vampiro de la colonia Roma*, 42.

13 Zapata, *El vampiro de la colonia Roma*, 15.

14 Zapata, *El vampiro de la colonia Roma*, 96. The original Spanish reads "todo un señor," which would translate to a respectable gentleman, presentable for society. Other translations have used "a real gentleman."

15 Hernandez, "Appreciation."

16 For an extensive sociological history of this type of migratory sexual behavior, see Lionel Cantú's work on sexual tourism at the US/Mexico border, which can also be put into conversations about similar tourisms today in Mexico City, Puerto Vallarta, and Zipolite, for example, to be explored elsewhere. See Cantú, *The Sexuality of Migration*.

17 Pérez, *A Taste for Brown Bodies*, 95.

18 Pérez, *A Taste for Brown Bodies*, 99.

19 Pérez, *A Taste for Brown Bodies*, chap. 4.

20 Pérez, *A Taste for Brown Bodies*, 104.

21 For an in-depth history of these North Mexican masculinities and the performance of their sexualities, see Núñez Noriega, *Just between Us*.

22 Zapata, *El vampiro de la colonia Roma*, 15.

23 Zapata, *El vampiro de la colonia Roma*, 20–21, 27, 31–32, 45.

24 Zapata, *El vampiro de la colonia Roma*, 45.

25 This is not a nod toward the homophobic laws that surrounded the events of Mexico's infamous Baile de los 41, in which a party of forty-one gay and gender-variant individuals were arrested for deviance and indecency (it is rumored that there was a forty-second, the president's son-in-law, now made popular by the 2021 Netflix original movie by the same title). To the point, this trap leads to a construction of a queer Mexican as a national subject. In contrast, what I am describing here exceeds any forms of national belonging or subject formation, since I look to Mexicanness defined by the features of one's sexual experiences that allow them to *feel* Mexican.

26 Hernandez, "Appreciation."

27 For an extensive study on the mapping and cartographic gestures of the novel, see Schulenburg, "El Vampiro de La Colonia Roma."

28 Both the Ángel and the damn Sanborns are both still standing (touché, Daniel!). It is worth noting, interestingly enough, that my own apartment building in the Zona Rosa collapsed as a result of the Puebla earthquake. Even the Zona Rosa *I* knew in my twenties does not exist anymore. The geography and its topology are permanently changed.

29 See Berlant, *Cruel Optimism*; and Muñoz, *The Sense of Brown*.

30 See Schulenburg, "El Vampiro de La Colonia Roma."

31 Muñoz, *Cruising Utopia*, 37.

32 Muñoz, *Cruising Utopia*, 38. Here Muñoz is describing the global AIDS epidemic, which stems from his extended meditation on Douglas Crimp, which he describes as "a testimony to a queer lifeworld in which the transformative potential of queer sex and public manifestations of such sexuality were both a respite from the abjection of homosexuality and a reformatting of that very abjection" (34). In many ways, we can even extend this argument into our reading of Adonis García's own first-person stream of consciousness: it is a sexual testimony about a sexual world.

33 Osorno, *Tengo que morir todas las noches*, chap. 7.

34 Dick, Kofman, and Derrida, *Derrida: Screenplay and Essays*, 53.

35 Derrida, "Psyche," 42, 61.

36 Derrida, "Psyche," 60, 62.

37 Zapata, *El vampiro de la colonia Roma*, 51.

38 Zapata, *El vampiro de la colonia Roma*, 65.

39 Zapata, *El vampiro de la colonia Roma*, 67.

40 Zapata, *El vampiro de la colonia Roma*, 57.

41 Robert McKee Irwin describes this history of the acceptance of homosexuality in Mexican cultural production. He writes, "Homosexuality was quickly made safe (in the 19th century) by equating it with effeminacy in men. . . . Homosocial relations among men remained key to literary Mexicanness in novels of the revolution. But by the fifties, Paz had cast suspicion on male-male relations of all kinds by implying that all Mexican men engage in symbolic *chingar* battles, homosexualizing half of them in every instance. The queer side of hypermasculinity was revealed." Irwin, *Mexican Masculinities*, 227.

42 Zapata, *El vampiro de la colonia Roma*, 77.

43 Zapata, *El vampiro de la colonia Roma*, 77.

44 Zapata, *El vampiro de la colonia Roma*, 77.

45 For Irwin, Adonis's sexual practices call into question the reliability of Paz's reading of homosexuality, which he argues disproves Paz's claims; this can be seen through Adonis's self-identification as a homosexual, but also his choices of being both top and bottom during sex. See *Mexican Masculinities*.

46 Zapata, *El vampiro de la colonia Roma*, 77.

47 Alberto Fuguet made his mark with his first novel, *Mala onda* (1991), introducing a new genre of writing about the Latinx American world and its current affairs. With a prolific writing career through the early 2000s, he defined a new literary stylistic approach in the Latinx American aesthetic imaginary that emphasized a very confrontational and assertive experience with the sensorial. After a five-year hiatus from writing fiction, the author returned to the novel, and this time to the theme of homosexuality and erotic masculinities with his 2015 novel *No ficción* and his 2016 novel *Sudor* (a book that takes place over the Grindr application, with the transcripts printed for the reader). It is befitting, then, that the next step in his creative oeuvre would be film, specifically gay film. Each of these remarkable texts could be given a chapter of its own, but they extend beyond the scope of this book. The current chapter is also not necessarily interested in the literary history of the McOndo movement (the condensation of McDonald's into Macondo, both signifying the same global capitalist project); rather, I provide here a brief context to the aesthetic literary devices that made their way into the visual aesthetics of Alberto Fuguet's *Siempre Sí*.

48 Zapata, *El vampiro de la colonia Roma*, 81.

49 Paz, *El laberinto*, 59.

50 Paz, *El laberinto*, 64–65.

51 De Man, "Autobiography as De-Facement," 921.

52 De Man, "Autobiography as De-Facement," 921–22.

53 In a close reading of Nietzsche's exordium, the French philosopher describes how at one time Nietzsche looked with pleasure upon both the life left behind and the one to come; Nietzsche writes, "I love what I am living and I desire what is coming. I recognize it gratefully and I desire it to return eternally. I desire whatever comes my way to come to me, to come back to me eternally." Derrida, *The Ear of the Other*, 88.

54 Derrida, *The Ear of the Other*, 49.

55 Blanchot and Derrida, *The Instant of My Death*, 43.

56 Blanchot and Derrida, *The Instant of My Death*, 47.

57 Derrida roots this in how he traces the various implications of what "passion" signifies, in its Christian-Roman context and even beyond. Derrida contends that passion "implies an engagement that is assumed in pain and suffering, experience without mastery and thus without active subjectivity." Blanchot and Derrida, *The Instant of My Death*, 26–27.

58 Zapata, *El vampiro de la colonia Roma*, 160.

59 Zapata, *El vampiro de la colonia Roma*, 176.

CHAPTER 3. BRUNO RAMRI AND THE CORRUPTION OF A MECOS STATE

1 Peña Nieto, "Decreto por el que se deroga el diverso."

2 Peña Nieto, "#MéxicoIncluyente por la igualdad."

3 López, "Al menos 5 muertos."

4 "Detienen a sujeto implicado en ataque."

5 This is according to data provided by the National Statistics and Geography Institute (INEGI) in Mexico. See www.inegi.org.mx.

6 In the Orlando mass shooting, forty-nine people were killed, and over fifty injured.

7 In 2013 the Señorita Durango Gay pageant was interrupted when tear gas was thrown at competitors who were on stage in front of an audience of about six hundred. An anti-gay undercurrent was also present during the recent uproar in the soccer community when Guillermo Cantú, director of Mexico's national teams, responded to the outcry over Mexico fans chanting "puto" during the World Cup, by positing that the term is not homophobic and he hopes to convey that to the FIFA officials. See "Lanzan gases lacrimógenos durante Señorita Durango Gay 450 Durango," *Periódico Zócalo*, July 10, 2013, www.zocalo.com.mx; Sahid Hernández Rosete, "Grito de 'eh . . . puto' podría costar un Mundial: Cantú," *Medio Tiempo*, June 7, 2016, www.mediotiempo.com.

8 Muñoz, *Disidentifications*, 11–12.

9 *OED Online*, s.v. "Pornography, n.," accessed January 11, 2020, www.oed.com.

10 For a very critical study and theorization of the relationship between sex work and Latina narrative cultural production in pornography and other forms of sex work, see Rodríguez, *Puta Life*. Juana María Rodríguez has greatly informed the ability to do this work in queer ways in Latinx studies.

11 Scott, *Extravagant Abjection*, 9.

12 Nash, *The Black Body in Ecstasy*, 86.

13 Alvarado, *Abject Performances*, 4.

14 Rodríguez, *Sexual Futures*, 71.

15 Museo Universitario del Chopo, "XXVII Festival."

16 Audio file recorded by Bruno Ramri during the performance, provided courtesy of the artist.

17 Cruz, *The Color of Kink*, 196.

18 See Hart-Johnson, "A Graham Technique Class."

19 Rodríguez, *Sexual Futures*, 155.

20 See Mecos Films, http://mecosfilms.com.

21 UK-based Venezuelan scholar Gustavo Subero has written extensively on Mecos Films, and in this vein, he argues, "The company's ethos is to exalt images of male Mexicanness that have been ignored in other media and filmic accounts that feed the national popular imaginary." While there is certainly a vast treatment of Mexican drug trafficking and corrupt politics in cinema and television, the extent to which these themes are queer in nature is due to their toxic obsessions and attachments with masculinity. Here, the realities of the abuse of power, drug trafficking, kidnapping, extortion, and anti-indigenous racism are loaded and imbricated with erotic fantasy in a way that does not make light of the situations, or overly turn to camp aesthetics common to role-play porn genres. As Paul Julian Smith contends, "Yet rather than reading this move as frivolous evasion of social problems, I see it as an exorcism or catharsis of genuine dangers that Mexican viewers, whether

gay or not, have good reason to fear in everyday life." While I agree with Smith on the perceivable reality of the threat of violence that exists in the quotidian life of Mexicans that informs the film, I'm hesitant to overly praise Mecos Films and *Corrupción mexicana* as romanticizable entities that rescue the representations of queer masculinities. See Subero, *Queer Masculinities*; and Smith, *Queer Mexico*.

22 Subero, *Queer Masculinities*, 180.

23 Subero, "Gay Pornography," 217.

24 Lauren Berlant writes, "Optimism manifests in attachments and the desire to sustain them: attachment is a structure of relationality. But the experience of affect and emotion that attaches to those relations is as extremely varied as the contexts of life in which they emerge. An optimistic attachment is invested in one's own or the world's continuity, but might feel any number of ways, from the romantic to the fatalistic to the numb to the nothing." Berlant, *Cruel Optimism*, 13.

25 Berlant, *Cruel Optimism*, 95.

26 Berlant, *Cruel Optimism*, 97.

27 Miller-Young, *A Taste for Brown Sugar*, 16.

28 Rodríguez, *Sexual Futures*, 152.

29 Musser, *Sensational Flesh*, 2.

30 Domínguez-Ruvalcaba, *Nación criminal*, 18.

31 Domínguez-Ruvalcaba, *Nación criminal*, 166.

32 Domínguez-Ruvalcaba, *Nación criminal*, 179.

CHAPTER 4. ALTARS FOR *LOS HIJOS DE LA CHINGADA*

1 Malinche is known by several names across history; historians have been able to document Malinche, Malintzín, and Doña Marina. I use them interchangeably in my discussion of her history.

2 For a well-researched and documented historical account of Malinche's life, which I draw on for creating this narrative about Malinche's historical background, see Townsend, *Malintzin's Choices*.

3 Townsend, *Malintzin's Choices*, 22–26.

4 Townsend, *Malintzin's Choices*, 32–36.

5 Townsend, *Malintzin's Choices*, 42.

6 Townsend, *Malintzin's Choices*, 169–71.

7 Paz, *El laberinto*, 94.

8 Paz, *El laberinto*, 83.

9 Anzaldúa, *Borderlands*, 25.

10 Anzaldúa, *Borderlands*, 100–101.

11 Moraga, *The Last Generation*, 150.

12 Moraga, *The Last Generation*, 153.

13 Moraga, *The Last Generation*, 172.

14 Moraga, *The Last Generation*, 173.

15 Ricardo L. Ortíz, "Diaspora," in Vargas, Mirabal, and La Fountain-Stokes, *Keywords for Latina/o Studies*, 48.

16 Gopinath, *Unruly Visions*, 3.
17 Gopinath, *Unruly Visions*, 6.
18 Gopinath, *Unruly Visions*, 88.
19 Gopinath, *Unruly Visions*, 21.
20 Gopinath, *Unruly Visions*, 85.
21 Sharpe, *In the Wake*, 18, emphasis in original.
22 Ruiz, *Ricanness*, 3.
23 Althaus-Reid, *Indecent Theology*, 146.
24 Reyes, *For Colored Boys Who Speak Softly*, 36.
25 Reyes, *For Colored Boys Who Speak Softly*, 36.
26 Reyes, *For Colored Boys Who Speak Softly*, 36.
27 *Online Etymology Dictionary*, s.v. "Prophecy," accessed July 2, 2019, www.etymon-line.com.
28 Reyes, *For Colored Boys Who Speak Softly*, 37.
29 Althaus-Reid, *The Queer God*, 8.
30 Muñoz, *Cruising Utopia*, 1.
31 Muñoz, "Feeling Brown," 680.
32 Reyes, *For Colored Boys Who Speak Softly*, 37.
33 Reyes, *For Colored Boys Who Speak Softly*, 37.
34 Ruiz, *Ricanness*, 3.
35 Sharpe, *In the Wake*, 16, emphasis in original.
36 A *vitrolero* is a large glass container used commonly in Mexico to prepare and serve *aguas frescas*, such as horchata, lemonade, etc.
37   "Well, today is the big day, in which I share with you my secret recipe.
            This recipe has been passed down by the mother, of my mother, of my
                mother, of my mother.
            So, pay close attention, because today, it's for you!
            The ingredients are:
            Limes, water, sugar, and . . ."
38 Yanina Orellana's *Todos somos hijos de la Chingada* premiered in 2017 at the New Shoes Showcase at Highways Performance Space in Santa Monica, California. The piece has been presented in various versions and media as a way of establishing a performance that functions as an archive that cannot be captured in just one medium or expression.
39 Vicente is my name in Spanish prior to 2020. Here it is used in the place of my name and referred to in the third person with they/them/their pronouns to distinguish between that former manifestation of myself and my authorial voice reading this work.
40   "First, carefully choose your lime.
            Now that you have your lime, stroke the peel with a constant touch
            Then, squeeze the lime juice until it's moist and wet
            Repeat until you achieve the desired consistency."

41 "I'm ready for you to eat me, like a fucking piece of meat
    Devour me with your gaze, tear off a piece of me
    And taste me with your catcalls, dumbass
    But be careful, because if you drink for too long
    You'll get burned, asshole!"
42 Of course this is if we accepted Diana Taylor's conceptualization of "performance" as rooted in "acts of transfer." This book is interested in taking on that assumption to understand its limits and problematize and extend how we study stories of history when they are performed. See Taylor, *The Archive and the Repertoire*.
43 Lepecki, *Singularities*, 16.
44 Lepecki, *Singularities*, 15.
45 Yanina Orellana, conversation with author, July 12, 2019.
46 Foster, *Choreography and Narrative*, 107.
47 Yanina Orellana, conversation with author, July 12, 2019.
48 MacKendrick, "Embodying Transgression," 141.
49 MacKendrick, "Embodying Transgression," 147–48.
50 Foster, *Choreography and Narrative*, 113.
51 Orellana, conversation with author.
52 Foster, *Choreography and Narrative*, 121.
53 Alvarado, *Abject Performances*, 55.
54 Foster, *Choreography and Narrative*, 121.

CHAPTER 5. STUCK ON CARLOS MARTIEL
1 Martiel, *Monumento I*.
2 Muñoz, *Disidentifications*, 7.
3 Vazquez, *Listening in Detail*, 270.
4 Chambers-Letson, *After the Party*, 15–16.
5 Macharia, *Frottage*, 5.
6 Macharia, *Frottage*, 5.
7 Macharia, *Frottage*, 5–7.
8 Young, *Embodying Black Experience*, 2, 15.
9 Martiel, *Monumento I*.
10 Carlos Martiel, interview with author, March 12, 2021.
11 Mitchell, *Living with Lynching*, 60.
12 Martiel, interview.
13 Schneider, *Performing Remains*, 100, emphasis in original.
14 Schneider, *Performing Remains*, 101, emphasis in original.
15 Schneider, *Performing Remains*, 102, emphasis in original.
16 Young, *Embodying Black Experience*, 2, 27–28.
17 Young, *Embodying Black Experience*, 50–63.
18 Young, *Embodying Black Experience*, 91.
19 Johnson, "Sorrow's Swing," 130.

20 Johnson is particularly analyzing "Never Catch Me," performed by Will Simmons and Angela Gibbs. Johnson, "Sorrow's Swing," 137.

21 Martiel, interview.

22 Jones, *Body Art*, 31.

23 See Taylor, *Performance*.

24 Jones, *Body Art*, 34–35.

25 Spillers, "Mama's Baby, Papa's Maybe," 67.

26 See Ruiz, *Ricanness*.

27 Butler, "Performative Acts," 523.

28 See Freeman, "Packing History"; Schneider, *Performing Remains*; and Halberstam, *In a Queer Time and Place*.

29 Schneider, *Performing Remains*, 6, 7, 10.

30 Taylor, *The Archive and the Repertoire*, 277

31 Taylor, *The Archive and the Repertoire*, 277.

32 Sharpe, *In the Wake*, 15.

33 Sharpe, *In the Wake*, 23.

34 Jackson, *Becoming Human*, 208.

35 Martiel, interview.

36 Norma Gutierrez, "Mexico: Law on National Symbols Amended."

37 Martiel, interview.

38 Martiel, interview.

39 Reid-Pharr, *Black Gay Man*, 103.

40 Reid-Pharr, *Black Gay Man*, 103–4.

41 Reid-Pharr, *Black Gay Man*, 104.

42 Spillers, "Mama's Baby, Papa's Maybe," 67.

43 Hartman, *Scenes of Subjection*.

44 Snorton, *Black on Both Sides*, 12.

45 Snorton, *Black on Both Sides*, 56.

46 Martiel, interview.

CODA

1 cárdenas, *Poetic Operations*, 33.

2 In this regard, cárdenas contends, "The travesti's ability to shift between gender challenges the Western conception of identity, where one must have a single, static body and gender." cárdenas, *Poetic Operations*, 6.

3 Muñoz, *The Sense of Brown*, 63.

4 Galarte, *Brown Trans Figurations*, 13.

5 Muñoz, "Feeling Brown," 676.

6 Muñoz, "Feeling Brown," 679.

7 Muñoz, "Feeling Brown," 680.

8 Alvarado, *Abject Performances*, 165.

BIBLIOGRAPHY

Althaus-Reid, Marcella. *Indecent Theology: Theological Perversions in Sex, Gender and Politics*. London: Routledge, 2000.

———. *The Queer God*. London: Routledge, 2003.

Alvarado, Leticia. *Abject Performances: Aesthetic Strategies in Latino Cultural Production*. Durham, NC: Duke University Press, 2018.

Anzaldúa, Gloria. *Borderlands/ La Frontera: The New Mestiza*. 3rd ed. San Francisco: Aunt Lute, 2007.

Athey, Ron. *Four Scenes in a Harsh Life*. 1994. Video available at Hemispheric Institute. https://hemisphericinstitute.org. Accessed June 23, 2023.

Bataille, Georges. *Erotism: Death and Sensuality*. San Francisco: City Lights Books, 1986.

Benjamin, Walter. *The Work of Art in the Age of Mechanical Reproduction*. Edited by Hannah Arendt. Translated by Harry Zohn. New York: Schocken/Random House, 2016.

Berlant, Lauren. *Cruel Optimism*. Durham, NC: Duke University Press, 2011.

Bersani, Leo. "Is the Rectum a Grave?" *October* 43 (1987): 197–222. https://doi.org/10.2307/3397574.

Blanchot, Maurice, and Jacques Derrida. *The Instant of My Death; Demeure: Fiction and Testimony*. Translated by Elizabeth Rottenberg. Stanford: Stanford University Press, 2000.

Bolaños, Claudia. "Presumen narco tras crimen en Zona Rosa." *El Universal*, February 16, 2013. https://archivo.eluniversal.com.mx.

Butler, Judith. "Performative Acts and Gender Constitution: An Essay in Phenomenology and Feminist Theory." *Theatre Journal* 40, no. 4 (1988): 519–31. https://doi.org/10.2307/3207893.

———. *Precarious Life: The Powers of Mourning and Violence*. New York: Verso, 2006.

———. *The Psychic Life of Power: Theories in Subjection*. Stanford: Stanford University Press, 1997.

Cantú, Lionel. *The Sexuality of Migration: Border Crossings and Mexican Immigrant Men*. New York: New York University Press, 2009.

cárdenas, micha. *Poetic Operations: Trans of Color Art in Digital Media*. Durham, NC: Duke University Press, 2022.

Chambers-Letson, Joshua Takano. *After the Party: A Manifesto for Queer of Color Life*. New York: New York University Press, 2018.

Chen, Mel Y. *Animacies: Biopolitics, Racial Mattering, and Queer Affect*. Durham, NC: Duke University Press, 2012.

Cruz, Ariane. *The Color of Kink: Black Women, BDSM, and Pornography.* New York: New York University Press, 2016.

Day, Stuart A., ed. *Modern Mexican Culture: Critical Foundations.* Tucson: University of Arizona Press, 2017.

Dean, Tim. *Unlimited Intimacy: Reflections on the Subculture of Barebacking.* Chicago: University of Chicago Press, 2009.

de Man, Paul. "Autobiography as De-Facement." *MLN* 94, no. 5 (1979): 919–30. https://doi.org/10.2307/2906560.

Derrida, Jacques. *Dissemination.* Translated by Barbara Johnson. Reissue, Chicago: University of Chicago Press, 2017.

———. *The Ear of the Other: Otobiography, Transference, Translation.* Edited by Christie McDonald and Claude Levesque. Translated by Peggy Kamuf. Lincoln: University of Nebraska Press, 1988.

———. "Psyche: Inventions of the Other." In *Reading de Man Reading*, edited by Lindsay Waters and Wlad Godzich. Minneapolis: University of Minnesota Press, 1989.

"Detienen a sujeto implicado en ataque a bar gay 'Madame' en Veracruz." *Imagen de Veracruz*, May 27, 2016. https://imagendeveracruz.mx.

Dick, Kirby, Amy Ziering Kofman, and Jacques Derrida. *Derrida: Screenplay and Essays on the Film.* Manchester: Manchester University Press, 2005.

Domínguez-Ruvalcaba, Héctor. *Modernity and the Nation in Mexican Representations of Masculinity: From Sensuality to Bloodshed.* New York: Springer, 2007.

———. *Nación criminal: Narrativas del crimen organizado y el estado mexicano.* México, DF: Editorial Ariel, 2015.

———. *Translating the Queer: Body Politics and Transnational Conversations.* London: Zed Books, 2016.

Doyle, Jennifer. *Hold It against Me: Difficulty and Emotion in Contemporary Art.* Durham, NC: Duke University Press, 2013.

Dreamers Adrift. *Behind the Image: 'Quiero Que Me Llames Joto' (with Yosimar Reyes).* Video. October 16, 2013. www.youtube.com/watch?v=qZCFLkglGbQ&t=22s.

Edelman, Lee. *No Future: Queer Theory and the Death Drive.* Durham, NC: Duke University Press, 2004.

Foster, Susan Leigh. *Choreography and Narrative: Ballet's Staging of Story and Desire.* Bloomington: Indiana University Press, 1998.

Foucault, Michel. *The History of Sexuality.* Vol. 1. New York: Vintage, 1988.

Freeman, Elizabeth. "Packing History, Count(er)ing Generations." *New Literary History* 31, no. 4 (2000): 727–44. https://doi.org/10.1353/nlh.2000.0046.

Galarte, Francisco J. *Brown Trans Figurations: Rethinking Race, Gender, and Sexuality in Chicanx/Latinx Studies.* Austin: University of Texas Press, 2021.

Gallo, Rubén. *New Tendencies in Mexican Art: The 1990s.* New York: Palgrave Macmillan, 2004.

Giménez Gatto, Fabián. "Pospornografía." *Estudios visuales: Ensayo, teoría y crítica de la cultura visual y el arte contemporáneo*, no. 5 (2008): 96–105.

Gómez-Peña, Guillermo. "In Defense of Performance Art." Pocha Nostra, n.d. www.
  pochanostra. Accessed October 19, 2019.
Gopinath, Gayatri. *Unruly Visions: The Aesthetic Practices of Queer Diaspora*. Durham,
  NC: Duke University Press, 2018.
Gutiérrez, Laura G. *Performing Mexicanidad: Vendidas y Cabareteras on the Transna-
  tional Stage*. Austin: University of Texas Press, 2010.
Gutierrez, Norma. "Mexico: Law on National Symbols Amended." Library of Congress
  web page, March 2, 2008. www.loc.gov.
Guzmán, Joshua Javier, and Christina A. León. "Cuts and Impressions: The Aes-
  thetic Work of Lingering in Latinidad." *Women & Performance: A Journal of
  Feminist Theory* 25, no. 3 (September 2015): 261–76. https://doi.org/10.1080/07407
  70X.2015.1136477.
Halberstam, Jack. *In a Queer Time and Place: Transgender Bodies, Subcultural Lives*.
  New York: New York University Press, 2005.
———. *The Queer Art of Failure*. Durham, NC: Duke University Press, 2011.
Halperin, David M., and Valerie Traub, eds. *Gay Shame*. Chicago: University of Chi-
  cago Press, 2009.
Hart-Johnson, Diana. "A Graham Technique Class." *Journal for the Anthropological
  Study of Human Movement* 9, no. 4 (Fall 1997): 193–214.
Hartman, Saidiya V. *Scenes of Subjection: Terror, Slavery, and Self-Making in
  Nineteenth-Century America*. New York: Oxford University Press, 1997.
Hernandez, Daniel. "Appreciation: Why Luis Zapata's Breakthrough Gay Mexican
  Novel Demands a New Translation." *Los Angeles Times*, November 18, 2020. www.
  latimes.com.
Huffer, Lynne. *Are the Lips a Grave? A Queer Feminist on the Ethics of Sex*. New York:
  Columbia University Press, 2013.
Irwin, Robert McKee. *Mexican Masculinities*. Minneapolis: University of Minnesota
  Press, 2003.
Jackson, Zakiyyah Iman. *Becoming Human: Matter and Meaning in an Antiblack
  World*. New York: New York University Press, 2020.
Johnson, Jasmine. "Sorrow's Swing." In *Race and Performance after Repetition*, edited
  by Soyica Diggs Colbert, Douglas A. Jones, and Shane Vogel, 127–41. Durham, NC:
  Duke University Press, 2020. https://doi.org/10.2307/j.ctv153k5r4.9.
Jones, Amelia. *Body Art/Performing the Subject*. Minneapolis: University of Minnesota
  Press, 1998.
Kristeva, Julia. *Powers of Horror: An Essay on Abjection*. Translated by Leon S. Roudiez.
  New York: Columbia University Press, 1982.
Lepecki, André. *Singularities: Dance in the Age of Performance*. New York: Routledge, 2016.
Levinas, Emmanuel. *Basic Philosophical Writings*. Edited by Adriaan T. Peperzak, et al.
  Bloomington: Indiana University Press, 1996.
———. *On Escape/De l'évasion*. Stanford: Stanford University Press, 2003.
———. *Otherwise Than Being, or Beyond Essence*. Translated by Alphonso Lingis. Pitts-
  burgh: Duquesne University Press, 1998.

Lim, Eng-Beng. *Brown Boys and Rice Queens: Spellbinding Performance in the Asias.* New York: New York University Press, 2013.

Long, Ryan F. *Fictions of Totality: The Mexican Novel and the National-Popular State.* West Lafayette, IN: Purdue University Press, 2008.

López, Lourdes. "Al menos 5 muertos en ataques a dos bares en Xalapa y Orizaba." *Excelsior,* May 23, 2016. www.excelsior.com.mx.

Macharia, Keguro. *Frottage: Frictions of Intimacy across the Black Diaspora.* New York: New York University Press, 2019.

MacKendrick, Karmen. "Embodying Transgression." In *Of the Presence of the Body: Essays on Dance and Performance Theory,* edited by André Lepecki, 140–56. Middletown, CT: Wesleyan University Press, 2004.

Magaloni, Beatriz. *Voting for Autocracy: Hegemonic Party Survival and Its Demise in Mexico.* Cambridge: Cambridge University Press, 2008.

Martiel, Carlos. *Monumento I.* www.carlosmartiel.net. Accessed February 20, 2021.

Mbembe, Achille. "Necropolitics." *Public Culture* 15, no. 1 (January 2003): 11–40. https://doi.org/10.1215/08992363-15-1-11.

Miller-Young, Mireille. *A Taste for Brown Sugar: Black Women in Pornography.* Durham, NC: Duke University Press, 2014.

Mitchell, Koritha. *Living with Lynching: African American Lynching Plays, Performance, and Citizenship, 1890–1930.* Urbana: University of Illinois Press, 2011.

Moraga, Cherríe. *The Last Generation.* Boston: South End, 1993.

Moreiras, Alberto. *The Exhaustion of Difference: The Politics of Latin American Cultural Studies.* Durham, NC: Duke University Press, 2001.

Muñoz, José Esteban. *Cruising Utopia: The Then and There of Queer Futurity.* New York: New York University Press, 2009.

———. *Disidentifications: Queers of Color and the Performance of Politics.* Minneapolis: University of Minnesota Press, 1999.

———. "Feeling Brown, Feeling Down: Latina Affect, the Performativity of Race, and the Depressive Position." *Signs* 31, no. 3 (2006): 675–88. https://doi.org/10.1086/499080.

———. *The Sense of Brown.* Edited by Tavia Nyong'o and Joshua Chambers-Letson. Durham, NC: Duke University Press, 2020.

Museo Universitario del Chopo. "XXVII Festival Internacional por La Diversidad Sexual." 2014. www.chopo.unam.mx.

Musser, Amber Jamilla. *Sensational Flesh: Race, Power, and Masochism.* New York: New York University Press, 2014.

———. *Sensual Excess: Queer Femininity and Brown Jouissance.* New York: New York University Press, 2018.

Nash, Jennifer C. *The Black Body in Ecstasy: Reading Race, Reading Pornography.* Durham, NC: Duke University Press, 2014.

Nguyen, Tan Hoang. *A View from the Bottom: Asian American Masculinity and Sexual Representation.* Durham, NC: Duke University Press, 2014.

"The Nobel Prize in Literature 1990." NobelPrize.org, n.d. www.nobelprize.org. Accessed October 27, 2018.

Núñez Noriega, Guillermo. *Just between Us: An Ethnography of Male Identity and Intimacy in Rural Communities of Northern Mexico*. Tucson: University of Arizona Press, 2014.

Osorno, Guillermo. *Tengo que morir todas las noches: Una crónica de los ochenta, el underground y la cultura gay*. México, DF: Debate, 2014.

Paz, Octavio. *El laberinto de la soledad; Posdata; Vuelta a El laberinto de la soledad*. México: Fondo de cultura económica, 1999.

Peña Nieto, Enrique. "Decreto por el que se deroga el diverso por el que se declara Día de la Tolerancia y el Respeto a Las Preferencias, el 17 de mayo de cada año, y se declara Día Nacional de la Lucha contra la Homofobia, el 17 de mayo de cada año." Diario Oficial de la Federación, March 21, 2014. www.dof.gob.mx.

———. (@PresidenciaMX). "#MéxicoIncluyente por la igualdad y la no discriminación. 17 de Mayo, Día Nacional de la Lucha contra la Homofobia." Twitter, March 22, 2014. https://twitter.com/presidenciamx/status/447175445138530304.

Pérez, Hiram. *A Taste for Brown Bodies: Gay Modernity and Cosmopolitan Desire*. New York: New York University Press, 2015.

Phelan, Peggy. *Unmarked: The Politics of Performance*. London: Routledge, 1993.

Poniatowska, Elena. *La noche de Tlatelolco*. 2nd ed. México: Ediciones Era, 1998.

Quiroga, José. *Understanding Octavio Paz*. Columbia: University of South Carolina Press, 1999.

Reid-Pharr, Robert F. *Black Gay Man: Essays*. New York: New York University Press, 2001.

Reyes, Yosimar. *For Colored Boys Who Speak Softly*. Self-published, 2009.

Rivera-Servera, Ramón H. *Performing Queer Latinidad: Dance, Sexuality, Politics*. Ann Arbor: University of Michigan Press, 2012.

Rodríguez, Juana María. *Puta Life: Seeing Latinas, Working Sex*. Durham, NC: Duke University Press, 2023.

———. *Queer Latinidad: Identity Practices, Discursive Spaces*. New York: New York University Press, 2003.

———. *Sexual Futures, Queer Gestures, and Other Latina Longings*. New York: New York University Press, 2014.

Ruiz, Sandra. *Ricanness: Enduring Time in Anticolonial Performance*. New York: New York University Press, 2019.

Schneider, Rebecca. *The Explicit Body in Performance*. London: Routledge, 1997.

———. *Performing Remains: Art and War in Times of Theatrical Reenactment*. New York: Routledge, 2011.

Schulenburg, Chris T. "El Vampiro de La Colonia Roma: Mexico City's Maps and Gaps." *Chasqui* 39, no. 2 (2010): 85–98.

Scott, Darieck. *Extravagant Abjection: Blackness, Power, and Sexuality in the African American Literary Imagination*. New York: New York University Press, 2010.

Secretaría de Cultura. "Fallece el escritor Luis Zapata, referente de la literatura contemporánea." November 4, 2020. www.gob.mx.

Sharpe, Christina Elizabeth. *In the Wake: On Blackness and Being*. Durham, NC: Duke University Press, 2016.

Sifuentes-Jáuregui, Ben. *The Avowal of Difference: Queer Latino American Narratives.* Albany: State University of New York Press, 2014.

Smith, Paul Julian. *Queer Mexico: Cinema and Television since 2000.* Detroit: Wayne State University Press, 2017.

Snorton, C. Riley. *Black on Both Sides: A Racial History of Trans Identity.* Minneapolis: University of Minnesota Press, 2017.

Sommer, Doris. *Foundational Fictions: The National Romances of Latin America.* Berkeley: University of California Press, 1991.

Spillers, Hortense J. "Mama's Baby, Papa's Maybe: An American Grammar Book." *Diacritics* 17, no. 2 (1987): 65–81. https://doi.org/10.2307/464747.

Steinberg, Samuel. *Photopoetics at Tlatelolco: Afterimages of Mexico, 1968.* Austin: University of Texas Press, 2016.

Subero, Gustavo. "Gay Pornography as Latin American Queer Historiography." In *LGBT Transnational Identity and the Media,* edited by Christopher Pullen, 213–30. Basingstoke, Hampshire: Palgrave Macmillan, 2012.

———. *Queer Masculinities in Latin American Cinema: Male Bodies and Narrative Representations.* London: I.B. Tauris, 2014.

Taylor, Diana. *The Archive and the Repertoire: Performing Cultural Memory in the Americas.* Durham, NC: Duke University Press, 2003.

———. *Performance.* Durham, NC: Duke University Press, 2016.

Téllez-Pon, Sergio. *La síntesis rara de un siglo loco: Poesía homoerótica en México.* Ciudad de México: Secretaría de Cultura, Dirección General de Publicaciones, 2017.

Townsend, Camilla. *Malintzin's Choices: An Indian Woman in the Conquest of Mexico.* Albuquerque: University of New Mexico Press, 2006.

Trimegisto, Lechedevirgen. "Cantos Xenobinarixs." *Hysteria Revista,* July 2021. https://hysteria.mx.

———. "Concepto." *Inferno Varieté* (blog), n.d. www.lechedevirgen.com. Accessed November 8, 2019.

———. "El día que no me dejaron sangrar en el foro, que paradójicamente, lleva por nombre 'Juan José Gurrola.'" Facebook, June 21, 2015. https://www.facebook.com/lechedevirgen/photos/a.485803228112986.131708.485795451447097/1167844996575469.

———. "Pensamiento puñal." May 21, 2013. https://pensamientopunal.tumblr.com.

Valencia, Sayak. *Capitalismo gore.* Barcelona: Editorial Melusina, 2010.

———. "Necropolitics, Postmortem/Transmortem Politics, and Transfeminisms in the Sexual Economies of Death." Translated by Olga Arnaiz Zhuravleva. *TSQ: Transgender Studies Quarterly* 6, no. 2 (May 2019): 180–93. https://doi.org/10.1215/23289252-7348468.

Vargas, Deborah R., Nancy Raquel Mirabal, and Lawrence M. La Fountain-Stokes, eds. *Keywords for Latina/o Studies.* New York: New York University Press, 2017.

Vazquez, Alexandra T. *Listening in Detail: Performances of Cuban Music.* Durham, NC: Duke University Press, 2013.

Weheliye, Alexander G. *Habeas Viscus: Racializing Assemblages, Biopolitics, and Black Feminist Theories of the Human*. Durham, NC: Duke University Press, 2014.

Wilderson, Frank B. *Red, White & Black: Cinema and the Structure of US Antagonisms*. Durham, NC: Duke University Press, 2010.

Young, Harvey. *Embodying Black Experience: Stillness, Critical Memory, and the Black Body*. Ann Arbor: University of Michigan Press, 2010.

Zapata, Luis. *Las aventuras, desventuras y sueños de Adonis García, el vampiro de la colonia Roma*. México, DF: Debolsillo Mexico, 2012.

INDEX

ABOUT THE AUTHOR

XIOMARA VERENICE CERVANTES-GÓMEZ is Assistant Professor of Spanish and Portuguese at the University of Illinois at Urbana-Champaign.